CAMBRIDGE TEXTBOOKS IN LINGUISTICS

General editors: S. R. ANDERSON, J. BRESNAN, B. COMRIE,
W. DRESSLER, C. EWEN, R. HUDDLESTON, R. LASS,
D. LIGHTFOOT, J. LYONS, P. H. MATTHEWS, R. POSNER,
S. ROMAINE, N. V. SMITH, N. VINCENT

Word-Formation in English

In this series

This book is an intro... ~re levied for the late return of items.
which new words are built on the ...
focusing on English. The book's dida... plication, in writing or by telephoning
or no prior linguistic knowledge to do their barcode number below.
words. Readers are familiarized with the necessary ...
and analyze relevant data and are shown how to relate the   Date Due
problems and debates. The book is not written in the persp...
theoretical framework and draws on insights from various rese...
reflecting important methodological and theoretical developments in
is a textbook directed towards university students of English and Lin...
all levels. It can also serve as a source book for teachers and advanced st...
and as an up-to-date reference concerning many word-formation process...
English.

INGO PLAG is Professor of English Linguistics at the University of Siegen. He has published extensively in various linguistics journals and is a member of the editorial board of the *Journal of Pidgin and Creole Languages*. His most recent books include *Morphological Productivity: Structural Constraints in English Derivation* (1999) and *Phonology and Morphology of Creole Languages* (ed., 2003).

WORD-FORMATION
IN ENGLISH

INGO PLAG

University of Siegen

PUBLISHED BY THE PRESS SYNDICATE OF THE UNIVERSITY OF CAMBRIDGE
The Pitt Building, Trumpington Street, Cambridge, United Kingdom

CAMBRIDGE UNIVERSITY PRESS
The Edinburgh Building, Cambridge CB2 2RU, UK
40 West 20th Street, New York NY 10011–4211, USA
477 Williamstown Road, Port Melbourne, VIC 3207, Australia
Ruiz de Alarcón 13, 28014 Madrid, Spain
Dock House, The Waterfront, Cape Town 8001, South Africa

http://www.cambridge.org

First published 2003

Printed in the United Kingdom at the University Press, Cambridge

Typefaces Times 10/13 pt. and Formata   *System* LATEX 2$_\varepsilon$ [TB]

A catalogue record for this book is available from the British Library

Library of Congress Cataloguing in Publication data
Plag, Ingo.
Word-formation in English / Ingo Plag.
    p.   cm. – (Cambridge textbooks in linguistics)
Includes bibliographical references (p.) and indexes.
ISBN 0 521 81959 8 (hardback) – ISBN 0 521 52563 2 (paperback)
1. English language – Word formation.   I. Title.   II. Series.
PE1175.P58   2003
425 – dc21   2003048479

ISBN 0 521 81959 8 hardback
ISBN 0 521 52563 2 paperback

Contents

Preface

This book could not have been written without the support of many people. Numerous colleagues have provided critical comments at various stages of this project, some of them even reading subsequent versions of the same chapter. Their feedback was simply invaluable and has made me reformulate my ideas and arguments over and over again. Whoever commented on the text contributed very special insights and taught me that a text can be read and understood (and, yes, also misread and misunderstood) in many different ways. The following friends and colleagues have generously put in their time and energy: Birgit Alber, Harald Baayen, Maria Braun, Hartmut Gembries, Christiane Dalton-Puffer, Sabine Lappe, Martin Neef, and Jörg Meibauer. Needless to say, they are not to blame for the remaining flaws and inadequacies.

I also have to thank my student assistants Guido Bongard and Karina Lückoff, who read chapters, worked on the exercises and helped in various ways in the preparation of the manuscript. Special thanks go to Maria Braun for her meticulous work on the exercises, which made clear to me where things could go wrong and needed revision. Gisela Schwung made life much easier for me during the past two years by her efficient handling of all kinds of organizational matters.

I am also grateful to the people involved with Cambridge University Press (in order of appearance): Andrew Winnard for his support, assistance, and efficient handling of this project; three anonymous readers for supporting the book proposal and for providing constructive feedback at an early stage; and, finally, Ulli Dressler for his close reading of and insightful remarks on the pre-final version of the manuscript.

In 1999 I came across a review article on Katamba's morphology textbook (Nevis and Stonham 1999). This article is a goldmine for textbook writers and I have tried to incorporate as many of the authors' recommendations as possible. I am indebted to Joel Nevis and John Stonham for their having written this article, and for having done so at the right time.

Joseph Beuys once claimed that "everyone is an artist." I am convinced that everyone is a linguist, even if it is sometimes hard work (for both teachers and students) to unearth this talent. I have to thank the students who have participated in my seminars on word-formation, prosodic morphology, and psycholinguistics. They have not only served as guinea-pigs for my didactic experiments (even long before I ever conceived of writing a textbook), but have also always forced me to explain complicated matters in a way that makes them accessible. My students have made teaching an enjoyable experience, even though I may not always have been as successful as I would have liked to be.

Thanks are also due to Claudia, Jonas, Hannah, and Leo, who have supported me in all conceivable (and inconceivable) respects. Special thanks to Leo for forcing me to lock the door of my study while writing the final chapters. That really kept me going.

Finally, I thank my academic teacher, mentor and friend, Professor Rüdiger Zimmermann, who has set a great example for me as an ever-enthusiastic, ever-curious and extremely knowledgeable teacher. This book is dedicated to him.

Abbreviations and notational conventions

A	adjective
AP	adjectival phrase
Adv	adverb
C	consonant
n_1	hapax legomenon
N	noun *or* number of observations
NP	noun phrase
P	productivity in the narrow sense
P*	global productivity
PP	prepositional phrase
PrWd	prosodic word
V	verb *or* vowel
V	extent of use
VP	verb phrase
WFR	word-formation rule
#	word boundary
·	syllable boundary
|	in the context of
< >	orthographic representation
/ /	phonological (i.e. underlying) representation
[ ]	phonetic representation *or* structural boundary
*	impossible word
!	possible, but unattested word
´	main stress
`	secondary stress
σ	syllable
( )	foot boundaries

Introduction: what this book is about and how it can be used

The existence of words is usually taken for granted by the speakers of a language. To speak and understand a language means – among many other things – knowing the words of that language. The average speaker knows thousands of words, and new words enter our minds and our language on a daily basis. This book is about words. More specifically, it deals with the internal structure of complex words, i.e. words that are composed of more than one meaningful element. Take, for example, the very word *meaningful*, which could be argued to consist of two elements, *meaning* and *-ful*, or even three, *mean, -ing*, and *-ful*. We will address the question of how such words are related to other words and how the language allows speakers to create new words. For example, *meaningful* seems to be clearly related to *colorful*, but perhaps less so to *awful* or *plentiful*. And, given that *meaningful* may be paraphrased as 'having (a definite) meaning,' and *colorful* as 'having (bright or many different) colors,' we could ask whether it is also possible to create the word *coffeeful*, meaning 'having coffee.' Under the assumption that language is a rule-governed system, it should be possible to find meaningful answers to such questions.

This area of study is traditionally referred to as 'word-formation' and the present book is mainly concerned with word-formation in one particular language, English. As a textbook for an undergraduate readership it presupposes very little or no prior knowledge of linguistics and introduces and explains linguistic terminology and theoretical apparatus as we go along. Technical terms usually appear in bold print when first mentioned. Definitions of terms can be easily located via the subject index, in which the respective page numbers are given in bold print.

The purpose of the book is to enable the students to engage in (and enjoy!) their own analyses of English (or other languages') complex words. After having worked with the book, the reader should be familiar with the necessary and most recent methodological tools to obtain relevant data (introspection, electronic text collections, various types of dictionaries, basic psycholinguistic experiments, internet resources), and able to systematically analyze their data and to relate their findings to theoretical problems and debates. The book is not written from the perspective of a particular theoretical framework and draws on insights from various research traditions.

Word-formation in English can be used as a textbook for a course on word-formation (or the word-formation parts of morphology courses), as a source-book for teachers, for student research projects, as a book for self-study by more advanced students (e.g. for their exam preparation), and as an up-to-date reference concerning selected word-formation processes in English for a more general readership.

For each chapter there are a number of basic and more advanced exercises, which are suitable for in-class work or as students' homework. The more advanced exercises include proper research tasks, which also give the students the opportunity to use the different methodological tools introduced in the text. Students can control their learning success by comparing their results with the answer key provided at the end of the book. The answer key features two kinds of answers. Basic exercises always receive definite answers, while for the more advanced tasks sometimes no 'correct' answers are given. Instead, methodological problems and possible lines of analysis are discussed. Even readers not interested in working on the exercises may find it fruitful to read the answer key texts for the advanced exercises, since they broaden and deepen the discussion of certain questions raised in the pertinent chapters.

Those who consult the book as a general reference on English word-formation may check subject, affix, and author indexes and the list of references in order to quickly find what they need.

Chapters 3 and 4 introduce the reader to most recent developments in research methodology, while short descriptions of individual affixes are located in chapter 4. Each chapter is also followed by a list of recommended further reading.

As every reader knows, English is spoken by hundreds of millions of people and there exist numerous varieties of English around the world. The variety that has been taken as a reference for this book is General American English. The reason for this choice is purely practical: it is the variety the author knows best. With regard to most of the phenomena discussed in this book, different varieties of English pattern very much alike. However, especially concerning aspects of pronunciation there are sometimes remarkable, though perhaps minor, differences observable between different varieties. Mostly for reasons of space, but also due to the lack of pertinent studies, these differences will not be discussed here. However, I hope that the book will enable the readers to adapt and relate the findings presented with reference to American English to the variety of English they are most familiar with.

The structure of the book is as follows. Chapters 1 through 3 introduce the basic notions needed for the study and description of word-internal structure (chapter 1), the problems that arise with the implementation of the said notions in the actual analysis of complex words in English (chapter 2), and one of the central problems in word-formation, productivity (chapter 3). The descriptively oriented chapters 4 through 6 deal with the different kinds of word-formation processes that can be found in English: chapter 4 discusses affixation, chapter 5 non-affixational processes, chapter 6 compounding. Chapter 7 is devoted to two theoretical issues, the role of phonology in word-formation and the nature of word-formation rules.

The author welcomes comments and feedback on all aspects of this book, especially from students. Without students telling their teachers what is good for them (i.e. for the students), teaching cannot become as effective and enjoyable as it should be for both teachers and teachees (oops, was that a possible word of English?).

1

Basic concepts

Outline

This chapter introduces basic concepts needed for the study and description of morphologically complex words. Since this is a book about the particular branch of morphology called word-formation, we will first take a look at the notion of 'word.' We will then turn to a first analysis of the kinds of phenomena that fall into the domain of word-formation, before we finally discuss how word-formation can be distinguished from the other sub-branch of morphology, inflection.

1.1   What is a word?

It has been estimated that average speakers of a language know from 45,000 to 60,000 words. This means that we as speakers must have stored these words somewhere in our heads, our so-called **mental lexicon**. But what exactly is it that we have stored? What do we mean when we speak of 'words'?

In non-technical everyday talk, we speak about 'words' without ever thinking that this could be a problematic notion. In this section we will see that, perhaps contra our first intuitive feeling, the 'word' as a linguistic unit deserves some attention, because it is not as straightforward as one might expect.

If you had to define what a word is, you might first think of the word as a unit in the writing system, the so-called **orthographic word**. You could say, for example, that a word is an uninterrupted string of letters which is preceded by a blank space and followed either by a blank space or a punctuation mark. At first sight, this looks like a good definition that can be easily applied, as we can see in the sentence in example (1):

(1)   Linguistics is a fascinating subject.

We count five orthographic words: there are five uninterrupted strings of letters, all of which are preceded by a blank space, four of which are also followed by a blank space, one of which is followed by a period. This count is also in accordance with our intuitive feeling of what a word is. Even without this somewhat formal and technical definition, you might want to argue, you could have told that the sentence in (1) contains five words. However, things are not always that straightforward. Consider the following example, and try to determine how many words there are:

(2)   Benjamin's girlfriend lives in a high-rise apartment building

Your result depends on a number of assumptions. If you consider apostrophes to be punctuation marks, *Benjamin's* constitutes two (orthographic) words. If not, *Benjamin's* is one word. If you consider a hyphen a punctuation mark, *high-rise* is two (orthographic) words, otherwise it's one (orthographic) word. The last two strings, *apartment building*, are easy to classify, they are two (orthographic) words, whereas *girlfriend* must be considered one (orthographic) word. However, there are two basic problems with our orthographic analysis. The first one is that orthography is often variable. Thus, *girlfriend* is also attested with the spellings <girl-friend> and even <girl friend> (fish brackets are used to indicate spellings, i.e. letters). Such variable spellings are quite common (cf. *word-formation*, *word formation*, and *wordformation*, all of them attested), and even where the spelling is conventionalized, similar words are often spelled differently, as evidenced with *grapefruit* vs. *passion fruit*. For our problem of defining what a word is, such cases are rather annoying. The notion of what a word is, should, after all, not depend on the fancies of individual writers or the arbitrariness of the English spelling system. The second problem with the orthographically defined word is that it may not always coincide with our intuitions. Thus, most of us would probably agree that *girlfriend* is a word (i.e. one word) which consists of two words (*girl* and *friend*), a so-called **compound**. If compounds are one word, they should be spelled without a blank space separating the elements that together make up the compound. Unfortunately, this is not the case. The compound *apartment building*, for example, has a blank space between *apartment* and *building*.

To summarize our discussion of purely orthographic criteria of wordhood, we must say that these criteria are not entirely reliable. Furthermore, a purely orthographic notion of 'word' would have the disadvantage of implying that illiterate speakers would have no idea about what a word might be. This is plainly false.

What, might you ask, is responsible for our intuitions about what a word is, if not the orthography? It has been argued that the word could be defined in four other ways: in terms of sound structure (i.e. phonologically), in terms of its internal integrity, in terms of meaning (i.e. semantically), or in terms of sentence structure (i.e. syntactically). We will discuss each in turn.

You might have thought that the blank spaces in writing reflect pauses in the spoken language, and that perhaps one could define the word as a unit in speech surrounded by pauses. However, if you carefully listen to naturally occurring speech you will realize that speakers do not make pauses before or after each word. Perhaps we could say that words can be surrounded by potential pauses in speech. This criterion works much better, but it runs into problems because speakers can and do make pauses not only between words but also between syllables, for example for emphasis.

But there is another way in which the sound structure can tell us something about the nature of the word as a linguistic unit. Think of stress. In many languages (including English) the word is the unit that is crucial for the occurrence and distribution of stress. Spoken in isolation, every word can have only one **main stress**, as indicated by the acute accents (´) in the data presented in (3) below (note that we speak of linguistic 'data' when we refer to language examples to be analyzed).

(3)   cárpenter   téxtbook
        wáter   análysis
        féderal   sýllable
        móther   understánd

The main stressed syllable is the syllable which is the most prominent one in a word. Prominence of a syllable is a function of loudness, pitch and duration, with stressed syllables being pronounced louder, with higher pitch, or with longer duration than the neighboring syllable(s). Longer words often have additional, weaker stresses, so-called **secondary stresses**, which we ignore here for simplicity's sake. The words in (4) now show that the phonologically defined word is not always identical with the orthographically defined word.

(4)   Bénjamin's
        gírlfriend
        apártment building

While *apártment building* is two orthographic words, it is only one word in terms of stress behavior. The same holds for other compounds like *trável agency*, *wéather forecast*, *spáce shuttle*, etc. We see that in these examples the phonological definition of 'word' comes closer to our intuition of what a word should be.

We have to take into consideration, however, that not all words carry stress. For example, function words like articles or auxiliaries are usually unstressed (*a cár*, *the dóg*, *Máry has a dóg*) or even severely reduced (*Jane's in the garden*, *I'll be there*). Hence, the stress criterion is not readily applicable to function words and to words that hang on to other words, so-called **clitics** (e.g. *'ve*, *'s*, *'ll*).

Let us now consider the integrity criterion, which says that the word is an indivisible unit into which no intervening material may be inserted. If some modificational element is added to a word, it must be done at the edges, but never inside the word. For example, plural endings such as *-s* in *girls*, negative elements such as *un-* in *uncommon* or endings that create verbs out of adjectives (such as *-ize* in *colonialize*) never occur inside the word they modify, but are added either before or after the word. Hence, the impossibility of formations such as **gi-s-rl*, **com-un-mon*, **col-ize-onial* (note that the asterisk indicates impossible words, i.e. words that are not formed in accordance with the morphological rules of the language in question).

However, there are some cases in which word integrity is violated. For example, the plural of *son-in-law* is not **son-in-laws* but *sons-in-law*. Under the assumption that *son-in-law* is one word (i.e. some kind of compound), the plural ending is inserted inside the word and not at the end. Apart from certain compounds, we can find other words that violate the integrity criterion for words. For example, in creations like *abso-bloody-lutely*, the element *bloody* is inserted inside the word, and not, as we would expect, at one of the edges. In fact, it is impossible to add *bloody* before or after *absolutely* in order to achieve the same effect. *Absolutely bloody* would mean something completely different, and **bloody absolutely* seems utterly strange and, above all, uninterpretable.

We can conclude that there are certain, though marginal counterexamples to the integrity criterion, but surely these cases should be regarded as the proverbial exceptions that prove the rule.

The semantic definition of 'word' states that a word expresses a unified semantic concept. Although this may be true for most words (even for *son-in-law*, which is ill-behaved with regard to the integrity criterion), it is not sufficient in order to differentiate between words and non-words. The simple reason is that not every unified semantic concept corresponds to one word in a given language. Consider, for example, the smell of fresh rain in a forest in the fall. Certainly a unified concept, but we would not consider *the smell of fresh rain in a forest in the fall* a word. In fact, English simply has no single word for this concept. A similar problem arises with phrases like *the woman who lives next door*. This phrase refers to a particular person and should therefore be considered as something expressing a unified concept. This concept is however expressed by more than one word. We learn from this example that although a word may always express a unified concept, not every unified concept is expressed by one word. Hence the criterion is not very helpful in distinguishing between words and larger units that are not words. An additional problem arises from the notion of 'unified semantic concept' itself, which seems to be rather vague. For example, does the complicated word *conventionalization* really express a unified concept? If we paraphrase it as 'the act or result of making something conventional,' it is not entirely clear whether this should still be regarded as a 'unified concept.' Before taking the semantic definition of 'word' seriously, it would be necessary to define exactly what 'unified concept' means.

This leaves us with the syntactically oriented criterion of wordhood. Words are usually considered to be syntactic atoms, i.e. the smallest elements in a sentence. Words belong to certain syntactic classes (nouns, verbs, adjectives, prepositions, etc.), which are called **parts of speech, word classes,** or **syntactic categories**. The position in which a given word may occur in a sentence is determined by the syntactic rules of a language. These rules make reference to words and the class they belong to. For example, *the* is said to belong to the class called articles, and there are rules which determine where in a sentence such words, i.e. articles, may occur (usually before nouns and their modifiers, as in *the big house*). We can therefore test whether something is a word by checking whether it belongs to such a word class. If the item in question, for example, follows the rules for nouns, it should be a noun, hence a word. Or consider the fact that only words (and groups of words), but no smaller units, can be moved to a different position in the sentence. For example, in 'yes/no' questions, the auxiliary verb does not occur in its usual position but is moved to the beginning of the sentence (*You **can** read my textbook* vs. ***Can** you read my textbook?*). Thus syntactic criteria can help to determine the wordhood of a given entity.

To summarize our discussion of the possible definition of 'word' we can say that, in spite of the intuitive appeal of the notion of 'word,' it is sometimes not easy to decide whether a given string of sounds (or letters) should be regarded as a word or not. In the treatment above, we have concentrated on the discussion of such problematic cases. In most cases, however, the stress criterion, the integrity criterion and the syntactic criteria lead to sufficiently clear results. The properties of words are summarized in (5):

(5)   Properties of words
       – words are entities having a part of speech specification
       – words are syntactic atoms
       – words (usually) have one main stress
       – words (usually) are indivisible units (no intervening material possible)

Unfortunately, there is yet another problem with the word *word* itself, namely its ambiguity. Thus, even if we have unequivocally decided that a given string is a word, some insecurity remains about what exactly we refer to when we say things like

(6)   a. The word *be* occurs twice in the sentence.
       b. [ðəwɚdbiəkɚztwaɪsɪnðəsentəns]

The utterance in (6), given in both its orthographic and its phonetic representation, can be understood in different ways, it is ambiguous in a number of ways. First,

<be> or the sounds [bi] may refer to the letters or the sounds which they stand for. Then sentence (6) would, for example, be true for every written sentence in which the string <BLANK SPACE be BLANK SPACE> occurs twice. Referring to the spoken equivalent of (6a), represented by the phonetic transcription in (6b), (6) would be true for any sentence in which the string of sounds [bi] occurs twice. In this case, [bi] could refer to two different 'words,' e.g. *bee* and *be*. The next possible interpretation is that in (6) we refer to the grammatically specified form *be*, i.e. the infinitive, imperative or subjunctive form of the linking verb BE. Such a grammatically specified form is called the **grammatical word** (or **morphosyntactic word**). Under this reading, (6) would be true of any sentence containing two infinitive, two imperative or two subjunctive forms of *be*, but would not be true of a sentence which contains any of the forms *am, is, are, was, were*.

To complicate matters further, even the same form can stand for more than one different grammatical word. Thus, the **word-form** *be* is used for three different grammatical words, expressing subjunctive, infinitive or imperative, respectively. This brings us to the last possible interpretation, namely that (6) may refer to the linking verb BE in general, as we would find it in a dictionary entry, abstracting away from the different word-forms in which the word BE occurs (*am, is, are, was, were, be, been*). Under this reading, (6) would be true for any sentence containing any two word-forms of the linking verb, i.e. *am, is, are, was, were, be*, and *been*. Under this interpretation, *am, is, are, was, were, be*, and *been* are regarded as realizations of an abstract morphological entity. Such abstract entities are called **lexemes**. Coming back to our previous example of *be* and *bee*, we could now say that BE and BEE are two different lexemes that simply sound the same (usually small capitals are used when writing about lexemes). In technical terms, they are **homophonous** words, or simply **homophones**.

In everyday speech, these rather subtle ambiguities in our use of the term 'word' are easily tolerated and are often not even noticed, but when discussing linguistics, it is sometimes necessary to be more explicit about what exactly one talks about. Having discussed what we can mean when we speak of 'words,' we may now turn to the question of what exactly we are dealing with in the study of word-formation.

1.2 Studying word-formation

As the term 'word-formation' suggests, we are dealing with the formation of words, but what does that mean? Let us look at a number of words that fall into the domain of word-formation and a number of words that do not:

(7)	a. employee	b. apartment building	c. chair
	inventor	greenhouse	neighbor
	inability	team manager	matter
	meaningless	truck driver	brow
	suddenness	blackboard	great
	unhappy	son-in-law	promise
	decolonialization	pickpocket	discuss

In columns (7a) and (7b) we find words that are obviously composed by putting together smaller elements to form larger words with more complex meanings. We can say that we are dealing with morphologically **complex words**. For example, *employee* can be analyzed as being composed of the verb *employ* and the ending *-ee*, the adjective *unhappy* can be analyzed as being derived from the adjective *happy* by the attachment of the element *un-*, and *decolonialization* can be segmented into the smallest parts *de-, colony, -al, -ize,* and *-ation*. We can thus decompose complex words into their smallest meaningful units. These units are called **morphemes**.

In contrast to those in (7a) and (7b), the words in (7c) cannot be decomposed into smaller meaningful units, they consist of only one morpheme, they are mono-morphemic. *Neighbor*, for example, is not composed of *neighb-* and *-or*, although the word looks rather similar to a word such as *inventor*. *Inventor* ('someone who invents (something)') is decomposable into two morphemes, because both *invent-* and *-or* are meaningful elements, whereas neither *neighb-* nor *-or* carry any meaning in *neighbor* (a neighbor is not someone who neighbs, whatever that may be . . .).

As we can see from the complex words in (7a), some morphemes can occur only if attached to some other morpheme(s). Such morphemes are called **bound morphemes**, in contrast to **free morphemes**, which do occur on their own. Some bound morphemes, for example *un-*, must always be attached before the central meaningful element of the word, the so-called **root, stem,** or **base**, whereas other bound morphemes, such as *-ity, -ness,* or *-less*, must follow the root. Using Latin-influenced terminology, *un-* is called a **prefix**, *-ity* a **suffix**, with **affix** being the cover term for all bound morphemes that attach to roots. Note that there are also **bound roots**, i.e. roots that only occur in combination with some other bound morpheme. Examples of bound roots are often of Latin origin, e.g. *later-* (as in combination with the adjectival suffix *-al*), *circul-* (as in *circulate, circulation, circulatory, circular*), *approb-* (as in *approbate, approbation, approbatory, approbator*), *simul-* (as in *simulant, simulate, simulation*), but occasional native bound roots can also be found (e.g. *hap-*, as in *hapless*).

Before we turn to the application of the terms introduced in this section, we should perhaps clarify the distinction between 'root,' 'stem,' and 'base,' because these terms are not always clearly defined in the morphological literature and are therefore a potential source of confusion. One reason for this lamentable lack of clarity is that languages differ remarkably in their morphological make-up, so that different terminologies reflect different organizational principles in the different languages. The part of a word which an affix is attached to is called **base**. We will use the term **root** to refer to bases that cannot be analyzed further into morphemes. The term 'stem' is usually used for bases of inflections, and occasionally also for bases of derivational affixes. To avoid terminological confusion, we will avoid the use of the term 'stem' altogether and speak of 'roots' and 'bases' only.

The term 'root' is used when we want to explicitly refer to the indivisible central part of a complex word. In all other cases, where the status of a form as indivisible or not is not at issue, we can just speak of **bases** (or, if the base is a word, of **base words**). The derived word is often referred to as a **derivative**. The base of the suffix *-al* in the derivative *colonial* is *colony*, the base of the suffix *-ize* in the derivative *colonialize* is *colonial*, the base of *-ation* in the derivative *colonialization* is *colonialize*. In the case of *colonial* the base is a root, in the other cases it is not. The terminological distinctions are again illustrated in (8), using *colonialization* as an example:

(8)

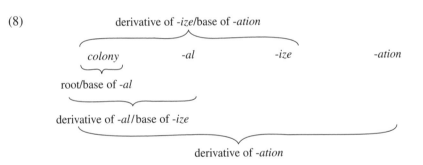

While suffixes and prefixes are very common in English, there are also rare cases of affixes that cannot be considered prefixes or suffixes, because they are inserted not at the boundary of another morpheme but right into another morpheme. Compare again our formation *abso-bloody-lutely* from above, where *-bloody-* interrupts the morpheme *absolute* (the base *absolutely* consists of course of the two morphemes *absolute* and *-ly*). Such intervening affixes are called **infixes**. Now, shouldn't we analyze *-al* in *decolonialization* also as an infix (after all, it occurs inside a word)? The answer is 'no.' True, *-al* occurs inside a complex word, but crucially it does not occur inside another morpheme. It follows one morpheme (*colony*), and precedes another one (*-ize*). Since it follows a base, it must be a suffix, which, in this particular case, is followed by another suffix.

One of the most interesting questions that arise from the study of affixed words is which mechanisms regulate the distribution of affixes and bases. That is, what exactly is responsible for the fact that some morphemes easily combine with each other, whereas others do not? For example, why can't we combine *de-* with *colony* to form **de-colony* or attach *-al* to *-ize* as in **summarize-al*? We will frequently return to this fundamental question throughout this book and learn that – perhaps unexpectedly – the combinatorial properties of morphemes are not as arbitrary as they may first appear.

Returning to the data in (7), we see that complex words need not be made up of roots and affixes. It is also possible to combine two bases, a process we already know as **compounding**. The words in (7b) (*apartment building, greenhouse, team manager, truck driver*) are cases in point.

So far, we have only encountered complex words that are created by **concatenation**, i.e. by linking together bases and affixes as in a chain. There are, however, also other, i.e. **non-concatenative**, ways to form morphologically complex words. For instance, we can turn nouns into verbs by adding nothing at all to the base. To give only one example, consider the noun *water*, which can also be used as a verb, meaning 'provide water,' as in *John waters his flowers every day*. This process is referred to as **conversion**, **zero-suffixation**, or **transposition**. Conversion is a rather wide-spread process, as is further illustrated in (9), which shows examples of verb-to-noun conversion:

(9)   *to walk*   take *a walk*
        to go   have *a go*
        to bite   have *a bite*
        to hug   give *a hug*

The term 'zero-suffixation' implies that there is a suffix present in such forms, only that this suffix cannot be heard or seen, hence *zero*-suffix. The postulation of zero elements in language may seem strange, but only at first sight. Speakers frequently leave out entities that are nevertheless integral, though invisible or inaudible, parts of their utterances. Consider the following sentences:

(10)   a. Jill has a car. Bob too.
        b. Jill promised Bob to buy him the book.

In (10a), *Bob too* is not a complete sentence, something is missing. What is missing is something like *has a car*, which can however be easily recovered by competent speakers on the basis of the rules of English grammar and the context. Similarly, in (10b) the verb *buy* does not have an overtly expressed subject. The logical subject (i.e. the buyer) can however be easily inferred: it must be the same person that is the logical subject of the superordinate verb *promise*. What these examples show us is that under certain conditions meaningful elements can indeed be left unexpressed on the surface, although they must still be somehow present at a certain level of analysis. Hence, it is not entirely strange to posit morphemes which have no overt expression. We will discuss this issue in more detail in section 2.1.2 and section 5.1.2 when we deal with non-affixational word-formation.

Apart from processes that attach something to a base (affixation) and processes that do not alter the base (conversion), there are processes involving the deletion of material, yet another case of non-concatenative morphology. English christian names, for example, can be shortened by deleting parts of the base word (see (11a)), a process also occasionally encountered with words that are not personal names (see (11b)). This type of word-formation is called **truncation**, with the term **clipping** also being used.

(11)   a. Ron (← Aaron)   b. condo (← condominium)
              Liz (← Elizabeth)   demo (← demonstration)
              Mike (← Michael)   disco (← discotheque)
              Trish (← Patricia)   lab (← laboratory)

Sometimes truncation and affixation can occur together, as with formations expressing intimacy or smallness, so-called **diminutives**:

(12)   Mandy (←Amanda)
             Andy (← Andrew)
             Charlie (← Charles)
             Patty (← Patricia)
             Robbie (← Roberta)

We also find so-called **blends**, which are amalgamations of parts of different words, such as *smog* (← *smoke/fog*) or *modem* (← *modulator/demodulator*). Blends based on orthography are called **acronyms**, which are coined by combining the initial letters of compounds or phrases into a pronounceable new word (*NATO, UNESCO*, etc.). Simple **abbreviations** like *UK* or *USA* are also quite common. The classification of blending either as a special case of compounding or as a case of non-affixational derivation is not so clear. In section 5.2.2 we will argue that it is best described as derivation.

In sum, there is a host of possibilities speakers of a language have at their disposal (or had so in the past, when the words were first coined) to create new words on the basis of existing ones, including the addition and subtraction of phonetic (or orthographic) material. The study of word-formation can thus be defined as the study of the ways in which new complex words are built on the basis of other words or morphemes. Some consequences of such a definition will be discussed in the next section.

1.3   Inflection and derivation

The definition of 'word-formation' in the previous paragraph raises an important problem. Consider the italicized words in (13) and think about the question whether *kicks* in (13a), *drinking* in (13b), or *students* in (13c) should be regarded as 'new words' in the sense of our definition.

(13)   a. She *kicks* the ball.
         b. The baby is not *drinking* her milk.
         c. The *students* are not interested in physics.

The italicized words in (13) are certainly complex words, all of them are made up of two morphemes. *Kicks* consists of the verb *kick* and the third-person-singular suffix *-s*, *drinking* consists of the verb *drink* and the participial suffix *-ing*, and *students* consists of the noun *student* and the plural suffix *-s*. However, we would not want to consider these complex words 'new' in the same sense as we would consider *kicker* a new word derived from the verb *kick*. Here the distinction between word-form and lexeme is again useful. We would want to say that suffixes like participial *-ing*, plural *-s*, or third-person-singular *-s* create new word-forms, i.e. grammatical words, but they do not create new lexemes. In contrast, suffixes like *-er* and *-ee* (both attached to verbs, as in *kicker* and *employee*), or prefixes like *re-* or *un-* (as in *rephrase* or *unconvincing*) do form new lexemes. On the basis of this criterion (i.e. lexeme formation), a distinction has traditionally been made between **inflection** (i.e. conjugation and declension in traditional grammar) as part of the grammar on the one hand, and **derivation** and compounding as part of word-formation (or rather: lexeme formation).

Let us have a look at the following data which show further characteristics by which the two classes of morphological processes, inflection vs. word-formation, can be distinguished. The derivational processes are on the left, the inflectional ones on the right.

(14)   a. **derivation**   b. **inflection**
            work*er*   (she) work*s*
            use*less*   (the) worker*s*
            *un*truth*fulness*   (is) colonializ*ing*
            *inter*view   (we) pick*ed*
            curios*ity*   (the) child*ren*
            passiv*ize*   John*'s* (house)
            terror*ism*   Emily*'s* (job)

As already indicated above, the most crucial difference is that inflectional morphemes encode grammatical categories such as plural (*workers*), person (*works*), tense (*picked*), or case (*John's*). These categories are relevant for the building of sentences and are referred to by the grammar. For example, there is a grammatical rule in English that demands that a third-person-singular subject is followed by a verb that is also marked as third-person-singular. This is called subject-verb agreement, which is also relevant for plural marking in sentences (*The flowers are/*is wonderful*). The plural and person suffixes are therefore syntactically relevant, hence inflectional.

One might argue that the suffix *-er* in *worker* is also syntactically relevant, in the sense that it is important for the syntax whether a word is a noun or a verb. That is of course true, but only in a very limited way. Thus, it is not relevant for the syntax whether the noun ends in *-er*, *-ee*, *-ion*, or whether the noun is morphologically complex at all. In that sense, derivational suffixes are not relevant for the syntax.

Let us turn to the next set of properties that unites the words on the left and differentiates them from the words on the right. These properties concern the position of the morphemes: in English derivational morphemes can occur at either end of the base words whereas regular inflection is always expressed by suffixes. Only irregular inflection makes use of non-affixational means, as for example in *mouse–mice* or *sing–sang*. There is no inflectional prefix in English. Furthermore, forms like *workers* or *colonializing* indicate that inflectional morphemes always occur outside derivational morphemes, they close the word for further (derivational) affixation (**workers-hood*, **colonializing-er*). As evidenced by derivatives like *un-truth-ful-ness* or the famous textbook example *dis-establish-ment-arian-ism*, derivational suffixes can and do occur inside other derivational suffixes.

Another interesting difference between the words in (14a) and (14b) concerns the part of speech. The suffixes in (14a) change the part of speech of the base word. For instance, the suffixation of *-less* makes an adjective out of a noun, the suffix *-ity* makes a noun out of an adjective, and the suffix *-ize* turns an adjective into a verb. The inflectional suffixes don't change the category of the base word. A plural marker on a noun does not change the category, nor does the past-tense marker on the verb. However, not all derivational affixes are category-changing, as is evidenced, for example, by most prefixes (as e.g. in *post-war*, *decolonialize*, *non-issue*), or by the nominal suffix *-ism*, which can attach to nouns to form nouns (e.g. *terrorism*).

The final property of derivation to be discussed here is exemplified by the two derivatives *interview* and *curiosity* in (14a), as against all inflectional forms. Both forms in (14a) show a property which is often found in derivation, but hardly ever in inflection, and which is called **semantic opacity**. If you consider the meaning of *interview* and the meaning of the ingredient morphemes *inter-* and *view*, you can observe that the meaning of *interview* is not the sum of the meaning of its parts. The meaning of *inter-* can be paraphrased as 'between,' that of (the verb) *view* as 'look at something' (definitions according to the *Longman Dictionary of Contemporary*

English), whereas the meaning of (the verb) *interview* is 'to ask someone questions, especially in a formal meeting.' Thus the meaning of the derived word cannot be inferred on the basis of its constituent morphemes; it is to some extent **opaque**, or **non-transparent**. The same holds for *curiosity*, a noun that has two related meanings: it can refer to a personal attribute 'the desire to know or learn about anything,' which is transparent, but it can also mean 'object of interest' (cf., for example, the definitions given in the *OED*), which is certainly less transparent. Non-transparent formations are quite common in derivational morphology, but rare in inflection.

Closely related to this generalization is the fact that inflectional categories tend to be fully **productive**, whereas derivational categories often show strong restrictions as to the kinds of possible combinations. What does 'fully productive' mean? A productive morpheme is one that can be attached regularly to any word of the appropriate class. For example, the morpheme expressing past tense can occur on all regular main verbs. And the morpheme expressing plural on nouns can be said to be fully productive, too, because all count nouns can take plural endings in English (some of these endings are irregular, as in *ox-en*, but the fact remains that plural morphology as such is fully productive). Note that the 'appropriate class' here is the class of count nouns; non-count nouns (such as *rice* and *milk*) regularly do not take plural. In contrast to the inflectional verbal and nominal endings just mentioned, not all verbs take the adjectival suffix *-ive*, nor do all count nouns take, say, the adjectival suffix *-al*:

(15)   a. *walk-ive   exhaust → exhaustive
            *read-ive   operate → operative
            *surprise-ive   assault → assaultive
        b. *computer-al   colony → colonial
            *desk-al   department → departmental
            *child-al   phrase → phrasal

The nature of the restrictions that are responsible for the impossibility of the asterisked examples in (15) (and in derivational morphology in general) are not always clear, but are often a complex mixture of phonological, morphological, and semantic mechanisms. The point is that, no matter what these restrictions in derivational morphology turn out to be, inflectional domains usually lack such complex restrictions.

As a conclusion to our discussion of derivation and inflection, I have summarized the differences between inflection and derivation in (16). Exercise 1.6 below focuses on the problems in the application of these criteria and on the general nature of the dichotomy of inflection and derivation:

(16)   **derivation**   **inflection**
   – encodes lexical meaning   – encodes grammatical categories
   – is not syntactically relevant   – is syntactically relevant
   – can occur inside derivation   – occurs outside all derivation
   – often changes the part of speech – does not change part of speech
   – is often semantically opaque   – is rarely semantically opaque
   – is often restricted in its productivity – is fully productive
   – is not restricted to suffixation – always suffixational (in English)

Based on these considerations we can conclude this sub-section by schematically conceptualizing the realm of morphology, as described so far:

(17)

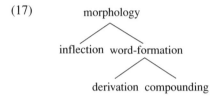

The formal means employed in derivational morphology and discussed so far can be classified in the following way:

(18)

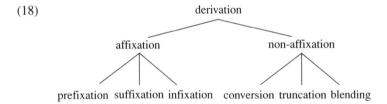

1.4   Summary

In this chapter we have looked at some fundamental properties of words and the notion of 'word' itself. We have seen that words can be composed of smaller units, called morphemes, and that there are many different ways to create new words from existing ones by affixational, non-affixational and compounding processes. Furthermore, it became clear that there are remarkable differences between different types of morphological processes, which has led us to postulate the distinction between inflection and word-formation.

We are now equipped with the most basic notions necessary for the study of complex words, and can turn to the investigation of more (and more complicated) data in order to gain a deeper understanding of these notions. This will be done in the next chapter.

Further reading

Introductions to the basics of morphological analysis can also be found in other textbooks, such as the more elementary Bauer (1983, 1988), Katamba (1993), and Haspelmath (2002), and the more advanced Matthews (1991), Spencer (1991), and Carstairs-McCarthy (1992). All of these contain useful discussions of the notion of 'word' and introduce basic terminology needed for the study of word-formation. There are also two handbooks of morphology available, which contain useful state-of-the-art articles on all aspects of word-formation: Spencer and Zwicky (1998) and Booij et al. (2000).

Those interested in a more detailed treatment of the distinction between inflection and derivation can consult the following primary sources: Bybee (1985, ch. 4), Booij (1993), Haspelmath (1996). Note that these are not specifically written for beginners and as a novice you may find them harder to understand (this also holds for some of the articles in the above-mentioned handbooks).

Exercises

Basic level

Exercise 1.1

Explain the notions of grammatical word, orthographic word, word-form and lexeme. Use the italicized words in the following examples to show the differences between these notions:

a.   Franky *walked* to Hollywood every morning.
b.   You'll never *walk* alone.
c.   Patricia had a new *walking stick*.

Exercise 1.2

Define the following terms and give three examples illustrating each term:

morpheme	prefix	suffix	affix
compound	root	truncation	

Exercise 1.3

Identify the individual morphemes in the words given below and determine whether they are free or bound morphemes, suffixes, prefixes or roots:

computerize	*bathroom*	*numerous*
unthinkable	*intersperse*	*actors*

Exercise 1.4

Consider the following sentence:

Textbook writers are sometimes grateful for comments and scholarly advice.

a.   List all morphemes in this sentence. How many morphemes can you detect?

b.   List all complex words and state for each of them which type of morphological process (inflection, derivation, or compounding) it is an example of.

Advanced level

Exercise 1.5

Consider again the notions of orthographic word, grammatical word, and lexeme as possible definitions of 'word.' Apply each of these notions to the words occurring in the following example and show how many words can be discerned on the basis of a given definition of 'word':

My birthday party's cancelled because of my brother's illness.

How and why does your count vary according to which definition you apply? Discuss the problems involved.

Exercise 1.6

Consider the status of the adverbial suffix *-ly* in English. Systematically apply the criteria summarized in (16) in chapter 1 and discuss whether *-ly* should be considered an inflectional suffix or a derivational one. You may want to take the following data into account:

slowly   aggressively   smoothly   hardly
rarely   intelligently   purposefully

2

Studying complex words

Outline

This chapter discusses in some detail the problems that arise with the implementation of the basic notions introduced in chapter 1 in the actual analysis of word structure in English. First the notion of the morpheme is scrutinized with its problems of the mapping of form and meaning. Then the phenomenon of base and affix allomorphy is introduced, followed by a discussion of the notion of word-formation rule. Finally, cases of multiple affixation and compounding are analyzed.

2.1 Identifying morphemes

In the previous chapter we introduced the crucial notion of the morpheme as the smallest meaningful unit. We have seen that this notion is very useful in accounting for the internal structure of many complex words (recall our examples *employ-ee*, *invent-or*, *un-happy*, etc.). In this section, we will look at more data and see that there are a number of problems involved with the morpheme as the central morphological unit.

2.1.1 The morpheme as the minimal linguistic sign

The most important characteristic of the traditional morpheme is that it is conceived of as a unit of form and meaning. For example, the morpheme *un-* (as in *unhappy*) is an entity that consists of the content or meaning on the one hand, and the sounds or letters which express this meaning on the other hand. It is a unit of form and meaning, a **sign**. The notion of sign may be familiar to most readers from non-linguistic contexts. A red traffic light, for instance, is also a kind of sign in the above sense: it has a meaning ('stop!'), and it has a form which expresses this meaning. In the case of the traffic light, we could say that the form consists of the well-known shape of the traffic light (a simple torch with a red bulb would not be recognized as a traffic light) and, of course, the red light it emits. Similarly, morphemes have a meaning that is expressed in the physical form of sound waves (in speech) or by the black marks on paper which we call letters. In the case of the prefix *un-*, the unit of form and meaning can be schematically represented as in (1). The part of the morpheme we have referred to as its 'form' is also called **morph**, a term coined on the basis of the Greek word for 'form, figure.'

(1)   The morpheme *un-*

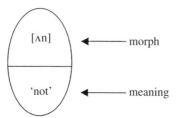

The pairing of certain sounds with certain meanings is essentially arbitrary. That the sound sequence [ʌn] stands for the meaning 'not' is a pure convention of English, and in a different language (and speech community) the same string of sounds may represent another meaning or no meaning at all.

In complex words at least one morpheme is combined with another morpheme. This creates a derived word, a new complex sign, which stands for the combined meaning of the two morphemes involved. This is schematically shown in (2):

(2)

[ʌn]		[hæpɪʲ]		[ʌnhæpɪʲ]
'not'	+	'happy'	=	'not happy'

The meaning of the new complex sign *unhappy* can be predicted from the meanings of its parts. Linguistic expressions such as *unhappy*, whose meaning is a function of the meaning of its parts, are called **compositional**. Not all complex words and expressions, however, are compositional, as can be seen from idiomatic expressions such as *kick the bucket* 'die.' And pairs such as *view* and *interview*, or *late* and *lately*, show that not even all complex words have compositional, i.e. completely transparent, meanings. As we have already seen in the previous chapter, the meaning of the prefix *inter-* can be paraphrased as 'between,' but the verb *interview* does not mean 'view between' but something like 'have a (formal) conversation.' And while *late* means 'after the due time,' the adverb *lately* does not have the compositional meaning 'in a late manner' but is best paraphrased as 'recently.'

2.1.2   Problems with the morpheme: the mapping of form and meaning

One of the central problems with the morpheme is that not all morphological phenomena can be accounted for by a neat one-to-one mapping of form and meaning. Of the many cases that could be mentioned here and that are discussed in the linguistic literature, I will discuss some that are especially relevant to English word-formation.

The first phenomenon which appears somewhat problematic for our notion of the morpheme is conversion, the process by which words are derived from other words without any visible marking (*to walk – a walk, to throw – a throw, water – to water, book – to book*). This would force us to recognize morphemes which have *no* morph, which is impossible according to our basic definition of morpheme. We have, however, already seen that this problem can be solved by assuming that zero-forms are also possible elements in language. In this view, the verb *water* is derived from the noun *water* by adding to the base noun *water* a zero-form with the meaning 'apply X.' Thus we could speak of the presence of a **zero-morph** in the case of conversion (hence the competing term **zero-derivation** for conversion). Note that it would be misleading to talk about a zero-*morpheme* in this case because it is only the outward expression, but not the meaning, which is zero.

More serious problems for the morpheme arise when we reconsider the non-affixational processes mentioned in the previous chapter. While affixational processes usually make it easy to find the different morphemes and determine their meaning and form, non-affixational processes do not lend themselves to a straight-forward analysis in terms of morphemes. Recall that we found a set of words that are derived from other words by truncation (e.g. *Ron, Liz, lab, demo*). Such derivatives pose the question of what exactly the morph is (and where it is) that – together with the base word – forms the derived word in a compositional manner. Perhaps the most natural way to account for truncation would be to say that it is the process of deleting material itself which is the morph. Under this analysis we would have to considerably extend our definition of morpheme ('smallest meaningful element') to allow processes of deletion to be counted as 'elements' in the sense of the definition. Additionally, the question may arise of what meaning is associated with truncations. What exactly is the semantic difference between *Ronald* and *Ron, laboratory* and *lab*? Although maybe not particularly obvious, it seems that the truncations, in addition to the meaning of the base, signal the familiarity of the speaker with the entity s/he is referring to. The marking of familiarity can be seen as the expression of a type of social meaning through which speakers signal their belonging to a certain group. In sum, truncations can be assigned a meaning, but the nature of the morph expressing that meaning is problematic.

In order to save the idea of morphemes as 'things,' one could also propose a different analysis of truncation, assuming the existence of a truncation morpheme which has no phonetic content but which crucially triggers the deletion of phonetic material in the base. Alternatively, we could conceptualize the formal side of the truncation morpheme as an empty morph which is filled with material from the base word.

A similar problem for the morpheme-is-a-thing view emerges from cases like the two verbs *to fall* 'move downwards' and *to fell* 'make fall.' It could be argued that *fell* is derived from *fall* by the addition of a so-called **causative** morpheme 'make X.' This idea is not far-fetched, given that the formation of causative verbs is quite common in English, but usually involves affixes, such as *-ify* in *humidify* 'make humid,' or *-en* in *blacken* 'make black.' But where is the causative morpheme in *to fell*? Obviously, the causative meaning is expressed merely by the vowel change in *fall* vs. *fell* ([ɔ] → [ɛ]) and not by any affix. A similar kind of process, i.e. the addition of meaning by means of **vowel alternation**, is evidenced in English in certain cases of past-tense formation and of plural marking on nouns, as illustrated in (3):

(3)　　 a. stick – stuck　 b. foot – feet
　　　　　 sing – sang　　　 goose – geese
　　　　　 take – took　　　 mouse – mice

Again, this is a problem for those who believe in morphemes as elements. And again, a redefinition in terms of processes can save the morpheme as a morphological entity, but seriously weakens the idea that the morpheme is a minimal sign, given that signs are not processes, but physical entities signifying meaning.

Another problem of the morpheme is that in some expressions there is more than one form signifying a certain meaning. A standard example from inflectional morphology is the progressive form in English, which is expressed by the combination of the verbal suffix *-ing* and the auxiliary verb BE preceding the suffixed verb form. A similar situation holds for English *-y* diminutives, which are marked by a combination of truncation and suffixation, i.e. the absence of parts of the base word on the one hand and the presence of the suffix *-y* on the other hand. Such phenomena are instances of so-called **extended exponence**, because the forms that represent the morpheme extend across more than one element. Extended exponence is schematically illustrated in (4):

(4)   a. progressive in English

        progressive + go

        Gill *is* go*ing* home

        b. *-y* diminutives in English

            diminutive

        And-*rew*   -*y*
            Andy

To account for cases of extended exponence we have to allow morphemes to be **discontinuous**. In other words, we have to allow for the meaning of a morpheme to be realized by more than one morph, e.g. by a form of BE and *-ing* in the case of the progressive, and by truncation and *-y* in the case of diminutives.

Another oft-cited problem of the morpheme is that there are frequently parts of words that invite morphological segmentation, but do not carry any meaning, hence do not qualify for morpheme status. Consider for example the following words, and try to determine the morphemes which the words may be composed of:

(5)   infer   confer   prefer   refer   transfer

A first step in the analysis of the data in (5) may be to hypothesize the existence of a morpheme *-fer* (a bound root) with a number of different prefixes (*in-*, *con-*, *pre-*, *re-*, *trans-*). However, if *-fer* is a bound root, it should have the same (or at least sufficiently similar) meanings in all the words in which it occurs. If you check the meanings these words have in contemporary English in a dictionary, you may end up with paraphrases similar to those found in the *OED*:

(6)   infer   'to draw a conclusion'
        confer   'to converse, talk together'
        prefer   'to like better'
        refer   'to send or direct (one) to a person, a book . . . for information'
        transfer   'to convey or take from one place, person, etc. to another'

Those readers who know some Latin may come up with the hypothesis that the words are borrowed from Latin (maybe through French), and that therefore *-fer* means 'carry,' which is the meaning of the Latin root. This works for *transfer*, which can be analyzed as consisting of the prefix *trans-* 'across' and the bound root *-fer* 'carry.' *Transfer* has then the compositional meaning 'carry across, carry over,' which is more or less the same as what we find in the *OED*. Unfortunately, this does not work for the other words in (5). If we assume that *in-* is a prefix meaning 'in, into' we would predict that *infer* would mean 'carry into,' which is not even close to the real meaning of *infer*. The meaning of *con-* in *confer* is impossible to discern, but again Latin experts might think of the Latin preposition *cum* 'with, together' and the related Latin prefix *con-/com-/cor-*. However, this yields the hypothetical compositional meaning 'carry with/together' for *confer*, which is not a satisfactory solution. Similar problems arise with *prefer* and *refer*, which we might be tempted to analyze as 'carry before' and 'carry again,' on the grounds that the prefixes *pre-* 'before' and *re-* 'again, back' might be involved. There are two problems with this analysis, though. First, the actual meanings of *prefer* and *refer* are quite remote from the hypothesized meanings 'carry before' and 'carry again/back,' which means that our theory makes wrong predictions. Second, our assumption that we are dealing with the prefixes *pre-* and *re-* is highly questionable not only on semantic grounds. Think a moment about the pronunciation of *prefer* on the one hand, and *pre-war* and *pre-determine* on the other, or of *refer* in comparison to *retry* and *retype*. There is a remarkable difference in pronunciation, which becomes also visually clear if we look at the respective phonetic transcriptions:

(7)   prefer   [prɪ'fɜr]   refer   [rɪ'fɜr]
        pre-war   [ˌpriː'wɔːr]   retry   [ˌriː'traɪ]
        predetermine   [ˌpriːdɪ'tɜːrmɪn] retype   [ˌriː'taɪp]

We can see that the (real) prefixes in *pre-war*, *predetermine*, *retry*, and *retype* carry secondary stress and have a vowel which is longer and qualitatively different from the vowel of the pseudo-prefix in *prefer* and *refer*, which is also unstressed. In other words, the difference in meaning goes together with a remarkable difference in phonetic shape.

The evidence we have collected so far amounts to the conclusion that at least *infer*, *confer*, *prefer*, and *refer* are **monomorphemic words**, because there are no meaningful units discernible that are smaller than the whole word. What we learn from these examples is that we have to be careful not to confuse morphology with etymology. Even though a morpheme may have had a certain meaning in the past, this does not entail that it still has this (or any other) meaning and can thus be considered a morpheme in today's language.

There is, however, one set of facts that strongly suggest that *-fer* is a kind of unit that is somehow relevant to morphology. Consider the nouns that can be derived from the verbs in (8):

(8)   **verb:**   infer   confer   prefer   refer   transfer
        noun: inference   conference   preference   reference   transference

The correspondences in (8) suggest that all words with the bound root *-fer* take *-ence* as the standard nominalizing suffix. In other words, even if *-fer* is not a well-behaved morpheme (it has no meaning), it seems that a morphological rule makes reference to it, which in turn means that *-fer* should be some kind of morphological unit. It has therefore been suggested, for example by Aronoff (1976), that it is not important that the morpheme has meaning, and that the traditional notion of the morpheme should be redefined as "a phonetic string which can be connected to a linguistic entity outside that string" (1976: 15). In the case of verbs involving the phonetic string [fɜr], the "linguistic entity outside that string" to which it can be connected is the suffix *-ence*. A similar argument would hold for many verbs of Latinate origin featuring the would-be morphemes *-ceive* (*receive, perceive, conceive*, etc.), *-duce* (*reduce, induce, deduce*, etc.), *-mit* (*transmit, permit, emit*, etc.), *-tain* (*pertain, detain, retain*, etc.). Each set of these verbs takes its own nominalizing suffix (with specific concomitant phonetic changes, cf. *-ceive* → *-ception*, *-duce* → *-duction*, *-mit* → *-mission*, *-tain* → *-tention*), which can again be seen as an argument for the morphological status of these strings.

Such arguments are, however, not compelling, because it can be shown that the above facts can equally well be described in purely phonetic terms. Thus we can simply state that *-ence* attaches to words ending in the *phonetic* string [fɜr] and not to words ending in the bound root *-fer*. How can we test which analysis is correct? We would need to find words that end in the phonetic string, but do not possibly contain the root in question. One such example that has been suggested to confirm the morphological status of *-mit* is *vomit*. This verb cannot be nominalized by adding *-ion* (cf. **vomission*), hence does not contain morphemic *-mit*. However, this argument is flawed, since *vomit* is also phonetically different from the verbs containing the putative root *-mit*: *vomit* has stress on the first syllable, whereas *transmit, permit, emit*, etc. have stress on the final syllable. Thus, instead of necessarily saying 'attach *-ion* to verbs with the root *-mit* (accompanied by the change of base-final [t] to [ʃ]),' we could generalize 'attach *-ion* to verbs ending in the stressed phonetic string [mɪt] (accompanied by the change of final [t] to [ʃ]).' In other words, the morphology works just as well in this case when it makes reference to merely phonetic information. We can therefore state that there is no compelling evidence so far that forces us to redefine the morpheme as a morphological unit that can be without meaning.

To summarize our discussion of the morpheme so far, we have seen that it is a useful unit in the analysis of complex words, but not without theoretical problems. These problems can, however, be solved in various ways by redefining the morpheme appropriately. For the purposes of this book it is not necessary to adhere to any particular theory of the morpheme. In most cases morpheme status is uncontroversial, and in controversial cases we will use more neutral terminology. In section 7.3 we will return to the theoretical issues touched upon above.

2.2   Allomorphy

So far we have assumed that morphemes have invariable realizations. That is, we have assumed that one meaning is expressed by a certain morph or a certain string of morphs and not by variable morphs whose exact shape differs according to the context in which they occur. However, this is exactly the kind of situation we find with many morphemes, be they bound or free. For instance, the definite and indefinite articles in English take on different shapes, depending on the kind of word which they precede:

(9)   The shape of articles in English
       a. the indefinite article *a*
       [ə] question   [ən] answer
       [ə] book   [ən] author
       [ə] fence   [ən] idea
       in isolation: ['eɪ]
       b. the definite article *the*
       [ðə] question   [ði] answer
       [ðə] book   [ði] author
       [ðə] fence   [ði] idea
       in isolation: ['ði]

The data clearly show that there are three distinct realizations of the indefinite article and three distinct realizations of the definite article. When not spoken in isolation, the indefinite article *a* has two different morphs [ə] and [ən], and the definite article *the* equally has two morphs, [ðə] and [ði]. When spoken in isolation (or sometimes when speakers hesitate, as in *I saw a . . . a . . . a unicorn*), each article has a third, stressed, variant, ['eɪ] and ['ði] respectively. Such different morphs representing the same morpheme are called **allomorphs**, and when different morphs realize one and the same morpheme the phenomenon is known as **allomorphy**.

How do speakers know when to use which allomorph? In the case of the articles, the answer is fairly straightforward. One of the two allomorphs occurs when a consonant follows, the other when a vowel follows. The third allomorph occurs if nothing follows. On a more abstract level, we can say that it is the sound structure that **conditions** the **distribution** of the allomorphs, i.e. determines which allomorph has to be used in a given linguistic context. This is called **phonological**

conditioning. We will shortly see that there are also other kinds of conditioning factors involved in allomorphy.

Allomorphy is also rather frequent in English derivation, and both bases and affixes can be affected by it. Consider first a few cases of base allomorphy and try to determine how many allomorphs the lexemes EXPLAIN, MAINTAIN, COURAGE have:

(10)   explain   maintain   courage
        explanation   maintenance   courageous
        explanatory

To make things more transparent, let us look at the actual pronunciations, given in phonetic transcription in (11) below. Primary stress is indicated by a super-script prime preceding the stressed syllable, secondary stress by a subscript prime preceding the stressed syllable.

(11)   [ɪkˈspleɪn]   [ˌmeɪnˈteɪn, mənˈteɪn]   [ˈkʌrɪdʒ]
        [ˌɛkspləˈneɪʃn]   [ˈmeɪntⁿnəns]   [kəˈreɪdʒəs]
        [ɪkˈsplænəˌtɔrɪ]

Let us first describe the allomorphy of the bases in (10) and (11). Obviously, the pronunciation of the base EXPLAIN varies according to the kind of suffix attached to it. Let us start with the attachment of *-ation*, which causes three different effects. First, stress is shifted from the second syllable of the base *plain* to the first syllable of the suffix. Second, the first syllable of the base is pronounced [ɛk] instead of [ɪk], and, third, the first syllable of the base receives secondary stress. The attachment of *-atory* to *explain* leads to a different pronunciation of the second syllable of the base ([æ] instead of [eɪ]). Similar observations can be made with regard to *maintain* and *courage*, which undergo vowel changes under attachment of *-ance* and *-ous*, respectively. In all cases involving affixes, there is more than one base allomorph, and the appropriate allomorph is dependent on the kind of suffix attached to it. We can thus state that the allomorphy in these cases is **morphologically conditioned**, because it is the following morpheme that is responsible for the realization of the base. Furthermore, we see that there are not only **obligatorily bound morphemes**, i.e. affixes, but also **obligatorily bound morphs**, i.e. specific realizations of a morpheme that only occur in contexts where the morpheme is combined with another morpheme. *Explain* has thus a free allomorph, the morph [ɪkˈspleɪn], and several bound allomorphs, [ˌɛksplən] and [ɪkˈsplæn]. In chapter 4 we will investigate in more detail the systematic phonological changes which affixes can inflict on their bases.

Let us turn to suffix allomorphy. The data in (12) show some adjectives derived from nouns by the suffixation of *-al/-ar*. Both suffixes mean the same thing and their phonetic resemblance strongly suggests that they are allomorphs of one morpheme. Think a minute about what conditions their distribution before you read on.

(12)   The allomorphy of adjectival *-al/-ar*

cause+al → causal   pole+al → polar
inflection+al → inflectional   nodule+al → nodular
distribution+al → distributional   cellule+al → cellular

Obviously, all derivatives ending in *-ar* are based on words ending in [l], whereas the derivatives ending in *-al* are based on words ending in sounds other than [l]. We could thus say that our suffix surfaces as *-ar* after [l], and as *-al* in all other cases (but see Raffelsiefen 1999: 239f for a more detailed analysis of a larger set of pertinent words). This is a case of the phonological conditioning of a suffix, with the final segment of the base triggering a **dissimilation** of the final sound of the suffix. The opposite process, **assimilation**, can also be observed, for example with the regular English past-tense ending, which is realized as [d] after voiced sounds (*vowed, pinned*) and [t] after unvoiced sounds (*kissed, kicked*). Conversely, the insertion of [ə] with words ending in [t] and [d] (*mended, attempted*) can be analyzed as a case of dissimilation.

Such a state of affairs, where one variant (*-ar*) is exclusively found in one environment, whereas the other variant (*-al*) is exclusively found in a different environment, is called **complementary distribution**. Complementary distribution is always an argument for the postulation of a two-level analysis with an underlying and a surface level. On the underlying level, there is one element from which the elements on the second level, the surface level, can be systematically derived (e.g. by phonological rules). The idea of complementary distribution is used not only in science, but also in everyday reasoning. For example, in the famous novel *The Strange Case of Dr. Jekyll and Mr. Hyde*, both men are the surface realizations of one underlying schizophrenic personality, with one realization appearing by night, the other by daylight. Dr. Jekyll and Mr. Hyde are complementarily distributed; in morphological terms they could be said to be allomorphs of the same morpheme.

In the case of the above suffix an analysis makes sense that assumes an underlying form /əl/, which surfaces as [ər] after base-final [l] and as [əl] in all other cases. This is formalized in (13):

(13)   A morpho-phonological rule

/əl/ → [ər] | [l]# —
/əl/ → [əl] elsewhere

(read: 'the underlying phonological form /əl/ is phonetically realized as [ər] after base-final [l], and is realized as [əl] elsewhere')

Such predictable changes in the realization of a morpheme are called **morpho-phonological alternations**.

To summarize this section, we have seen that morphemes can appear in different phonetic shapes and that it can make sense to analyze systematic alternations in terms of morpho-phonological rules. Such rules imply the existence of two levels of representation, with underlying representations being systematically related to and transformed into surface forms.

Having clarified the most important problems raised by the smallest morphological units, we can now turn to the question of how these minimal signs are combined to form larger units.

2.3   Establishing word-formation rules

So far, we have seen that words can be composed of smaller meaningful elements, and we have detected these elements largely by following our intuition. While our intuition works nicely with rather unproblematic complex words like *unhappy* or *girl-friend*, other data (such as those in (5) above) require more systematic investigation. The ultimate aim of such investigations is of course to determine the rules that underlie the make-up of complex words in English. For example, if a speaker knows the words *unhappy, unkind, unfaithful, untrue, uncommon,* and *analyzable*, s/he can easily identify the meaning of *unanalyzable*, even if s/he has never seen that word before. There must be some kind of system in speakers' minds that is responsible for that. In the following we will see how this system, or rather parts thereof, can be described.

As a first step, let us try to find the rule (the so-called **word-formation rule**) according to which *un-* can be attached to another morpheme in order to form a new word. Consider the morphemes in the left-hand column of (14), and what happens when the prefix *un-* is attached, as in the right-hand column. What does the behavior of the different words tell us about our word-formation rule?

(14)	a.	table	*untable
		car	*uncar
		pillow	*unpillow
	b.	available	unavailable
		broken	unbroken
		aware	unaware
	c.	(to) sing	(to) *unsing
		(to) walk	(to) *unwalk
		(to) tell	(to) *untell
	d.	post-	*unpost-
		mega-	*unmega-
		-ize	*unize
		-ness	*unness

The most obvious observation is that *un-* cannot attach to just any other morpheme, but only to certain ones. In those cases where it can attach, it adds a negative meaning to the base. However, only the morphemes in (14b) can take *un-*, while those in (14a), (14c), and (14d) cannot. The straightforward generalization to account for this pattern is that *un-* attaches to adjectives (*available*, *broken*, and *aware* are all adjectives), but not to nouns or verbs (see (14a) and (14c)). Furthermore, *un-* can only attach to words, not to bound morphemes (see (14d)).

We can summarize these observations and formulate a word-formation rule as in (15) below. In order to be applied correctly, the rule must at least contain information about the phonology of the affix, what kind of affix it is (prefix or suffix), its semantics, and possible base morphemes ('X' stands for the base):

(15) Word-formation rule for the prefix *un-*
      phonology: /ʌn/X
      semantics: 'not X'
      base: X = adjective

This rule already looks quite workable, but how can we tell that it is really correct? After all, it is only based on the very limited data set given in (14). We can verify the accuracy of the rule by testing it against further data. The rule makes the interesting prediction that all adjectives can be prefixed with *un-*, and that no verb and no noun can take *un-*. If there are words that do not behave according to the hypothesized rule, the hypothesis is falsified and we must either abandon our rule or refine it in such a way that it makes more accurate predictions.

How can we find more data? Especially with prefixes, the easiest way is to look up words in a dictionary. There are also other ways, some of which we will discuss later in the book (section 4.2), but for the present purposes any large desk dictionary is just fine. And, indeed, among the very many well-behaved deadjectival *un-* derivatives we can find apparent exceptions such as those in (16). While the vast majority of *un-* derivatives behave according to our word-formation rule, there are a number of words that go against it:

(16)   a. **nouns**   b. **verbs**
          unbelief   undo   unearth
          unease   unfold   unsaddle
          untruth   undress   unplug
                            unmask

Two kinds of exceptions can be noted, the nouns in (16a) and the verbs in (16b). The number of nouns is quite small, so that it is hard to tell whether this group consists of really idiosyncratic exceptions or is systematic in nature. Semantically, the base words *belief*, *ease*, and *truth* are all abstract nouns, but not all abstract nouns can take *un-* (cf. the odd formations ?*unidea*, ?*unthought*, ?*uninformation*, etc.), which suggests that the words in (16) are perhaps individual exceptions to our rule. However, the meaning of *un-* in all three forms can be paraphrased as 'lack of,' which is a clear generalization. This meaning is slightly different, though, from the meaning of *un-* which is given in (15) as 'not.' Additional data would be needed to find out more about such denominal *un-* formations and how they can possibly be related to de-adjectival ones. The fact that the interpretation 'lack of X' occurs with nouns and the interpretation 'not X' with adjectives might however be taken as a hint that the two cases can be unified into one, with slightly different interpretations following from the difference in the part of speech of the base. This possibility is explored further below, after we have looked at deverbal *un-* derivatives.

The second set of derivatives apparently violating the rule as formulated in (15) are the verbs in (16b). The list above is not exhaustive and the overall number of pertinent derivatives is quite large. It seems that it is even possible to create new forms. For example, the *OED* provides the following verbs as being coined in the twentieth century:

(17)   unditch   unspool
        unquote   unstack
        unscramble   untack
        unsnib   unzip

A closer look at the derived *un-* verbs reveals, however, that they deviate from the rule in (15) not only in terms of part of speech of the base (i.e. verbs instead of adjectives), but also in terms of meaning. The verb *undo* does not mean 'not do,' the verb *unfold* does not mean 'not fold,' the verb *unfasten* does not mean 'not fasten.' Rather, the verbs can all be characterized by the fact that they denote reversal or deprivation. The derivative *unearth* nicely illustrates both meanings, because it can refer either to the removal of something from the earth, or to the removal of earth from something. In the first case, we are dealing with a reversative meaning, in the second with the privative meaning. Given the systematicity of the data, one is tempted to postulate another word-formation rule for *un-*, this time deverbal, with a reversative and privative meaning.

The dictionary data have been very helpful in determining which words and patterns exist. However, the dictionary did not tell us anything about which patterns are systematically excluded, which means that concerning one of our predictions we did not find any evidence. This prediction has been that all adjectives take *un-*. In order to test this prediction we would have to find adjectives that crucially do not take *un-*. But dictionaries only list existing words, not impossible ones. Nevertheless, the dictionary can still be useful for the investigation of this question. We could, for instance, extract all adjectives from the dictionary and then see which of these have derived forms with *un-* in the dictionary, and which ones have no such derived form. From the list of adjectives without corresponding *un-* derivative we could perhaps infer whether there are any systematic restrictions at work. However, this list would have the serious disadvantage that it would not tell us whether the lack of derived forms is simply an accident or represents a systematic gap. For example, the dictionary may not list *unaligned* simply because it is a word that is not used very often. However, it is certainly a possible formation.

One way out of this trap is introspective or experimental evidence. Introspection means that we simply use our own intuition as competent speakers to decide whether certain formations are possible or impossible. However, sometimes such judgments may be quite subjective or controversial so that it is much better to set up a regular experiment, in which the intuitions of a larger number of speakers are systematically tested. For example, we could set up a random list of all kinds of adjectives and have people (so-called **subjects, informants**, or **participants**) tell us whether they think it is possible to attach *un-* to the words in the list. Such experiments work best if one already has some kind of hypothesis concerning what kind of restriction may be at work. In such cases testable data sets can be constructed in such a way that one data set has the property in question and the other data set does not have it. If this property is indeed relevant, the experimental hypothesis would be that the subjects treat the data in set 1 differently from the data in set 2. An example of such an experiment is given in exercise 2.6 at the end of this chapter.

But let us return from these methodological considerations to the solution of the problem of *un-*. For the present purposes, I have used introspection to arrive at a number of words that are impossible *un-* formations and which are therefore not to be found even in the largest dictionary of all, the *OED* (with roughly 500,000 entries). These examples show that not all adjectives can take *un-*.

(18)   a. *ungreen   b. *unbad
            *unblack   *unnaked
            *unred   *unsilly

It seems, however, that the words in (18) are not just arbitrary exceptions, but that they show a systematic gap in the pattern. Thus, color adjectives (18a) do not take *un-*, neither do the adjectives in (18b) for as yet unclear reasons. In other words, the rule in (15) needs to be further restricted, excluding certain semantically definable classes of adjectives such as color adjectives.

And indeed there is one semantic restriction on *un-* often mentioned in the literature (e.g. in Zimmer 1964, Adams 2001) that may also be responsible for the exclusion of color adjectives. It has been observed that *un-* attachment mostly creates derivatives that express a contrary contrast on a bi-dimensional scale of 'more or less,' i.e. a contrast between gradable adjectives and their respective opposites, as in *happy–unhappy, clear–unclear, comfortable–uncomfortable*. Thus there are two other kinds of opposites that are usually not expressible through *un-* prefixation, namely contradictories and complementaries. Contradictory expressions exclude one another, and there is no room in between. For example, something is either *artificial* or *genuine*, either *unique* or *multiple*. Complementarity is a semantic relation in which one expression stands in a complementary contrast to a whole set of other, related expressions. Thus, if something is *green*, it is *not red, not blue, not brown, not white*, etc.; and if it is *not green*, it may be *red, blue, brown, white*, etc. From the generalization that *un-* prefixation does not readily form complementaries, it follows naturally that color adjectives are not legitimate bases for this prefix.

One important caveat needs to be mentioned. The said restriction seems to hold only for *un-* adjectives that are based on simplex bases. Derived adjectives such as *publicized, available*, or *married* may take *un-* regardless of the semantic nature of the oppositeness expressed. Thus *unpublicized, unavailable*, and *unmarried* are not contraries, but are nevertheless possible *un-* derivatives.

Another problem with the semantic restriction to contraries is that adjectives often have more than one meaning, and that they can therefore belong to more than one semantic group. For example, *unique* can mean 'the only one of its kind,' in which case it is non-gradable and therefore not eligible as a base for *un-* prefixation. But *unique* is also used in the sense of 'exceptionally good,' in which case it can be prefixed by *un-*. If complex base words are ambiguous in this way, we can see the effect of the preference for contrary interpretations. For example, *un-American* is necessarily interpreted as referring to the qualitative meaning of the adjective (with *American* designating a gradable property), and not to the classifying meaning (with *American* being used as a geographic term in complementary opposition to other geographic terms like *Canadian, Mexican*, etc.). The complementary antonym of *American* would normally be formed by attachment of the neighboring prefix *non-*, giving us *non-American*. Thus, Britons are not necessarily *un-American* people, but they are certainly *non-American*.

What are the overall consequences of the foregoing analyses for the word-formation rule in (15)? Contrary to the first impression, it turned out that the rule makes basically correct predictions and that the data in (16) do not constitute sufficient evidence against (15). Rather, we have detected that there are probably three *un-* prefixes. The first is de-adjectival and has the meaning 'not,' the second is denominal and has the meaning 'lack of,' and the third is deverbal and has reversative or privative meaning. We arrived at this conclusion by testing our initial hypothesis against further data, collected from dictionaries and by introspection.

Given that different meanings of *un-* go together with bases of different parts of speech, and given that the meanings of de-adjectival, denominal, and deverbal derivatives all have a strong negative element, one might also think of a radical alternative analysis. Let us assume the existence of only one prefix *un-*, with a very general negative meaning that interacts with the meaning of the base word. This interaction is characterized by very general inferencing procedures. Let us further assume that there is no restriction concerning the part of speech of possible base words, i.e. nouns, verbs, and adjectives are all allowed.

Now, when the prefix is attached to an adjective, the general negative meaning of the prefix interacts in such a way with the meaning of the base X that the meaning 'not X' naturally emerges. The only interpretation possible for a combination of negation and adjectival meaning is that the derived form denotes the absence of the property denoted by the adjective. With abstract nouns, a similar inferencing procedure applies. The derivative is automatically interpreted as 'lack of X' because this is the only way to make sense out of the composition of general negative meaning and the meaning of the abstract noun. With verbs denoting a goal-oriented action, negation is automatically interpreted as reversal or removal. Although not unattractive because of its elegance, this unitary account of *un-* is not entirely convincing. If *un-* has indeed a general negative meaning, why don't we say *unwalk to signify *not walk*, *unsleep to signify *not sleep*? Obviously, there must be a restriction at work that only allows as bases verbs that denote an action which can be reversed or which involves a participant that can be removed. But allowing a restriction that is exclusively pertinent for verbs destroys the elegance of unitary *un-* and boils down to acknowledging a deverbal *un-* prefix with its own special restrictions. Similar arguments would hold for the relevant restrictions on nominal and adjectival bases. In essence, the postulation of only one *un-* prefix does not solve the problem of the part-of-speech-specific restrictions we have detected.

To summarize our discussion of how to establish a word-formation rule, we have seen that this is not an easy task, even with affixes that look relatively straightforward. Complex restrictions are at work that need to be incorporated in the rules. The revised – but still tentative – word-formation rules for *un-* are given in (19)–(21):

(19)   Word-formation rule *un-₁*
        phonology: /ʌn/-X
        base: X = adjective
        semantics: 'not X'
        restrictions: – derivatives with simplex bases must be
                            interpretable as contraries
                            – some further unclear restrictions on possible base
                            words

(20)   Word-formation rule *un-₂*
        phonology: /ʌn/-X
        base: X = abstract noun
        semantics: 'lack of X'
        restrictions: unclear restrictions on possible base words

(21)   Word-formation rule *un-₃*
       phonology: /ʌn/-X
       base: X = verb
       semantics: reversative/privative
       restrictions: only bases whose meaning allows reversative and
                                   privative manipulation

The word-formation rules in (19) through (21) are of course only tentative and still quite rudimentary representations of the competent speakers' tacit knowledge of how to form and understand *un-* derivatives. The task of the morphologist would be to find out more about the exact nature of the restrictions mentioned in the rules. How this could be done is exemplified in exercise 2.5 below.

We will now turn to another affix and try to establish the pertinent word-formation rule. (22) is a collection of nouns featuring the suffix *-th*, which derives from an adjectival base an abstract noun denoting a state (we ignore here deverbal formations such as *growth*):

(22)   broad+th   →   breadth
       deep+th   →   depth
       long+th   →   length
       strong+th →   strength
       true+th   →   truth
       warm+th   →   warmth
       wide+th   →   width

From this pattern we can tentatively deduce the following word-formation rule:

(23)   word-formation rule for *-th* (tentative)
       phonology: X-/θ/, with various base alternations
       base: X = adjective
       semantics: 'state or property of being X'

While the pattern is quite clear, the number of forms derived by the rule is very limited. In fact, there seem to exist no other transparent forms than those in (22), and it seems generally impossible to create new words on the basis of the pattern. In technical terms, the rule is totally unproductive. In order to form state nouns from adjectives, suffixes like *-ness* or *-ity* are attached, and only the adjectives listed in (22) take *-th*. Thus, the attachment of nominal *-th* can be said to be **lexically conditioned** (or **lexically governed**), which means that the possibility to take *-th* must be listed with each individual lexical item that has this possibility. It is impossible to define the class of *-th*-taking adjectives by some independent property that all possible bases have and all impossible bases don't have. Strictly speaking then, we are not dealing with a rule that can be used to form new words, but with a rule that simply generalizes over the structure of a set of existing complex words. Such rules are sometimes referred to as **redundancy rules** or **word-structure rules**. The redundancy rule for *-th* could look like this:

(24)   redundancy rule for *-th*
        phonology: X-/θ/, X = allomorph of base
        base: {*broad, deep, long, strong, true, warm*}
        semantics: 'state or property of being X'

In most cases, it is not necessary to make the distinction between rules that can be used to coin new words and rules that cannot be used in this way, so that we will often use the term 'word-formation rule' or 'word-formation process' to refer to both kinds of rule.

Before finishing our discussion of word-formation rules, we should address the fact that sometimes new complex words are derived without an existing word-formation rule, but formed on the basis of a single (or very few) model words. For example, *earwitness* 'someone who has heard a crime being commited' was coined on the basis of *eyewitness*, *cheeseburger* on the basis of *hamburger*, and *air-sick* on the basis of *sea-sick*. The process by which these words came into being is called **analogy**, which can be modeled as a proportional relation between words, as illustrated in (25):

(25)   a. a : b :: c : d
        b. eye : eyewitness :: ear : earwitness
        c. ham : hamburger :: cheese : cheeseburger
        d. sea : sea-sick :: air : air-sick

The essence of a proportional analogy is that the relation between two items (a and b in the above formula) is the same as the relation between two other, corresponding items (c and d in our case). The relation that holds between *eye* and *eyewitness* is the same as the relation between *ear* and *earwitness*, *ham* and *hamburger* relate to each other in the same way as do *cheese* and *cheeseburger*, and so on. Quite often, words are analogically derived by deleting a suffix (or supposed suffix), a process called **back-formation**. An example of such a back-formation is the verb *edit* which was derived from the word *editor* by deleting *-or* on the basis of a proportional analogy with word pairs such as *actor–act*. Another example of back-formation is the verb *escalate*, which occurs with two meanings, each of which is derived from a different model word. The first meaning can be paraphrased as 'To climb or reach by means of an escalator . . . To travel on an escalator' (*OED*), and is modeled on *escalator*. The second meaning of *escalate* is roughly synonymous with 'increase in intensity,' which is back-formed from *escalation* which can be paraphrased as 'increase of development by successive stages.'

The words in (25) can be called regular in the sense that their meaning can readily be discerned on the basis of the individual forms which obviously have served as their models. They are, however, irregular, in the sense that no larger pattern, no word-formation rule existed on the basis of which these words could have been coined. Sometimes it may happen that such analogical formations can give rise to larger patterns, as, for example, in the case of *hamburger, cheeseburger, chickenburger, fishburger, vegeburger*, etc. In such cases, the dividing line between analogical patterns and word-formation rules is hard to draw. In fact, if we look at rules we could even argue that analogical relations hold for words that are coined on the basis of rules, as evidenced by the examples in (26):

(26)   big : bigger :: great : greater
        happy : unhappy :: likely : unlikely
        read : readable :: conceive : conceivable

Based on such reasoning, some scholars (e.g. Becker 1990, Skousen 1995) have developed theories that abandon the concept of rule entirely and replace it by the notion of analogy. In other words, it is claimed that there are no morphological rules, but there are analogies across larger or smaller sets of words. Two major theoretical problems need to be solved under such a radical approach. First, it is unclear how the systematic structural restrictions emerge that are characteristic of derivational processes and which in a rule-based framework are an integral part of the rule. Second, it is unclear why certain analogies are often made while others are never made. In a rule-based system this follows from the rule itself.

We will therefore stick to the traditional idea of word-formation rules and to the traditional idea of analogy as a local mechanism, usually involving some degree of unpredictability.

2.4   Multiple affixation

So far, we have mainly dealt with complex words that consist of two elements. However, many complex words contain more than two morphemes. Consider, for example, the adjective *untruthful* or the compound *textbook reader*. The former combines three affixes and a base (*un-*, *tru(e)*, *-th*, and *-ful*), the latter three roots and one suffix (*text*, *book*, *read*, and *-er*). Such multiply affixed or compounded words raise the question of how they are derived and what their internal structure might be. For example, are both affixes in *unregretful* attached in one step, or is *un-* attached to *regretful*, or is *-ful* attached to *unregret*? The three possibilities are given in (27):

(27)   a. *un + regret + ful*
        b. *un + regretful*
        c. *unregret + ful*

The relationship between the three morphemes can also be represented by brackets or by a tree diagram, as in (28):

(28)   a.   [un-regret-ful]

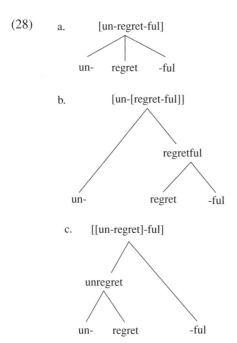

   b.   [un-[regret-ful]]

   c.   [[un-regret]-ful]

How can one decide which structure is correct? The main argument may come from the meaning of the word *unregretful*. The most common paraphrase of this word would probably be something like 'not regretful.' Given that meaning is compositional in this word, such an analysis would clearly speak against structure (28a) and for structure (28b): first, *-ful* creates an adjective by attaching to *regret*, and then the meaning of this derived adjective is manipulated by the prefix *un-*. If *un-* in *unregretful* was a prefix to form the putative noun ?*unregret*, the meaning of *unregretful* should be something like 'full of unregret.' Given that it is not clear what 'unregret' really means, such an analysis is much less straightforward than assuming that *un-* attaches to the adjective *regretful*. Further support for this analysis comes from the general behavior of *un-*, which, as we saw earlier, is a prefix that happily attaches to adjectives, but not so easily to nouns.

Let us look at a second example of multiple affixation, *unaffordable*. Perhaps you agree if I say that of the three representational possibilities, the following is the best:

(29)   [un-[afford-able]]

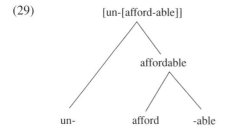

This structure is supported by the semantic analysis ('not affordable'), but also by the fact that *-un* only attaches to verbs if the action or process denoted by the verb can be reversed (cf. again *bind–unbind*). This is not the case with *afford*. Thus *un-afford* is an impossible derivative because it goes against the regular properties of the prefix *un-*. The structure (29), however, is in complete accordance with what we have said about *un-*.

   Sometimes it is not so easy to make a case for one or the other analysis. Consider the following words, in which *-ation* and *re-/de-* are the outermost affixes (we ignore the verbal *-ize* for the moment):

(30)

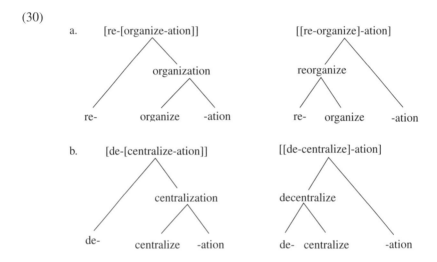

In both cases, the semantics does not really help to determine the structure. *Reorganization* can refer to the organization being redone, or it can refer to the process of reorganizing. Both are possible interpretations with only an extremely subtle difference in meaning (if detectable at all). Furthermore, the prefix *re-* combines with both verbs and nouns (the latter if they denote processes), so that on the basis of the general properties of *re-* no argument can be made in favor of either structure. A similar argumentation holds for *decentralization*.

   To complicate matters further, some complex words with more than one affix seem to have come into being through the **simultaneous** attachment of two affixes. A case in point is *decaffeinate*, for which, at the time of creation, neither *caffeinate* was available as a base word (for the prefixation of *de-*), nor *decaffein* (as the basis for *-ate* suffixation). Such forms are called **parasynthetic** formations, and the process of simultaneous multiple affixation is **parasynthesis**.

2.5   Summary

This chapter started out with a discussion of the various problems involved with the notion of the morpheme. It was shown that the mapping of form and meaning is not always a straightforward matter. For example, extended exponence and subtractive morphology pose serious challenges to traditional morphemic analyses, and morphs with no (or a hard-to-pin-down) meaning are not infrequent. Further complications arise when the variable shape of morphemes, known as allomorphy, is taken into account. We have seen that the choice of the appropriate allomorph can be determined by phonological, morphological, or lexical conditions. Then we have tried to determine two of the many word-formation rules of English, which involved the exemplary discussion of important empirical, theoretical and methodological problems. One of these problems was whether a rule can be used to form new words or whether it is a mere redundancy rule. This is known as the problem of productivity, which will be the topic of the next chapter.

Further reading

For different kinds of introductions to the basic notions and problems concerning morphemic analysis you may consult the textbooks already mentioned in the first chapter (Bauer 1983, 1988; Katamba 1993; Matthews 1991; Spencer 1991; Carstairs-McCarthy 1992). Critical discussion of the notions of morpheme and word-formation rule can be found in the studies by Aronoff (1976) and Anderson (1992). For strictly analogical approaches to morphology, see Becker (1990), Skousen (1995), or Krott et al. (2001).

Exercises

Basic level

Exercise 2.1

Describe three major problems involved in the notion of morpheme. Use the following word pairs for illustration:

a.   *(to) father – (a) father*
       (to) face – (a) face
b.   *David–Dave*
       Patricia–Trish
c.   *bring–brought*
       keep–kept

Exercise 2.2

Discuss the morphological structure of the following words. Are they morphologically complex? How many morphemes do they contain? Provide a meaning for each morpheme that you detect.

> *report   refrain   regard   retry   rest*
> *rephrase   reformat   retain   remain   restate*

Exercise 2.3

Explain the notion of base allomorphy using the following words for illustration. Transcribe the words in phonetic transcription and compare the phonetic forms.

> *active–activity   curious–curiosity   affect–affection   possess–possession*

Advanced level

Exercise 2.4

Determine the internal structure of the following complex words. Use tree diagrams for representing the structure and give arguments for your analysis.

> *uncontrollability   postcolonialism   anti-war-movement*

Exercise 2.5

Determine the allomorphy of the prefix *in-* on the basis of the data below. First, transcribe the prefix in all words below and collect all variants. Some of the variants are easy to spot, others are only determinable by closely listening to the words being spoken in a natural context. Instead of trying to hear the differences yourself you may also consult a pronunciation dictionary (e.g. Jones 1997). Group the data according to the variants and try to determine which kinds of base take which kinds of prefix allomorph and what kind of mechanism is responsible for the allomorphy. Formulate a rule. Test the predictions of your rule against some prefix-base pairs that are not mentioned below.

irregular	*incomprehensible*	*illiterate*
ingenious	*inoffensive*	*inharmonic*
impenetrable	*illegal*	*incompetent*
irresistible	*impossible*	*irresponsible*
immobile	*illogical*	*indifferent*
inconsistent	*innumerable*	*inevitable*

Exercise 2.6

In this chapter we have argued that the only verbs that can be prefixed with *un-* are those that express an action or process which can be reversed. Take this as your initial hypothesis and set up an experiment in which this hypothesis is systematically tested. Imagine that you have ten native speakers of English who volunteer as experimental subjects. There are of course many different experiments imaginable (there is no 'ideal' experiment). Be creative and invent a methodology which makes it possible to obtain results that could potentially falsify the initial hypothesis.

3

Productivity and the mental lexicon

Outline

In this chapter we will look at the mechanisms that are responsible for the fact that some affixes can easily be used to coin new words while other affixes can not. First, the notions of 'possible word' and 'actual word' are explored, which leads to the discussion of how complex words are stored and accessed in the mental lexicon. This turns out to be of crucial importance for the understanding of productivity. Different measures of productivity are introduced and applied to a number of affixes. Finally, some general restrictions on productivity are discussed.

3.1   Introduction: what is productivity?

We have seen in the previous chapter that we can distinguish between redundancy rules that describe the relationship between existing words and word-formation rules that can in addition be used to create new words. Any theory of word-formation would therefore ideally not only describe existing complex words but also determine which kinds of derivative could be formed by the speakers according to the regularities and conditions of the rules of their language. In other words, any word-formation theory should make predictions about which words are possible in a language and which words are not.

Some affixes are often used to create new words, whereas others are less often used, or not used at all, for this purpose. The property of an affix to be used to coin new complex words is referred to as the **productivity** of that affix. Not all affixes possess this property to the same degree; some affixes do not possess it at all. For example, in chapter 2 we saw that nominal -*th* (as in *length*) can only attach to a small number of specified words, but cannot attach to any other words beyond that set. This suffix can therefore be considered unproductive. Even among affixes that can in principle be used to coin new words, there seem to be some that are more productive than others. For example, the suffix -*ness* (as in *cuteness*) gives rise to many more new words than, for example, the suffix *-ish* (as in *apish*). The obvious question now is which mechanisms are responsible for the productivity of a word-formation rule. This is the question we want to address in this chapter. What makes some affixes productive and others unproductive?

3.2   Possible and actual words

A notorious problem in the description of the speakers' morphological competence is that there are quite often unclear restrictions on the possibility of forming (and understanding) new complex words. We have seen, for example, in chapter 2 that *un-* can be freely attached to most adjectives, but not to all, that *un-* occurs with nouns, but only with very few, and that *un-* can occur with verbs, but by no means with all verbs. In our analysis, we could establish some restrictions, but other restrictions remained mysterious. The challenge for the analyst, however, is to propose a word-formation rule that yields (only) the correct set of complex words. Often, word-formation rules that look straightforward and adequate at first sight turn out to be problematic upon closer inspection. A famous example of this kind (see, for example, Aronoff 1976) is the attachment of the nominalizing suffix *-ity* to adjectival bases ending in *-ous*, which is attested with forms such as *curious–curiosity*, *capacious–capacity*, *monstrous–monstrosity*. However, *-ity* cannot be attached to all bases of this type, as evidenced by the impossibility of *glorious–*gloriosity* or *furious–*furiosity*. What is responsible for this limitation on the productivity of *-ity*?

Another typical problem with many postulated word-formation rules is that they are often formulated in such a way that they prohibit formations that are nevertheless attested. For example, it is often assumed that person nouns ending in *-ee* (such as *employee, nominee*) can only be formed with verbs that take an object ('employ someone,' 'nominate someone'), so-called transitive verbs. Such *-ee* derivatives denote the object of the base verb, i.e. an employee is 'someone who is employed,' a nominee is 'someone who is nominated.' However, sometimes, though rarely, even intransitive verbs take *-ee* (e.g. *escape–escapee*, *stand–standee*), or even nouns (*festschrift–festschriftee* 'someone to whom a festschrift is dedicated'). Ideally, one would find an explanation for these apparently strange conditions on the productivity of these affixes.

A further problem that we would like to solve is why some affixes occur with a large number of words, whereas others are only attested with a small number of derivatives. What conditions these differences in proliferance? Intuitively, the notion of productivity must make reference to the speaker's ability to form new words and to the conditions the language system imposes on new words.

This brings us to a central distinction in morphology, the one between **possible** (or 'potential') and **actual words**.

A possible, or potential, word can be defined as a word whose semantic, morphological or phonological structure is in accordance with the rules and regularities of the language. It is obvious that before one can assign the status of 'possible word' to a given form, these rules and regularities need to be stated as clearly as possible. It is equally clear that very often the status of a word as possible is uncontroversial. For example, it seems that all transitive verbs can be turned into adjectives by the attachment of *-able*. Thus, *affordable*, *readable*, *manageable* are all possible words. Notably, these forms are also semantically transparent, i.e. their meaning is predictable on the basis of the word-formation rule according to which they have been formed. Predictability of meaning is therefore another property of potential words.

In the case of the potential words *affordable*, *readable*, *manageable*, these words are also actual words, because they have already been coined and used by speakers. But not all possible words are existing words, because, to use again the example of *-able*, the speakers of English have not coined *-able* derivatives on the basis of each and every transitive verb of English. For instance, neither the *OED* nor any other source I consulted lists *cannibalizable*. Hence this word is not an existing word, in the sense that it is used by the speakers of English. However, it is a possible word of English because it is in accordance with the rules of English word-formation, and if speakers had a practical application for it they could happily use it.

Having clarified the notion of a possible word, we can turn to the question of what an actual (or existing) word is. A loose definition would simply say that actual words are those words that are in use. However, when can we consider a word as being 'in use'? Does it mean that some speaker has observed it being used somewhere? Or that the majority of the speech community is familiar with it? Or that it is listed in dictionaries? The problem is that there is variation between individual speakers. Not all words one speaker knows are also known by other speakers, i.e. the mental lexicon of one speaker is never completely identical to any other speaker's mental lexicon. Furthermore, it is even not completely clear when we can say that a given word is 'known' by a speaker, or 'listed' in her/his mental lexicon. For example, we know that the more frequent a word is the more easily we can memorize it and retrieve it later from our lexicon. This entails, however, that 'knowledge of a word' is a gradual notion, and that we know some words better than others. Note that this is also the underlying assumption in foreign language learning where there is often a distinction made between the so-called 'active' and 'passive' vocabulary. The active vocabulary obviously consists of words that we know 'better' than those that constitute our passive vocabulary. The same distinction holds for native speakers, who also actively use only a subset of the words that they are familiar with. Another instance of graded knowledge of words is the fact that, even as native speakers, we often only know that we have heard or read a certain word before, but do not know what it means.

Coming back to the individual differences between speakers and the idea of 'actual words,' it seems nevertheless clear that there is a large overlap between the vocabularies of the individual native speakers of a language. It is this overlap that makes it possible to speak of 'the vocabulary of the English language,' although, strictly speaking, this is an abstraction from the mental lexicons of the speakers. To come down to a manageable definition of 'actual word' we can state that if we find a word attested in a text, or used by a speaker in a conversation, and if there are other speakers of the language that can understand this word, we can say with some confidence that it is an actual word. The class of actual words contains of course both morphologically simplex and complex words, and among the complex words we find many that do behave according to the present-day rules of English word-formation. However, we also find many actual words that do not behave according to these rules. For example, *affordable* ('can be afforded'), *readable* ('can be (easily) read'), and *manageable* ('can be managed') are all actual words in accordance with the word-formation rule for *-able* words, which states that *-able* derivatives have the meaning 'can be Xed,' whereas *knowledgeable* (*'can be knowledged') or *probable* (*'can be probed') are actual words which do not behave according to the word-formation rule for *-able*. The crucial difference between actual and possible words is then that only actual words may be idiosyncratic, i.e. not in accordance with the word-formation rules of English, whereas possible words are never idiosyncratic.

We have explored the difference between actual and possible words and may now turn to the mechanisms that allow speakers to form new possible words. We have already briefly touched upon the question of how words are stored in the mental lexicon. In the following section, we will discuss this issue in more detail, because it has important repercussions on the nature of word-formation rules and their productivity.

3.3   Complex words in the lexicon

Idiosyncratic complex words must be stored in the mental lexicon, be-cause they cannot be derived on the basis of rules. But what about complex words that are completely regular, i.e. words that are in complete accordance with the word-formation rule on the basis of which they are formed? There are differ-ent models of the mental lexicon conceivable. In some approaches to morphol-ogy the lexicon is seen "like a prison – it contains only the lawless" (Di Sciullo and Williams 1987: 3). In this view the lexicon would contain only information which is not predictable, which means that in this type of lexicon only simplex words, roots, and affixes would have a place, but no regular complex words. This is also the principle that is applied to regular dictionaries, which, for example, do not list regular past-tense forms of verbs, because these can be generated by rule and need not be listed. The question is, however, whether our brain really follows the organizational principles established by dictionary makers. There is growing psycholinguistic evidence that it does not and that both simplex and complex words, regular and idiosyncratic, can be listed in the lexicon (in addition to the word-formation rules and redundancy rules that relate words to one another).

But why would one want to bar complex words from being listed in the lexicon in the first place? The main argument for excluding these forms from the lexicon is economy of storage. According to this argument, the lexicon should be minimally **redundant**, i.e. no information should be listed more than once in the mental lexicon, and everything that is predictable by rule need not be listed. This would be the most economical way of storing lexical items. Although non-redundancy is theoretically elegant and economical, there is a lot of evidence that the human brain does not strictly avoid redundancy in the representation of lexical items, and that the way words are stored in the human brain is not totally economical. The reason for this lack of economy of storage is that apart from storage, the brain must also be optimized with regard to the processing of words. What does 'processing' mean in this context?

In normal speech, speakers utter about three words per second, and given that this includes also the planning and articulation of the message to be conveyed, speakers and hearers must be able to access and retrieve words from the mental lexicon within fragments of seconds. As we will shortly see, sometimes this necessity of quick access may be in conflict with the necessity of economical storage, because faster processing may involve more storage and this potential conflict is often solved in favor of faster processing.

For illustration, consider the two possible ways of representing the complex adjective *affordable* in our mental lexicon. One possibility is that this word is decomposed in its two constituent morphemes *afford* and *-able* and that the whole word is not stored at all. This would be extremely economical in terms of storage, since the verb *afford* and the suffix *-able* stored anyway, and the properties of the word *affordable* are entirely predictable on the basis of the properties of the verb *afford* and the properties of the suffix *-able*. However, this kind of storage would involve rather high processing costs, because each time a speaker wanted to say or understand the word *affordable*, her/his language processor would have to look up both morphemes, put them together (or decompose them) and compute the meaning of the derivative on the basis of the constituent morphemes. An alternative way of storage would be to store the word *affordable* without decomposition, i.e. as a whole. Since the verb *afford* and the suffix *-able* and its word-formation rule are also stored, whole-word storage of *affordable* would certainly be more costly in terms of storage, but it would have a clear advantage in processing: whenever the word *affordable* needs to be used, only one item has to be retrieved from the lexicon, and no rule has to be applied. This example shows how economy of storage and economy of processing must be counter-balanced to achieve maximum functionality. But how does that work in detail? Which model of storage is correct? Surprisingly, there is evidence for both kinds of storage, whole-word and decomposed, with frequency of occurrence playing an important role.

In most current models of morphological processing access to morphologically complex words in the mental lexicon works in two ways: by direct access to the whole-word representation (the so-called **whole-word route**) or by access to the decomposed elements (the so-called **decomposition route**). This means that each incoming complex word is simultaneously processed in parallel in two ways. On the decomposition route it is decomposed in its parts and the parts are being looked up individually; on the whole-word route the word is looked up as a whole in the mental lexicon. The faster route wins the race and the item is retrieved in that way. The two routes are schematically shown in (1):

(1)

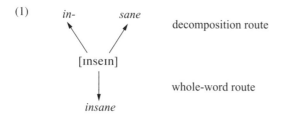

How does frequency come in here? As mentioned above, there is a strong tendency that more frequent words are more easily stored and accessed than less frequent words. Psycholinguists have created the metaphor of **resting activation** to account for this phenomenon (and other phenomena). The idea is that words are sitting in the lexicon, waiting to be called up or 'activated' when the speaker wants to use them in speech production or perception. If such a word is retrieved at relatively short intervals, it is thought that its activation never completely drops down to zero in between. The remaining activation is called 'resting activation,' and this becomes higher the more often the word is retrieved. Thus, in psycholinguistic experiments it can be observed that more frequent words are more easily activated by speakers, such words are therefore said to have a higher resting activation. Less frequent words have a lower resting activation.

Other experiments have also shown that when speakers search for a word in their mental lexicon, not only the target word is activated but also semantically and phonologically similar words. Thus lexical search can be modeled as activation spreading through the lexicon. Usually only the target item is (successfully) retrieved, which means that the activation of the target must have been strongest.

Now assume that a low-frequency complex word enters the speech-processing system of the hearer. Given that low-frequency items have a low resting activation, access to the whole-word representation of this word (if there is a whole-word representation available at all) will be rather slow, so that the decomposition route will win the race. If there is no whole-word representation available, for example in the case of newly coined words, decomposition is the only way to process the word. If, however, the complex word is extremely frequent, it will have a high resting activation, will be retrieved very fast and can win the race, even if decomposition is also in principle possible.

Let us look at some complex words and their frequencies for illustration. The first problem we face is to determine how frequently speakers use a certain word. This methodological problem can be solved with the help of large electronic text collections, so-called 'corpora.' Such corpora are huge collections of spoken and written texts which can be used for studies of vocabulary, syntax, semantics, etc., or for making dictionaries. In our case, we will make use of the **British National Corpus** (BNC). This is a very large representative collection of texts and conversations from all kinds of sources, which is available on the internet. The corpus amounts to about 100 million words, c. 90 million of which are taken from written sources, c. 10 million of which represent spoken language. For reasons of clarity we have to distinguish between the number of different words (the so-called **types**) and the overall number of words in a corpus (the so-called **tokens**). The 100 million words of the BNC are tokens, which represent about 940,000 types. We can look up the frequency of words in the BNC by checking the word-frequency list provided by the corpus compilers. The two most frequent words in English, for example, are the definite article *the* (which occurs about 6.1 million times in the BNC), followed by the verb BE, which (counting all its different forms *am*, *are*, *be*, *been*, *being*, *is*, *was*, *were*) has a frequency of c. 4.2 million, meaning that it occurs 4.2 million times in the corpus.

For illustrating the frequencies of derived words in a large corpus let us look at the frequencies of some of the words with the suffix *-able* as they occur in the BNC. In (2), I give the first twenty *-able* derivatives (in alphabetical order) from the word list for the written part of the BNC corpus. Note that the inclusion of the form *affable* in this list of *-able* derivatives may be controversial (see section

4.2, or exercise 4.1, for a discussion of the methodological problems involved in extracting lists of complex words from a corpus).

(2)   Frequencies of -*able* derivatives in the BNC (written corpus)

-*able* derivative	frequency	-*able* derivative	frequency
abominable	84	actionable	87
absorbable	1	actualizable	1
abstractable	2	adaptable	230
abusable	1	addressable	12
acceptable	3416	adjustable	369
accountable	611	admirable	468
accruable	1	admissable	2
achievable	176	adorable	66
acid-extractable	1	advisable	516
actable	1	affable	111

There are huge differences observable between the different -*able* derivatives. While *acceptable* has a frequency of 3416 occurrences, *absorbable*, *abusable*, *accruable*, *acid-extractable*, *actable*, and *actualizable* occur only once among the 90 million words of that sub-corpus. For the reasons outlined above, high-frequency words such as *acceptable* are highly likely to have a whole-word representation in the mental lexicon although they are perfectly regular.

To summarize, it was shown that frequency of occurrence plays an important role in the storage, access, and retrieval of both simplex and complex words. Infrequent complex words have a strong tendency to be decomposed. By contrast, highly frequent forms, be they completely regular or not, tend to be stored as whole words in the lexicon. On the basis of these psycholinguistic arguments, the notion of a non-redundant lexicon should be rejected.

But what has all this to do with productivity? This will become obvious in the next section, where we will see that (and why) productive processes are characterized by a high proportion of low-frequency words.

3.4   Measuring productivity

We have argued above that productivity is a gradual phenomenon, which means that some morphological processes are more productive than others. That this view is widespread is evidenced by the fact that in the literature on word-formation, we frequently find affixes being labeled as "quasi-," "marginally," "semi-," "fully," "quite," "immensely," and "very productive." Completely un-productive or fully productive processes thus only mark the end-points of a scale. But how can we find out whether an affix is productive, or how productive it is? How do we know where on that scale a given affix is to be located?

Assuming that productivity is defined as the *possibility* of creating a new word, it should in principle be possible to estimate or quantify the probability of the oc-currence of newly created words of a given **morphological category** (understood here as the set of words that share a crucial morphological property, e.g. the same suffix). This is the essential insight behind Bolinger's definition of productivity as "the statistical readiness with which an element enters into new combinations" (1948: 18). Since the formulation of this insight more than half a century ago, a number of productivity measures have been proposed.

There is one quantitative measure that is probably the most widely used and the most widely rejected at the same time. According to this measure, the productivity of an affix can be discerned by counting the number of attested different words with that affix at a given point in time. This has also been called the type frequency of an affix. The severe problem with this measure is that there can be many words with a given affix, but nevertheless speakers will not use the suffix to make up new words. An example of such a suffix is -*ment*, which in earlier centuries led to the coinage of hundreds of then new words. Many of these are still in use, but today's speakers hardly ever employ -*ment* to create a new word and the suffix should therefore be considered as rather unproductive (cf. Bauer 2001: 196). Thus the sheer number of types with a given affix does not tell us whether this figure reflects the productivity of that affix in the past or its present potential to create new words.

Counting derivatives can nevertheless be a fruitful way of determining the pro-ductivity of an affix, that is, if one does not count all derivatives with a certain affix in use at a given point in time, but only those derivatives that were newly coined in a given period, the so-called **neologisms**. In doing this, one can show that for instance an affix may have given rise to many neologisms in the eighteenth century but not in the twentieth century. The methodological problem with this measure is of course to reliably determine the number of neologisms in a given period. This can be done with the help of very good dictionaries. Students of English, for example, are in the advantageous position that there is a dictionary like the *Oxford English Dictionary* (*OED*). This dictionary has about 500,000 entries and aims at giving thorough and complete information on all words of the language and thus the development of the English vocabulary from its earliest attestations onwards. The CD version of the *OED* can be searched in various ways, so that it is possible to obtain lists of neologisms for a given period of time with only a few mouse-clicks (and some additional analytical work; see the discussion in the next chapter).

For example, for the twentieth century we find 284 new verbs in *-ize* (Plag 1999: ch. 5) in the *OED*, which shows that this is a productive suffix. The power of the *OED* as a tool for measuring productivity should however not be overestimated, because quite a number of new words escape the eyes of the *OED* lexicographers. For instance, the number of *-ness* neologisms listed in the *OED* for the twentieth century (N=279, Plag 1999: 98) roughly equals the number of *-ize* neologisms, although it is clear from many studies that *-ness* is by far the most productive suffix of English. Or consider the highly productive adverb-forming suffix *-wise* 'with regard to,' of which only eleven neologisms are listed in the *OED* (e.g. "Weatherwise the last week has been real nice," 1975). Thus, in those cases where the *OED* does not list many neologisms it may be true that the affix is unproductive, but it is also possible that the pertinent neologisms simply have been overlooked (or not included for some other, unknown reason). Only in those cases where the *OED* lists many neologisms can we be sure that the affix in question must be productive. Given these problems involved with dictionary-based measures (even if a superb dictionary like the *OED* is available) one should also look for other, and perhaps more reliable, measures of productivity.

There are measures that take Bolinger's idea of probability seriously and try to estimate how likely it is that a speaker or hearer meets a newly coined word of a certain morphological category. Unfortunately it is practically impossible to investigate the entirety of all utterances (oral and written) in a language in a given period of time. However, one can imagine investigating a representative sample of the language, as they are nowadays available in the form of the large text corpora already introduced above. One way to use such corpora is to simply count the number of types (i.e. the number of different words) with a given affix. This has, however, the disadvantage already discussed above, namely that this might reflect past rather than present productivity. This measure has been called **extent of use** (e.g. Baayen 1993). A more fruitful way of measuring productivity is to take into account how often derivatives are used, i.e. their token frequency. But why, might you ask, should the token frequency of words be particularly interesting for productivity studies? What is the link between frequency and the possibility of coining new words? The relationship between frequency and productivity has been explored in the writings of Harald Baayen and his collaborators (see, for example, Baayen 1993 and the references listed at the end of this chapter) and I will outline the main ideas in the following paragraphs.

In order to understand the relationship between frequency and productivity, we have to return to the insight that high-frequency words (e.g. *acceptable*) are more likely to be stored as whole words in the mental lexicon than are low-frequency words (e.g. *actualizable*). By definition, newly coined words have not been used before, they are low-frequency words and don't have an entry in our mental lexicon. But how can we understand these new words, if we don't know them? We can understand them in those cases where an available word-formation rule allows us to decompose the word into its constituent morphemes and compute the meaning on the basis of the meaning of the parts. The word-formation rule in the mental lexicon guarantees that even complex words with extremely low frequency can be understood. If, in contrast, words of a morphological category are all highly frequent, these words will tend to be stored in the mental lexicon, and a word-formation pattern will be less readily available for the perception and production of newly coined forms.

One other way of looking at this is the following. Each time a low-frequency complex word enters the processing system, this word will be decomposed, because there is no whole-word representation available. This decomposition will strengthen the representation of the affix, which will in turn make the affix readily available for use with other bases, which may lead to the coinage of new derivatives. If, however, only high-frequency complex words enter the system, there will be a strong tendency towards whole-word storage, and the affix will not be so strongly represented; it will therefore not be so readily available for new formations.

In sum, this means that unproductive morphological categories will be characterized by a preponderance of words with rather high frequencies and by a small number of words with low frequencies. With regard to productive processes, we expect the opposite, namely large numbers of low-frequency words and small numbers of high-frequency words.

Let us look at some examples to illustrate and better understand this rather theoretical reasoning. We will concentrate on the items with the lowest possible frequency, the so-called **hapax legomena**. Hapax legomena (or **hapaxes** for short) are words that occur only once in a corpus. For example, *absorbable* and *accruable* from the table in (2) above are hapaxes. The crucial point now is that, for the reasons explained in the previous paragraph, the number of hapaxes of a given morphological category should correlate with the number of neologisms of that category, so that the number of hapaxes can be seen as an indicator of productivity. Note that it is not claimed that a hapax legomenon *is* a neologism. A hapax legomenon is defined with respect to a given corpus, and could therefore simply be a rare word of the language (instead of a newly coined derivative) or some weird ad-hoc invention by an imaginative speaker, as sometimes found in poetry or advertisements. The latter kinds of coinages are, however, extremely rare and can be easily weeded out.

The size of the corpus plays an important role in determining the nature of hapaxes. When this corpus is small, most hapax legomena will indeed be well-known words of the language. However, as the corpus size increases, the proportion of neologisms among the hapax legomena increases, and it is precisely among the hapax legomena that the greatest number of neologisms appear.

In the following, we will show how this claim can be empirically tested. First, we will investigate whether words with a given affix that are not hapaxes are more likely to be listed in a very large dictionary than the hapaxes with that affix. Under the assumption that unlisted words have a good chance of being real neologisms, we should expect to find more words among the hapaxes that are not listed than among the more frequent words. We will use as a dictionary *Webster's Third New International Dictionary* (*Webster's Third* for short, 450,000 entries). As a second test, we will investigate how many of the hapaxes are listed in *Webster's Third* in order to see how great the chances are of encountering a real neologism among the hapaxes. In (3) I have taken again our *-able* derivatives from above as extracted from the BNC (remember that this was a randomly picked sample) and looked them up in *Webster's Third*. The words are ranked according to frequency.

(3)   *-able* derivatives: BNC frequency and listedness in *Webster's Third*

-able derivative	token frequency	listed in *Webster's Third*
absorbable	1	yes
abusable	1	**no**
accruable	1	**no**
acid-extractable	1	**no**
actable	1	yes
actualizable	1	yes
abstractable	2	**no**
admissable	2	**no**
addressable	12	**no**
adorable	66	yes
abominable	84	yes
actionable	87	yes
affable	111	yes
achievable	176	yes
adaptable	230	yes
adjustable	369	yes
admirable	468	yes
advisable	516	yes
accountable	611	yes
acceptable	3416	yes

Of the six hapaxes in (3), three are not listed. Furthermore, three other low-frequency forms (*abstractable, addressable, admissable*) are also not listed. The remaining eleven items have a frequency of 66 plus and are all listed in *Webster's Third*. Although the words in the table are only an extremely small, randomly picked sample, it clearly shows that indeed it is among the lowest-frequency items that we find the largest number of words not listed in a large dictionary, hence likely to be newly coined. For a much more detailed illustration of this point, see Baayen and Renouf (1996).

A second attempt to substantiate the claim that the number of hapaxes is indicative of the number of neologisms is made in (4). The first twenty hapaxes (in alphabetical order) among the BNC -*able* derivatives (written corpus) have been checked in *Webster's Third*.

(4)   BNC hapaxes and their entries in *Webster's Third*

-able derivative	Listed in *Webster's Third*	*-able* derivative	Listed in *Webster's Third*
absorbable	yes	amusable	**no**
abusable	**no**	annotatable	**no**
accruable	**no**	applaudable	yes
acid-extractable	**no**	approvable	**no**
actable	yes	arrangeable	**no**
actualizable	yes	assessionable	yes
affirmable	yes	auctionable	**no**
again-fashionable	**no**	biteable	yes
aidable	**no**	blackmailable	**no**
air-droppable	**no**	blameable	**no**

The table in (4) shows that the number of non-listed words is high among the hapaxes: thirteen out of twenty hapaxes are not listed in *Webster's Third*.

Our two tests have shown that we can use hapaxes to measure productivity. The higher the number of hapaxes with a given affix, the higher the number of neologisms, hence the higher the likelihood of meeting a newly coined word, i.e. the affix's productivity.

Now in order to return to our aim of estimating the probability of finding a neologism among the words of a morphological category, we calculate the ratio of the number of hapaxes with a given affix and the number of all tokens containing that affix. What does that mean? Metaphorically speaking, we go through all attested tokens with a given affix and pick out all words that we encounter only once. If we divide the number of these words (i.e. the hapaxes) by the number of all tokens, we arrive at the probability of finding a hitherto unattested word (i.e.

'new' in terms of the corpus) among all the words of that category. For example, if there are 100 tokens with only two hapaxes, the probability of encountering a new word is 2 percent. Statistically, every fiftieth word will be a hapax. This probability has been called 'productivity in the narrow sense,' and can be expressed by the following formula, where P stands for 'productivity in the narrow sense,' n_1^{aff} for the number of hapaxes with a given affix af and N^{aff} stands for the number of all tokens with that affix.

(5) $$P = \frac{n_1^{\text{aff}}}{N^{\text{aff}}}$$

The productivity P of an affix can now be precisely calculated and interpreted. A large number of hapaxes leads to a high value of P, thus indicating a productive morphological process. Conversely, large numbers of high-frequency items lead to a high value of N^{aff}, hence to a decrease of P, indicating low productivity. To understand this better, some sample calculations might be useful.

In (6) I have listed the frequencies of a number of suffixes as they occur in the BNC (written corpus, from Plag et al. 1999):

(6)   Frequencies of affixes in the BNC (written corpus)

Affix	V	N	n_1	P
-able	933	140627	311	0.0022
-ful 'measure'	136	2615	60	0.023
-ful 'property'	154	77316	22	0.00028
-ize	658	100496	212	0.0021
-ness	2466	106957	943	0.0088
-wise	183	2091	128	0.061

V = type frequency/'extent of use',
N = token frequency, n_1 = hapax frequency,
$P = n_1/N$ 'productivity in the narrow sense'

With regard to all four measures we can see enormous differences between suffixes. Looking at the column for N, we can state that some affixes have high token figures (see -able, -ness, and -ize), which means that at least some of the words with these suffixes are used very often. Other kinds of derivatives are not used very often and have rather low token frequencies (in particular -wise and -ful 'measure').

Let us discuss the significance of the figures in table (6) in an exemplary fashion using the two -ful suffixes which obviously – and perhaps surprisingly – differ from each other significantly. What is called 'measure -ful' here is a nominal suffix used to form so-called measure partitive nouns such as cupful, handful, *spoonful*, while what is called 'property -*ful*' here is an adjectival suffix used to form qualitative adjectives like *careful, forgetful*, etc. The two homophonous suffixes have a similar extent of use V (136 vs. 154 different types) but differ greatly in the other columns of the table. Thus, words with measure -*ful* are not used very often in comparison to words with property -*ful* (N=2615 vs. N=77316). Many of the adjectival derivatives are highly frequent, as is evidenced by the frequency spectrum of these words, illustrated in (7). I list the frequencies for the six most frequent items:

(7)   Frequencies of the most frequent adjectival -*ful* derivatives (BNC, written corpus)

derivative	frequency
successful	10366
useful	9479
beautiful	7964
powerful	7064
careful	4546
wonderful	4202

These items alone account for more than half of the tokens of adjectival -*ful*, and each individual item is much more frequent than all nominal, i.e. 'measure,' -*ful* derivatives together. Comparing the number of hapaxes and the *P* values, we find a high figure for nominal -*ful*, which is a sure sign of its productivity. For illustration of the potential of nominal -*ful* to be used for the creation of new forms, let us look at the two hapaxes *bootful* and *stickful* and the contexts in which they occur in the BNC:

(8)   We would have fished Tony out two or three kilometres down after the water had knocked him around a bit, and given him a dreadful **bootful** since he was wearing his Lundhags.

(9)   As the men at the windlass rope heaved and a long timber started to rise up and swing, the wheel on the pulley squealed like an injured dog and the man stationed at the top of the wall took a **stickful** of thick grease from a pot, leaned out, and worked it into the axle.

Returning to table (6), we have to state that the measures often seem to contradict each other. If we tried to rank the suffixes in terms of productivity, we would get different rankings depending on the type of measure we use, which may seem somewhat unsatisfactory. However, we have to keep in mind that each measure highlights a different aspect of productivity. In particular, these aspects are

- the number of forms with a given affix ('extent of use' V)
- the number of neologisms attested in a given period
- the number of hapaxes in a given corpus (as an indicator of the amount of newly coined derivatives)
- the probability of encountering new formations among all derivatives of a certain morphological category ('productivity in the narrow sense' *P*).

To summarize our discussion of how productivity can be measured, it should have become clear that the different measures have the great advantage that they make certain intuitive aspects of morphological productivity explicit and calculable. Furthermore, we have learned that productivity is largely a function of the frequency of words and that the reason for the connection between frequency and productivity lies in the nature of the storage and processing of (complex) words in the lexicon.

3.5   Constraining productivity

Having quantitatively assessed that a certain process is productive or more or less productive than another one, the obvious next question is which factors influence the relative productivity of a given process?

One factor that may first come to mind is of course the usefulness of a newly coined word for the speakers of the language. But what are new words good for anyway? Why would speakers want to make up new words in the first place? Basically, we can distinguish three major functions of word-formation. Consider the examples in (10) through (12), which illustrate the three functions:

(10)   a. The Time Patrol also had to *unmurder* Capistrano's great-grandmother, *unmarry* him from the pasha's daughter in 1600, and *uncreate* those three kids he had fathered. (from Kastovsky 1986: 594)

         b. A patient . . . was etherised, and had a limb amputated . . . without the infliction of any pain. (from the *OED* entry for *etherize*)

(11)   a. Faye usually *works* in a different department. She is such a good *worker* that every department wants to have her on their staff.

         b. Yes, George is extremely *slow*. But it is not his *slowness* that I find most irritating.

(12)   a. Come here, *sweetie*, let me kiss you.

         b. Did you bring your wonderful *doggie*, my darling?

In (10a), the writer needed three words to designate three new concepts, namely the reversal of the actions murdering, marrying, and creating. This is an example of the so-called labeling or referential function. In such cases, a new word is created in order to give a name to a new concept or thing. Another example of this function is given in (10b). After the discovery of ether as an anaesthetic substance, physicians needed a term that designated the action of applying ether to patients, and the word *etherize* was coined.

Examples (11a) and (11b) are instances of the second major function of word-formation, syntactic recategorization. The motivation for syntactic recategorization is often the condensation of information. Longer phrases and even whole clauses can be substituted by single complex words, which not only makes life easier for speakers and writers (cf. also *his clumsiness* vs. *that he was always so clumsy*), but can also serve to create stylistic variation, as in (11a), or text cohesion, as in (11b).

Finally, example (12) shows that speakers coin words to express an attitude (in this case fondness of the person or animal referred to by the derivative). No matter which function a particular derivative serves in a particular situation, intended usefulness is a necessary prerequisite for the emergence of productively formed derivatives.

But not all potentially useful words are actually created and used, which means that there must be certain restrictions at work. What kinds of restrictions are conceivable? We must distinguish between, on the one hand, the general possibility to apply a word-formation rule to form a new word and, on the other hand, the opportunity to use such newly coined derivatives in speech. Both aspects are subject to different kinds of restriction, namely those restrictions that originate in problems of language use (so-called **pragmatic restrictions**) and those restrictions that originate in problems of language structure (so-called **structural restrictions**). We will discuss each type of restriction in turn (using the terms 'restriction' and 'constraint' interchangeably).

3.5.1   Pragmatic restrictions

Perhaps the most obvious of the usage-based factors influencing productivity is fashion. The rise and fall of affixes like *mega-*, *giga-*, *mini-* or *-nik* is an example of the result of extra-linguistic developments in society which make certain words or morphological elements desirable to use.

Another pragmatic requirement new lexemes must meet is that they denote something nameable. Although the nameability requirement is rather ill-defined, it captures a significant insight: the concepts encoded by derivational categories are rather simple and general (e.g. adjectival *un-* 'not X,' verbal *-en* 'make X,' etc.) and may not be highly specific or complex, as illustrated in the example of an unlikely denominal verb-forming category given by Rose (1973: 516): "grasp NOUN in the left hand and shake vigorously while standing on the right foot in a 2.5 gallon galvanized pail of corn-meal-mush."

The problem with pragmatic restrictions is that, given a seemingly impossible new formation, it is not clear whether it is ruled out on structural grounds or on the basis of pragmatic considerations. A closer look at the structural restrictions involved often reveals that a form is impossible due to pertinent phonological, morphological, syntactic, or semantic restrictions. Pragmatic restrictions are thus best conceived as operating only on the set of structurally possible derivatives. Which kinds of restrictions can constrain this set will become clear in the next section.

3.5.2   Structural restrictions

Before we can say anything specific about the role of usage factors that may preclude the formation of a certain derivative we have to investigate which structural factors restrict the productivity of the rule in question. In other words, we should first aim at describing the class of possible derivatives of a given category as precisely as possible in structural terms, and then ask ourselves which pragmatic factors influence its application rate.

Structural restrictions in word-formation may concern the traditional levels of linguistic analysis, i.e. phonology, morphology, syntax, and semantics. A general question that arises from the study of such restrictions is which of these should be considered to be peculiar to the particular word-formation rule in question and which restrictions are of a more general kind that operates on all (or at least some classes of) morphological processes. In this section we will discuss restrictions that are only operative with a specific process and do not constrain derivational morphology in a principled way. More general constraints will be discussed in section 3.5.3.

Rule-specific constraints may concern the properties of the base or of the derived word. Let us start with phonological constraints, which can make reference to individual sounds and to phenomena beyond the individual sound, such as syllable structure or stress. Have a look at the examples in (13) and try to find out which phonological properties the respective derivatives or base words share:

(13)   Noun-forming *-al*

arrive	→	arrival	*but*	enter	→	*enteral
betray	→	betrayal	*but*	promise	→	*promiseal
construe	→	construal	*but*	manage	→	*manageal
deny	→	denial	*but*	answer	→	*answeral
propose	→	proposal	*but*	forward	→	*forwardal

The data in (13) illustrate a stress-related restriction. Nominal *-al* only attaches to verbs that end in a stressed syllable. Hence, verbs ending in an unstressed syllable are a priori excluded as possible bases. Note that this restriction does not mean that any verb ending in a stressed syllable can take -*al*. That such a generalization is wrong can be easily tested by trying to attach -*al* to stress-final verbs such as *deláy, expláin, applý, obtáin*. Obviously, this is not possible (cf. **delayal, *explainal, *applial, *obtainal*). So, having final stress is only one (of perhaps many) prerequisites that a base form must fulfill to become eligible for nominal -*al* suffixation.

A second example of phonological restrictions can be seen in (14), which lists typical verbal derivatives in -*en*, alongside impossible derivatives. Before reading on, try to state as clearly as possible the differences between the items in (14a) and (14b), and (14a) and (14c), paying specific attention to the sound (and not the letter!) immediately preceding the suffix, and the number of syllables:

(14)   Verb-forming -*en*
         a. blacken   ←   black
            fatten   ←   fat
            lengthen   ←   long/length
            loosen   ←   loose
            widen   ←   wide
         b. *finen   ←   fine
            *dullen   ←   dull
            *highen   ←   high
            *lo[ŋ]en   ←   long
            *lowen   ←   low
         c. *candiden   ←   candid
            *equivalenten   ←   equivalent
            *expensiven   ←   expensive
            *hilariousen   ←   hilarious
            *validen   ←   valid

(14a) and (14b) show that suffixation of verbal -*en* is subject to a segmental restriction. The last sound (or 'segment') of the base can be /k/, /t/, /θ/, /s/, /d/, but must not be /n/, /ŋ/, /l/, or a vowel. What may look like two arbitrary sets of sounds is in fact two classes that can be distinguished by the manner in which they are produced. Phonologists recognize the two classes as 'obstruents' and 'sonorants.' Obstruents are sounds that are produced by a severe obstruction of the airstream. Thus, with sounds such as /k/, /t/, and /d/ (the so-called stops), the airstream is completely blocked and then suddenly released; with sounds such as /θ/, /s/ (the so-called fricatives) the air has to pass through a very small gap, which creates a lot of friction (hence the term 'fricative'). With sonorants, the air coming out of the lungs is not nearly as severely obstructed, but rather gently manipulated, to the effect that the air pressure is the same everywhere in the vocal tract. The generalization concerning -*en* now is that this suffix only attaches to base-final obstruents. Looking at the data in (14c), a second restriction on -*en* derivatives emerges, namely that *-en* does not take bases that have more than one syllable.

Apart from being sensitive to phonological constraints, affixes can be sensitive to the morphological structure of their base words. An example of such a morphological constraint at work is the suffix combination *-ize-ation*. Virtually every word ending in the suffix *-ize* can be turned into a noun only by adding *-ation*. Other conceivable nominal suffixes, such as *-ment, -al, -age*, etc., are ruled out by this morphological restriction imposed on *-ize* derivatives (cf., for example, *colonization* vs. **colonizement, *colonizal* or **colonizage*).

If we consider the suffix *-ee* (as in *employee*) and its possible and impossible derivatives, it becomes apparent that there must be a semantic restriction that allows *squeezee* to be used in (15), but disallows it in (16):

(15)   I'd discovered that if I hugged the right side of the road, drivers would be more reluctant to move to their left thereby creating a squeeze play with me being the squeezee. (from the internet, http://www.atlantic.net/~tavaresv/pacweek3.htm)

(16)   After making himself a glass of grapefruit juice, John threw the *squeezees away. (from Barker 1998: 710)

The pertinent restriction is that *-ee* derivatives generally must refer to sentient entities. Squeezed-out grapefruits are not sentient, which prohibits the use of an *-ee* derivative to refer to them.

Finally, productivity restrictions can make reference to syntactic properties. One of the most commonly mentioned ones is the restriction of word-formation rules to members of a certain syntactic category. We have already introduced such restrictions in chapter 2, when we talked about the proper formulation of the word-formation rule for the prefix *un-*, which seems to be largely restricted to adjectives and (certain kinds of) verbs. Other examples would be the suffix *-able* which normally attaches to verbs, or the adjectival suffix *-al*, which attaches to nouns.

In summary, it is clear that rule-specific structural restrictions play a prominent role in restricting the productivity of word-formation rules. We will see many more examples of such restrictions in the following three chapters, in which we examine in detail the properties of numerous word-formation processes. But before we do that, let us look at one productivity restriction that is not rule-specific, but of a more principled kind, blocking.

3.5.3   Blocking

The term 'blocking' has been mainly used to refer to two different types of phenomena, shown in (17):

(17)   a. thief – *stealer
          b. liver 'inner organ' – ?liver 'someone who lives'

One could argue that *stealer is impossible because there is already a synonymous competing form *thief* available. In (17b) the case is different in the sense that the derived form *liver* 'someone who lives' is homonymous to an already existing non-complex form *liver* 'inner organ.' In both cases one speaks of 'blocking,' with the existing form blocking the creation of a semantically or phonologically identical derived form. I will first discuss briefly the latter type and then turn to the more interesting type of synonymy blocking.

Although frequently mentioned in the pertinent literature, homonymy blocking cannot be assigned real significance since in almost all cases cited, the would-be blocked derivative is acceptable if used in an appropriate context. With regard to the agent noun *liver*, for example, Jespersen (1942: 231) mentions the pun *Is life worth living? – It depends on the liver*, and *OED* has an entry "*liver n 2*," with the following quotation: "The country for easy livers, The quietest under the sun." In both cases we see that, provided the appropriate context, the putative oddness of the agent noun *liver* disappears. But why do we nevertheless feel that, outside appropriate contexts, something is strange about *liver* as an agent noun? The answer to this question lies in the semantics of *-er*, which is given by Marchand (1969: 273) as follows: "Deverbal derivatives (in *-er*, I. P.) are chiefly agent substantives . . . denoting the performer of an action, occasional or habitual." If this characterization is correct, the oddness of *liver* falls out automatically: *live* is neither a typical action verb, nor does it denote anything that is performed occasionally or habitually, in any reasonable sense of the definition. Notably, in the two quotations above, the derived form *liver* receives a more intentional, agentive interpretation than its base word *live* would suggest.

Plank (1981: 165–173) discusses numerous similar cases from different languages in which homonymy blocking does not provide a satisfactory solution. In essence, it seems that homonymy blocking serves as a pseudo-explanation for facts that appear to be otherwise unaccountable. In a broader perspective, homonymy blocking is only one instance of what some linguists have labeled the principle of ambiguity avoidance. However, this putative principle fails to explain why language tolerates innumerable ambiguities (which often enough lead to misunderstandings between speakers), but should avoid this particular one. In summary, homonymy blocking should be disposed of as a relevant morphological mechanism. Let us therefore turn to the more fruitful concept of synonymy blocking.

Rainer (1988) distinguishes between two forms of synonymy blocking, type-blocking and token-blocking. Type-blocking concerns the interaction of more or less regular rival morphological processes (for example *decency* vs. *decentness*) whereas token-blocking involves the blocking of potential regular forms by already existing synonymous words, an example of which is the blocking of *arrivement* by *arrival* or *stealer* by *thief*. I will first discuss the relatively uncontroversial notion of token-blocking and then move on to the problematic concept of type-blocking.

Token-blocking occurs under three conditions: synonymy, productivity, and frequency. The condition of synonymy says that an existing word can only block a newly derived one if they are completely synonymous. Thus doublets with different meanings are permitted. The condition of productivity states that the blocked word must be morphologically well-formed, i.e. it must be a potential word, derived on the basis of a productive rule. In other words, a word that is impossible to form out of independent reasons, e.g. *manageal*, see (13) above, cannot be argued to be blocked by a competing form, such as *management* in this example. These conditions may sound rather trivial, but they are nevertheless important to mention.

The last condition, frequency, is not at all trivial. The crucial insight provided by Rainer (1988) is that, contrary to earlier assumptions, not only idiosyncratic or simplex words (like *thief*) can block productive formations, but that stored words in general can do so. As already discussed in section 3.3 above, the storage of words is largely dependent on their frequency. This leads to the postulation of the frequency condition, which says that in order to be able to block a potential synonymous formation, the blocking word must be sufficiently frequent. This hypothesis is supported by Rainer's investigation of a number of rival nominalizing suffixes in Italian and German. In an experiment, native speakers were asked to rate rival forms (comparable to *decentness* vs. *decency* in English) in terms of acceptability, with the following result. The higher the frequency of a given word, the more likely it was that the word blocked a rival formation. Both idiosyncratic words and regular complex words are able to block other forms, provided that the blocking word is stored.

That such an account of blocking is on the right track is corroborated by the fact that occasionally really synonymous doublets do occur. This looks like a refutation of the blocking hypothesis at first, but upon closer inspection it turns out to speak in favor of the idea of token-blocking. Plank (1981: 181–182) already notes that blocking of a newly derived form does not occur in those cases where the speaker fails to activate the already existing alternative form. To take an example from inflectional morphology, we could say that the stored irregular form *brought* blocks the formation of the regular *bringed*. If, however, the irregular form is not available to the speaker, s/he is likely to produce the regular form *bringed*. This happens with children who might not have strong representations of the irregular forms yet, and therefore either produce only regular forms or alternate between the regular and the irregular forms. Adults have strong representations of the irregular form, but they may nevertheless produce speech errors like *bringed* whenever they fail to access the irregular past-tense form they have stored. One potential reason for such a failure is that regular rule application and access to the individual morphemes may be momentarily faster than access to the irregular form via the whole-word route.

For obvious reasons, the likelihood of failing to activate a stored form is negatively correlated to the frequency of the form to be accessed. In other words, the less frequent the stored word is, the more likely it is that the speaker will fail to access it (and apply the regular rule instead); and the more frequent the stored word is, the more likely it is that the speaker will successfully retrieve it, and the more likely it is, therefore, that it will block the formation of a rival word. With frequency and storage being the decisive factors for token-blocking, the theory can naturally account for the occasional occurrence even of synonymous doublets.

In the light of these considerations, token-blocking is not some kind of mysterious measure to avoid undesired synonymy, but the effect of word-storage and word-processing mechanisms, and thus a psycholinguistic phenomenon.

We may now move on to the notion of type-blocking, which has been said to occur when a certain affix blocks the application of another affix. Our example *decency* vs. *decentness* would be a case in point. The crucial idea underlying the notion of type-blocking is that rival suffixes (such as -*ness*, -*ity*, and -*cy*) are organized in such a way that each suffix can be applied to a certain domain. In many cases one can distinguish between affixes with an unrestricted domain, the so-called general case (e.g. -*ness* suffixation, which may apply to practically any adjective), and affixes with restricted domains, the so-called special cases (for example -*ity* suffixation). The latter are characterized by the fact that certain constraints limit the applicability of the suffixes to a lexically, phonologically, morphologically, semantically or otherwise governed set of bases. Type-blocking occurs when the more special affix precludes the application of the more general affix.

For an evaluation of this theory of type-blocking we will look in more detail at -*ness* suffixation and its rivals. Aronoff (1976: 53) regards formations involving nominal -*ness* as ill-formed in all those cases where the base adjective ends in -*ate*, -*ent*, or -*ant*, hence the contrast between *decency* and ?*decentness*. This could be a nice case of type-blocking, with the systematic special case -*cy* (*decency*) precluding the general case -*ness*. There are, however, three problems with this kind of analysis. The first one is that, on closer inspection, -*ness* and its putative rivals -*ity* or -*cy* are not really synonymous, so that blocking could – if at all – only occur in those cases where the meaning differences would be neutralized. Riddle (1985) shows that there is in fact a slight but consistent meaning difference observable between rival -*ness* and -*ity* derivatives. Consider the pairs in (18) and

(19) and try to figure out what this difference in meaning could be (examples from Riddle 1985: 438):

(18)   a. The lanterns demonstrated the *ethnicity* of the restaurant.
         b. The lanterns demonstrated the *ethnicness* of the restaurant.

(19)   a. Her *ethnicity* was not a factor in the hiring decision. We are an equal opportunity employer.
         b. Her *ethnicness* was certainly a big factor in the director's decision. He wanted someone who personified his conception of the prototypical Greek to play the part.

In (18a) the lanterns show to which ethnic group the restaurant belongs, whereas in (18b) the lanterns show that the restaurant has an ethnic appeal (as opposed to a non-ethnic appeal). A similar contrast emerges with (19a) and (19b), where *ethnicity* refers to nationality or race, and *ethnicness* to a particular personal trait. In general, *-ness* formations tend to denote an embodied attribute, property or trait, whereas *-ity* formations refer to an abstract or concrete entity. From the case of *-ity* and *-ness* we can learn that one should not call two affixes synonymous before having seriously investigated their ranges of meanings.

The second problem of the notion of type-blocking concerns the status of forms like *decentness*, for which it remains to be shown that they are indeed morphologically ill-formed. The occurrence of many attested doublets rather indicates that the domain of the general case *-ness* is not systematically curtailed by *-ity* or *-cy*. (20) presents a small selection of these doublets as attested in the *OED*:

(20)   Some attested doublets with *-ity/-ness*
         destructiveness   –   destructivity
         discoursiveness   –   discoursivity
         exclusiveness   –   exclusivity
         impracticalness   –   impracticality
         inventibleness   –   inventability
         naiveness   –   naivity
         ovalness   –   ovality
         prescriptiveness   –   prescriptivity

The final problem with putative cases of type-blocking is to distinguish them from token-blocking. Thus, the putative avoidance of *decentness* could equally well be a case of token-blocking, since one can assume that, for many speakers, the word *decency* is part of their lexicon, and is therefore capable of token-blocking.

To summarize our discussion of the notion of type-blocking, we have seen that it rests on false assumptions about the meaning of putatively rival affixes and that it cannot account for the empirical facts. The idea of type-blocking should therefore be abandoned. We have, however, also seen that another kind of blocking, namely token-blocking, can occur and does occur, when an individual stored lexical item prevents the formation of a complex rival synonymous form.

3.6   Summary

In this chapter we have looked at what it means when we say that a word-formation process is productive or not. The productivity of a given affix was loosely defined as the possibility to coin a new complex word with this affix. We have seen that possible words need to conform to the word-formation rules of a language whereas actual words are often idiosyncratic. We have then discussed how complex words are stored and accessed in the mental lexicon, which is crucial for an understanding of the notion of productivity in word-formation. Productive processes are characterized by many low-frequency words and thus do not depend on the storage of many individual words, whereas unproductive processes show a preponderance of high-frequency forms, i.e. stored words.

Differences in productivity between affixes raise the question of productivity restrictions. We have seen that apart from contraints on usage, structural constraints play an important role in word-formation. Possible words of a given morphological category need to conform to very specific phonological, morphological, semantic, and syntactic requirements. These requirements restrict the set of potential complex words, thus constraining productivity.

Finally, token-blocking was discussed, which is a general psycholinguistic mechanism which prevents complex forms from being formed if a synonymous word is already present in the speaker's lexicon.

In the next chapter we will turn to the details of affixational processes in English and see how we can implement the insights of the foregoing chapter to gain a deeper understanding of the properties of these processes.

Further reading

Storage of and access to complex words in the lexicon are explained in more detail in Baayen (1993), Frauenfelder and Schreuder (1992). For corpus-based studies of the productivity of English affixes see Baayen and Lieber (1991), Baayen and Renouf (1996), Plag (1999: ch. 5), or Plag et al. (1999). The methodological problems involved in corpus-based analyses of derivational morphology are discussed in considerable detail in Plag (1999: ch. 5). Book-length studies of mainly structural aspects of productivity are Plag (1999) and Bauer (2001), which also contain useful summaries of the pertinent literature. For further elaboration of the psycholinguistic aspects of productivity, see Hay (2001), Hay and Baayen (2002, 2003).

Exercises

Basic level

Exercise 3.1

This exercise is to test the hypothesis that among hapaxes there is a large proportion of neologisms. We will use derivatives in *-ize* as they occur in the 20-million-word Cobuild Corpus (as given in Plag 1999: 279). The data below are the first sixteen items from the alphabetical list of hapaxes in *-ize*.

academicize	*aerobicize*	*aerolize*	*aluminiumize*
anthologize	*anthropomorphize*	*apostasize*	*arabize*
archaize	*astrologize*	*attitudinize*	*austrianize*
bilingualize	*botanize*	*canadianize*	*carbonize*

Check these hapaxes in one or two large dictionaries for verification of their status as neologisms. How many of them are listed? Does your result support the hypothesis?

Exercise 3.2

Calculate the missing *P* measures for the following suffixes on the basis of the figures given in table 3.1:

Table 3.1 *Frequency of affixes in the BNC (from Plag et al. 1999) and* OED *(from Plag 2002)*

	V	N	n_1	P	OED neologisms
-able	933	140627	311	0.0022	185
-ful 'measure'	136	2615	60	0.023	22
-ful 'property'	154	77316	22	0.00028	14
-ion	2392	1369116	524		625
-ish	491	7745	262		101
-ist	1207	98823	354		552
-ity	1372	371747	341		487
-ize	658	100496	212	0.0021	273
-less	681	28340	272		103
-ness	2466	106957	943	0.0088	279
-wise	183	2091	128	0.061	12

Exercise 3.3

The nominal suffixes -*ation*, -*ication*, -*ion*, -*ance*, -*al*, -*age*, -*y*, and -*ment* are roughly synonymous. The obvious question is which mechanisms govern their distribution, i.e. which verb takes which suffix. We will try to answer this question only for a subset of verbs, namely those derived by the suffixation of -*ify*, -*ize*, and -*ate*. Consider the data below, which exemplify the nominalization of the pertinent verbs *magnify*, *verbalize*, and *concentrate* as examples. State the restrictions that constrain the selection of nominalizing suffixes with derived verbs of these types.

magnification	*verbalization*	*concentration*
*magnify-ation	**verbalize-cation*	**concentrate-ation*
*magnify-ion	**verbalize-ion*	**concentrate-cation*
*magnify-ance	**verbalize-ance*	**concentrate-ance*
*magnify-al	**verbalize-al*	**concentrate-al*
*magnify-age	**verbalize-age*	**concentrate-age*
*magnify-ment	**verbalize-ment*	**concentrate-ment*

Advanced level

Exercise 3.4

Go back to the table in (6) of this chapter, which was enlarged and completed in exercise 3.2 above. Order the suffixes in descending order of the values of the different measures to see which suffixes are more productive and which suffixes are less productive with regard to each measure. Compare the corpus-based measures for -*ion*, -*ist*, -*ity*, -*ish*, and -*less* with each other and with the results obtained by using the *OED*. Where do the results agree, where don't they? Comment on the productivity of the different suffixes in the light of the different measures and different data sources and discuss possible discrepancies.

Exercise 3.5

The verb-forming suffixes -*ify* and -*ize* impose severe phonological restrictions on their possible base words. There seem to be three classes of words involved, one class taking obligatorily -*ize*, one class taking obligatorily -*ify*, and one minor third class which can take both suffixes. Try to establish the pertinent phonological restriction as accurately as possible, using the following data, which are all twentieth-century neologisms from the *OED*. Hint: consider the number of syllables and the stress patterns for all derivatives and try to find the appropriate generalization.

a. *-ize* derivatives

academicize	accessorize	absolutize	acronymize	adjectivize
aerosolize	anodize	anthropologize	bacterize	Baskonize
Bolshevize	Bonderize	bovrilize	cannibalize	capsulize
*artize	*massize	*bourgeoisize	*Japanize	*speechize

b. *-ify* derivatives

artify	bourgeoisify	gentrify	jazzify	karstify
massify	mucify	mythify	Nazify	negrify
*randomify	*federalify	*activify	*modernify	*Germanify

4

Affixation

Outline

This chapter provides an overview of the affixational word-formation processes of English. First, it discusses how affixes can be distinguished from other entities. This is followed by an introduction to the methodological problems of data gathering for the study of affixation through dictionaries and electronic corpora. Then some general properties that characterize the system of English affixation are introduced, and a survey of a wide range of suffixes and prefixes is presented. Finally, we investigate cases of infixation.

4.1   What is an affix?

In chapter 1 we defined 'affix' as a bound morpheme that attaches to bases. Although this seems like a clear definition, there are at least two major problems. First, it is not always easy to say whether something is a bound morpheme or a free morpheme, and second, it is not always obvious whether something should be regarded as a base or an affix. We will discuss each problem in turn.

Consider the data in (1) through (4), which show the putative affixes *-free*, *-less*, *-like*, and *-wise* in a number of derivatives, illustrated with quotations from the BNC:

(1)   There was never an *error-free* text, Cropper said.
(2)   Now the lanes were *carless, lawless.*
(3)   Arriving on her broomstick at the *prison-like* school gates, Mildred peered through the railings into the misty playground.
(4)   She had been a teacher, and made sure the girl went to a good school: "my granny had more influence on me *education-wise.*"

Which of the four morphemes in question would you consider a bound morpheme, which of them free? Given that very many words are formed on the basis of the same pattern, one could think that we are dealing with suffixes in all four cases. We will see that things are not so clear upon closer inspection.

In chapter 1 we defined a bound morpheme as a morpheme that can only occur if attached to some other morpheme. When we apply this definition, it turns out that all four morphemes also occur on their own, and should therefore be classified as free morphemes, and not as affixes. However, we should also test whether the free element really has the same meaning as the bound element. For example, *error-free* can be paraphrased by *free of error(s)*, which means that *free* in *error-free* and *free* in *free of error(s)* are most probably the same lexical item, and not two different ones (a suffix and a free form). This would mean that *error-free* should be regarded as a compound and not as a derivative. An analogous argument can be made for *prison-like* (cf. *like a prison*). However, when we try to do the same thing with the words involving *-wise* and *-less*, we fail. The word *education-wise* can be paraphrased as 'in terms of education, with regard to education,' which shows that there is a difference between the morpheme *-wise* we find in complex words such as that in (4) and the morpheme *wise* 'clever.' The latter is a free morpheme, the former a form that only occurs attached to a base. A similar analysis holds for *-less*. While there is a free morpheme *less* denoting the opposite of *more*, *-less* in (2) means 'without,' and this meaning only occurs when *-less* is attached to a base. Furthermore, *-l*[ə]*ss* and *l*[ɛ]*ss* differ significantly in pronunciation. Thus we have good evidence that in the case of *-less* and *-wise*, we have two homographic morphemes in each case, one being a suffix, the other a free morpheme. This analysis is corroborated by the syntactic categories of the items. While the free morpheme *less* is an adverb, the suffix *-less* creates adjectives, and while the free morpheme *wise* is an adjective, the suffix *-wise* creates adverbs. Thus, in both cases, the suffix and the free morpheme do not only differ in meaning, but also in their syntactic category.

To summarize, we can say that an element can occur both as part of a complex word and as a free morpheme. In such cases, only a careful analysis of its linguistic properties can reveal whether the element in question is really the same in both cases. If (and only if) there are significant differences between the two usages we can safely assume that we are dealing with two different items. If there are no significant differences, the element should be treated as a free morpheme and the pertinent complex word as a compound.

We can now turn to the second problem concerning the notion of affix, namely the distinction between an affix and a bound root. Given that affixes are also obligatorily bound, it is not particularly obvious what the difference between a bound root and an affix may be. In chapter 1 we loosely defined a root as the central meaningful element of the word, to which affixes can attach. But when can we call an element central, when non-central? This problem is prominent with a whole class of words which are formed on the basis of morphemes that are called **neoclassical elements.** These elements are lexemes that are originally borrowed from Latin or Greek, but their combinations are of modern origin (hence the term N E Oclassical). Examples of neoclassical word-formation are given in (5):

(5)   a. *bio*chemistry   b. *photo*graph   c. geo*logy*
          *bio*rhythm   *photo*ionize   bio*logy*
          *bio*warfare   *photo*analysis   neuro*logy*

It is not obvious whether the italicized elements should be regarded as affixes or as bound roots. If the data in (5a) are taken as evidence for the prefix status of *bio-*, and the data in (5c) are taken as evidence for the suffix status of *-logy*, we are faced with the problem that words such as *biology* would consist of a prefix and a suffix. This would go against our basic assumptions about the general structure of words. Alternatively, we could assume that we are not dealing with affixes, but with bound roots, so that we are in fact talking about cases of compounding, and not of affixation. Speakers of English who are familiar with such words or even know some Greek would readily say that *bio-* has the meaning 'life,' and this insight would lead us to think that the words in (5a) behave exactly like compounds on the basis of native words. For instance, a *blackboard* is a kind of board, a *kitchen sink* is a kind of sink, a *university campus* is a kind of campus, etc. And *biochemistry* is a kind of chemistry, *biorhythm* is a kind of rhythm, etc. The same argument holds for the element *photo-* 'light,' which behaves like a first element in a compound in the forms in (5b), and for the forms in (5c) (*geo-* 'earth,' *neuro-* 'nerve,' *-logy* 'science of'). The only difference between the neoclassical forms and native compounds is that the non-native elements are obligatorily bound. This is also the reason why the neoclassical elements are often called **combining forms.** We can thus state that neoclassical formations are best treated as compounds, and not as cases of affixation. Further discussion of these forms will therefore be postponed until chapter 6.

To summarize our discussion of how to distinguish affixes from non-affixational morphemes, we can say that this distinction is not always straightforward, but that even in problematic cases it is possible to establish the nature of a complex word as either affixed or compounded on the basis of structural arguments.

4.2   How to investigate affixes: more on methodology

In the previous chapters, we have already seen that large dictionaries and computerized corpora can be used fruitfully to investigate properties of derived words and of the affixes by which they are derived. However, we did not discuss *how* word lists such as the ones we have used can be extracted from those sources, and what the problems are that one encounters in this endeavor. It is the purpose of this section to introduce the reader to these important aspects of empirical research on affixation.

Let us start with the simplest and rather traditional kind of data-base: reverse dictionaries such as Walker (1924), Lehnert (1971), or Muthmann (1999). These dictionaries list words in alphabetical order according to their spelling from right to left, to the effect that words *ending* in <a> come first, those ending in <z> come last. Thus *sofa* is among the first words in a reverse dictionary, *fuzz* among the last. This kind of organization is of course very convenient for the study of suffixes, whereas for prefixes any large dictionary will help the researcher to find pertinent forms. The reverse dictionary by Muthmann (1999) is the most convenient for morphological research because it does not list the words in strictly orthographical order, but groups them according to their pronunciation or morphology. For example, if one is interested in words with the suffix *-ion*, these words are found in one subsection, with no other words intervening. Thus, words ending in the same string of letters, such as *lion*, are found in a different subsection and do not spoil the list of words whose final string <ion> represents a suffix. Needless to say, this kind of dictionary is extremely practical for the analysis of word-formation patterns, but has the disadvantage of containing nothing but word-forms, hence not giving any additional information on these forms (e.g. meaning, first attestations, usage, etc.). Another disadvantage of reverse dictionaries is their comparatively small size. Muthmann (1999), for example, contains only 35,000 words, which, compared to the *OED*, is a small data-base.

The *OED* is not only much larger, but also offers detailed information on each word. An entry of a word in the *OED* is a rather complex text, which contains different kinds of information, such as pronunciation, part of speech, etymology, definitions, quotations, date of quotation, author of quotation, etc. The quotations illustrate the usage of a lexical item at a specific point in time, and since the *OED* aims at complete coverage of the English word stock, the earliest known attestation of a word is always given. This is very important in our context, because it allows us to trace neologisms for any given period in time. On the CD-ROM version of the *OED*, this wealth of information is organized not in serial form, but as a large data-base, which has the considerable advantage that the different kinds of information contained in the dictionary can be accessed separately. The modular organization of the data in the *OED* allows us, for example, to search all quotations for certain words that are first used in the quotations of a specific period in time, or we can search all entries for words containing a specific set of letters. How is this done in practice and how can it be employed for morphological research?

Assume that we want to investigate the properties of the suffix -*ment*. Let us further assume that we also want to know whether this suffix is still productive. Of course we can look up the suffix itself in the *OED*, but this does not satisfactorily answer all our questions (after all, the *OED* is a dictionary, not a reference book on English derivational morphology). But we can carry out our own investigation of all the -*ment* words contained in the *OED*. To investigate the properties of the suffix -*ment* we could extract all words containing the suffix, and, to answer the question whether -*ment* is still productive, we could, for example, extract all words containing the suffix that first occurred after 1950.

The words can be extracted by using a simple programming language that comes with the CD-ROM and running a small search program. Note that the procedures described here are valid for version 1 of the *OED on CD-ROM* (1994) and that later versions may have other (and often more easy to handle) search procedures. The programming language is explained in detail in the user's handbook of the *OED on CD-ROM*, but our simple -*ment* example will make clear how it works. By clicking on the menu 'file' and then 'Query Files: New' in the drop-down menu, we open a window ('New Query File') in which we must enter our search query. By typing 'ENT wd=(*ment) & fd=(1950–1985) into (ment.ent)' we tell the program to search all *OED* entries ('ENT') for all words ('wd=') that start in any string of letters ('*') and end in the letter string <ment>. The command '& fd=(1950–1985)' further tells the program to look only for those <*ment> words that are first attested ('fd' stands for 'first date of attestation') between 1950 and 1985 (where the *OED* coverage ends). When we run this query by clicking on 'Run' in the file menu, the program will write all relevant words into the file 'ment.ent.' This file can then always be reopened by clicking on the menu 'file' and then 'Result Files: Open.' Or the result file can be transformed into a text file by clicking 'Result Files: Output to text' in the file menu. After having clicked on the file, one can select in the following window which parts of the entries shall be written into the text file. Selecting only 'word,' we get the headwords of the entries that contain our -*ment* derivatives. Alternatively, one can also select other parts of the entry, which are then equally written into the text file. The text file can then be further processed with any suitable text-processing software.

The list of headwords from our search as described above is given in (6):

(6)
database	de-development	endistance, v.
Gedankenexperiment	hi-fi	macrosegment
microsegment	no comment	over-achiever
resedimentation	self-assessment	self-reinforcement
tracklement	under-achiever	underlayment
Wittig		

There are a number of problems with this list. First, and quite surprisingly, it contains items that do not feature *-ment* at all. The trick is that we have to search each entry of these words to find the *-ment* derivative we are looking for. For example, in the entry *database* we find *database management*. This is, however, not a new *-ment* derivative, but rather a new compound, in which *management* is the right element. Thus it should not remain on the list of *-ment* neologisms. Similar arguments hold for *de-development, hi-fi equipment* (as found in the entry for *hi-fi*), *over-achievement* (found in the entry for *over-achiever*), *resedimentation, self-assessment, self-reinforcement, under-achievement* (found in the entry for *under-achiever*), and *Wittig rearrangement* (found in the entry for *Wittig*). Furthermore, there are words on the list that end in the string *-ment* but which should certainly not be analyzed as belonging to this morphological category: *Gedanken-experiment, no comment, macrosegment, microsegment* (the latter two being prefixed forms of the simplex *segment* anyway). Eliminating all items that do not belong here, we end up with only three *-ment* neologisms for the relevant period, *endistancement, tracklement, underlayment* (the suffix was much more productive in earlier times, see, for example, Jucker 1994:151f).

We learn from this little exercise that each word has to be carefully checked before any further conclusions can be drawn. This perhaps disappointing result emerges from the fact that we cannot successfully search the *OED* for a given affix, but only for the string of letters corresponding to the affix. Thus we inevitably get words that only share the string of letters, but not the morpheme in question. Eliminating such irrelevant and undesired items is most often an unproblematic task, but sometimes involves difficult methodological decisions, which directly reflect certain theoretical assumptions.

For example, if we extract all words with the initial string <re> in order to investigate the properties of the prefix *re-* 'again' (as in *retry*), we end up with numerous words on our list in which the status of the string <re> is extremely problematic. Recall our discussion from chapter 2, where it was shown that there are arguments for and against analyzing <re> as a morpheme in words like *refer, recall*, etc. How should one deal with such messy data? The most important strategy is to state as clearly as possible the criteria according to which words are included in or excluded from the list. In the case of <re>, for example, we saw that only those words that have secondary stress on the prefix belong to the category of *re*-prefixed words. Or one could exclude all words where the base is not attested as a free morpheme. Both criteria are supported by our preliminary analysis of problematic <re> words in chapter 2. Of course we have to be very careful with such decisions, because we may run the risk of prejudging the analysis. For example, by a priori excluding all words where the base is not attested as a free morpheme or where the prefix is not stressed, we might exclude data that could potentially show us that the prefix *re-* 'again' can in fact sometimes occur attached to bound roots or can sometimes be unstressed. It is therefore a good strategy to leave items on our lists and see if they stand further scrutiny later, when we know more details about the morphological category under investigation.

Similar methodological problems hold for corpus-based morphological research. Here we usually start with a complete list of all words that occur in the corpus, from which we must extract the words that are of interest to us. Again, we need a software program that can search for words with the relevant string. This can be done with freely available specialized text retrieval software (such as TACT®) or with more generally applicable programming packages such as AWK, which are included in any UNIX or LINUX-based system. Given the BNC word list in a two-column format (with frequencies given in the first column, the word-forms given in the second column), the simple AWK script '$2 ∼ /.*ment$/ {print $1, $2}' would extract all words ending in the string <ment> ('∼ /.*ment$/') from the second column ('$2') and write them in a new file ('{ print $1, $2}') together with their respective frequencies, which are listed in the first column ('$1') of the word list. This gives us a list of raw data, which we then need to process further along the same lines as discussed for the *OED* raw data in order to filter out the derivatives of the pertinent morphological category.

To summarize, we have seen how data can be extracted from the *OED* and from word lists of large text corpora with the help of comparatively simple search procedures. However, it also became clear that the lists of raw data obtained in this way need to be further processed 'by hand' to arrive at sensible data sets, which can then be subjected to detailed structural analysis. Having clarified these methodological problems, we may turn to some general properties of affixes in English.

4.3   General properties of English affixation

Before we take a closer look at the properties of individual affixes in section 4.4, it seems desirable to discuss some of the properties that larger sets of affixes have in common, so that it becomes clear that even in this seemingly arbitrary and idiosyncratic domain of language called affixation certain larger patterns can be discerned. Dealing with these general properties before looking at individual affixes has the considerable advantage that certain properties of affixes need not be stated for each affix individually, because, as we will see, these properties are at least partially predictable on the basis of other properties that a given affix shares with certain other affixes.

These properties are mostly of a phonological nature, but they have serious consequences for the properties of derived words and the combinability of affixes with roots and other affixes.

An inspection of the phonological properties of a wider range of suffixes and prefixes reveals striking differences but also surprising similarities between subsets of affixes. One such difference is illustrated in the examples in (7):

(7)   a. prefixes
            contextualize   **de**contextualize
            organize   **re**organize
            modern   **post**modern
            modify   **pre**modify
            argument   **counter**argument
     b. suffixes
            féminine   fémin**ìze**
            mércury   mércur**àte**
            seléctive   sèlectí**vity**
            sígnify   sìgni**ficátion**
            emplóy   èmploy**ée**

If we analyze the pronunciation of the base words before and after the affixation of the morpheme printed in bold, we can see a crucial difference between the prefixes and the suffixes. While the prefixes in (7a) do not change anything in the pronunciation or shape of the base words, the suffixes in (7b) have such an effect. They lead either to the deletion of material at the end of the base or to a different stress pattern (in the examples in (7) and elsewhere, primary stress is indicated by an acute accent, secondary stress by a grave accent). Thus, *feminine* loses two sounds when *-ize* attaches, and *mercury* loses its final vowel when *-ate* is attached. The suffixes *-ity*, *-ation*, and *-ee* have an effect on the stress pattern of their base words, in that they either shift the main stress of the base to the syllable immediately preceding the suffix (as with *-ity*), or attract the stress to themselves, as is the case with *-ation* and *-ee*. Prefixes obviously have no effect on the stress patterns of their base words.

Of course not all suffixes inflict such phonological changes, as can be seen with suffixes like *-less* or *-ness*.

(8)   Phonologically neutral suffixes: *-less* and *-ness*

propagánda	propagándaless	advénturous	advénturousness
radiátion	radiátionless	artículate	artículateness
mánager	mánagerless	openmínded	openmíndedness

Apart from the deletion of base material at the end of the base (as in *feminine–feminize*), suffixes can also cause the reduction of syllables by other means.

Consider the difference in behavior between the suffixes *-ic* and *-ance* on the one hand, and *-ish* and *-ing* on the other, as illustrated with the examples in (9). Dots mark syllable boundaries:

(9)   cy.lin.der   cy.lin.de.rish   cy.lin.dric
           en.ter   en.te.ring   en.trance

The attachment of the suffixes *-ish* and *-ing* leads (at least in careful speech) to the addition of a syllable which consists of the base-final [r] and the suffix (*.rish* and *.ring*, respectively). The vowel of the last syllable of the base, [ə], is preserved when these two suffixes are added. The suffixes *-ic* and *-ance* behave differently. They trigger not only the deletion of the last base vowel but also the formation of a consonant cluster immediately preceding the suffix, which has the effect that the derivatives have as many syllables as the base (and not one syllable more, as with *-ish* and *-ing*).

In order to see whether it is possible to make further generalizations as to which kinds of suffix may trigger phonological alternations and which ones do not, I have listed a number of suffixes in table 4.1 according to their phonological properties. Try to find common properties of each set before you read on.

The first generalization that emerges from the two sets concerns the phonological structure of the suffixes. Thus, all suffixes that inflict phonological changes on their base words begin in a vowel. Among the suffixes that do not trigger any changes there is only one (*-ish*) which begins in a vowel, all others are consonant-initial. Obviously, vowel-initial suffixes have a strong tendency to trigger alternations, whereas consonant-initials have a strong tendency not to trigger alternations. This looks like a rather strange and curious state of affairs. However, if one takes into account findings about the phonological structure of words in general, the co-occurrence of vowel-initialness (another neologism!) and the triggering of

Table 4.1 *The phonological properties of some suffixes*

suffixes that trigger alternations	examples	suffixes that do not trigger alternations	examples
-(at)ion	alternation	-ness	religiousness
-y	candidacy	-less	televisionless
-al	environmental	-ful	eventful
-ic	parasitic	-hood	companionhood
-ize	hypothesize	-ship	editorship
-ous	monstrous	-ly	headmasterly
-ive	productive	-ish	introvertish
-ese	Japanese	-dom	martyrdom

morpho-phonological alternations is no longer mysterious. We will therefore take a short detour through the realm of **prosodic structure**.

The term **prosody** is used to refer to all phonological phenomena that concern phonological units larger than the individual sound. For example, we know that the word *black* has only one syllable, the word *sofa* two, we know that words are stressed on certain syllables and not on others, and we know that utterances have a certain intonation and rhythm. All these phenomena can be described in terms of phonological units whose properties and behavior are to a large extent rule-governed. What concerns us here in the context of suffixation are two units called **syllable** and **prosodic word**.

A syllable is a phonological unit that consists of one or more sounds and which, according to many phonologists, has the following structure (here exemplified with the words *strikes* and *wash*):

(10)

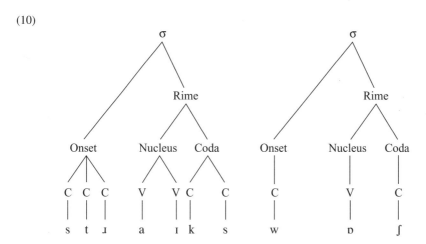

The so-called **onset** is the first structural unit of the syllable and contains the syllable-initial consonants. The onset is followed by the so-called **rime**, which contains everything but the onset, and which is the portion of the syllable that rimes (cf., for example, *show–throw*, *screw–flew*). The rime splits up into two constituents, the **nucleus**, which is the central part of the syllable and which usually consists of vowels, and the **coda**, which contains the syllable-final consonants. From the existence of monosyllabic words like *eye* and the non-existence and impossibility in English of syllables such as *[ptk] we can conclude that onset and coda are in principle optional constituents of the syllable, but that the nucleus of a syllable must be obligatorily filled.

What is now very important for the understanding of the peculiar patterning of vowel- vs. consonant-initial suffixes is the fact that syllables in general have a strong tendency to have onsets. Thus, a word like *banana* consists of three syllables with each syllable having an onset, and not of three syllables with only one of them having an onset. The tendency to create onsets rather than codas is shown in (11) for a number of words:

(11)   ba.na.na   *ban.an.a
        ho.ri.zon   *hor.iz.on
        a.gen.da   *ag.en.da
        sym.pa.thy   *symp.ath.y
        in.ter.pret   *int.erpr.et

The last examples show that things are more difficult if there is a cluster of consonants. In this case not all consonants of the cluster necessarily end up in onset position. Thus, in the clusters [mp] (in *sympathy*), [nt] (in *interpret*), and [rpr] (in *interpret*), the first consonant forms the coda of the preceding syllable, respectively, and the rest of the cluster forms the onset. The reason for this non-unitary behavior of consonants in a cluster is, among other things, that certain types of onset clusters are illegal in English (and many other languages). Thus,*mp, *nt, or *rp(r) can never form onsets in English, as can be seen from invented forms such as *ntick or *rpin, which are impossible words and syllables for English speakers. We can conclude our discussion by stating that word-internal consonants end up in onset position, unless they would form illegal syllable-initial combinations (such as *rp or *nt).

Having gained some basic insight into the structure of syllables and syllabification, the obvious question is what syllabification has to do with morphology. A lot, as we will shortly see. For example, consider the syllable boundaries in compounds such as those in (12). Syllable boundaries are marked by dots, word boundaries by '#':

(12)   a. back.#bone   *ba.ck#bone
           snow.#drift   *snow#d.rift
           car.#park   *ca.r#park
        b. back.#lash   *ba.ck#lash   *cf.*.**cl**ash.
           ship.#wreck   *shi.p#wreck   *cf.*.**pr**ice.
           rat.#race   *ra.t#race   *cf.*.**tr**ace.

Obviously, the syllable boundaries always coincide with the word boundaries. This is trivially the case when a different syllabification would lead to illegal onsets as in the words in (12a, right-hand column). However, the words in (12b, left-hand column) have their syllable boundaries placed in such a way that they coincide with the word boundaries, even though a different syllabification would be possible (and indeed obligatory if these were monomorphemic words, see the third column in (12b)). Obviously, the otherwise legal onsets [kl], [pr], and [tr] are impossible if they straddle a word boundary (*[.k#l], *[.p#r] and *[.t#r]). We can thus state that the domain of the phonological mechanism of syllabification is the word. Given that we are talking about phonological units here, and given that the word is also a phonological unit (see the remarks on the notion of word in chapter 1) we should speak of the **phonological** or **prosodic word** as the domain of syllabification (and stress assignment, for that matter).

Coming finally back to our affixes, we can make an observation parallel to that regarding syllabification in compounds. Consider the behavior of the following prefixed and suffixed words. The relevant affixes appear in bold print:

(13)   **mis**.#un.der.stand   ***mi.s**#un.der.stand
        dis.#or.ga.nize   ***di.s**#or.ga.**nize**
        help.#**less**   *hel.p#**less**
        carpet.#**wise**   *carpe.t#**wise**

Again, in the left-hand column the word boundaries coincide with syllable boundaries, and the right-hand column shows that syllabifications that are common and legal in monomorphemic words are prohibited across word boundaries. We can thus state that there must be a prosodic word boundary between the base and the affixes in (13), as indicated by brackets in (14):

(14)   **mis**[.un.der.stand]_{PrWd}   *mi.sun.der.stand
        dis[.or.ga.nize]_{PrWd}   *di.sor.ga.nize
        _{PrWd}[help.]**less**   *hel.pless
        _{PrWd}[carpet.]**wise**   *carpe.twise

In contrast to this, the suffixes in (15) attract base-final consonants as onsets:

(15)   alter.**nation**   candida.**cy**
        environmen.**tal**   parasi.**tic**
        hypothe.**size**   mon.str**ous**
        produc.**tive**   Japa.n**ese**

Notably, the suffixes in (14) are consonant-initial, whereas the suffixes in (15) are vowel-initial. This means that the vowel-initial suffixes integrate into the prosodic structure of the base word. In contrast to consonant-initial suffixes, they become part of the prosodic word, as shown in (16):

(16)   [alter.nation] _{PrWd}   [candida.cy] _{PrWd}
        [environmen.tal] _{PrWd}   [parasi.tic] _{PrWd}
        [hypothe.size] _{PrWd}   [mon.strous] _{PrWd}
        [produc.tive] _{PrWd}   [Japa.nese] _{PrWd}

By forming one prosodic word with the base, the suffixes in (16) can influence the prosodic structure of the derivative. Affixes outside the prosodic word obviously cannot do so. This prosodic difference between certain sets of affixes can also be illustrated by another interesting phenomenon. Both in compounding and in certain cases of affixation it is possible to coordinate two words by leaving out one element. This is sometimes called **gapping** and is illustrated in (17a–c). However, gapping is not possible with the suffixes in (17d):

(17)   a. possible gapping in compounds
                word and sentence structure
                computer and cooking courses
                word-structure and -meaning
                speech-production and -perception
         b. possible gapping with prefixes
                de- and recolonization
                pre- and post-war (fiction)
                over- and underdetermination
         c. possible gapping with suffixes
                curious- and openness
                computer- and internetwise
                child- and homeless
         d. impossible gapping with suffixes
                *productiv(e)- and selectivity (for *productivity and selectivity*)
                *feder- and local (for *federal and local*)
                *computer- and formalize (for *computerize and formalize*)

The contrast between (17a–c) and (17d) shows that gapping is only possible with affixes that do not form one prosodic word together with their base.

Apart from the phonological properties that larger classes of affixes share, it seems that the etymology of a suffix may also significantly influence its behavior. Have a look at the data in (18) and try first to discern the differences between the sets in (18a) and (18b) before reading on:

(18)   a. signify   identity   investigate   federal
            personify   productivity   hyphenate   colonial
         b. friendship   sweetness   helpful   brotherhood
            citizenship   attentiveness   beautiful   companionhood

The suffixes in (18a) are all of foreign origin, while the suffixes in (18b) are of native Germanic origin. What we can observe is that suffixes that have been borrowed from Latin or Greek (sometimes through intermediate languages such as French) behave differently from those of native Germanic origin. The data in (18) illustrate the general tendency that so-called **Latinate** suffixes (such as *-ify*, *-ate*, *-ity*, and *-al*) prefer Latinate bases and often have bound roots as bases, whereas native suffixes (such as *-ship*, *-ful*, *-ness*, and *-hood*) are indifferent to these kinds of distinctions. For example, *ident-* in *identity* is a bound root, and all the bases in (18a) are of Latin/Greek origin. In contrast, for each pair of derivatives with the same suffix in (18b) it can be said that the first member of the pair has a native base, the second a Latinate base, which shows that these suffixes tolerate both kinds of bases.

The interesting question now is, how do the speakers know whether a base or an affix is native or foreign? After all, only a small minority learn Latin or classical Greek at school yet those who do not still get their word-formation right. Thus, it can't be the case that speakers of English really know the origin of all these elements. But what is it then that they know? There must be other, more overt properties of Latinate words that allow speakers to identify them. It has been suggested that it is in fact phonological properties of roots and affixes that correlate strongly with the Latinate/native distinction. Thus, most of the Latinate suffixes are vowel-initial whereas the native suffixes tend to be consonant-initial. Most of the Latinate prefixes are secondarily stressed, whereas the native prefixes (such as *en-*, *be-*, *a-*) tend to be unstressed. Native roots are mostly monosyllabic (or disyllabic with an unstressed second syllable, as in *water*), while Latinate roots are mostly polysyllabic or occur as bound morphs (*investig-* illustrates both polysyllabicity and boundness). With regard to the combinability of suffixes we can observe that often Latinate affixes do not readily combine with native affixes (e.g. **less-ity*), but native suffixes are tolerant towards non-native affixes (cf. *-ive-ness*).

It should be clear that the above observations reflect strong tendencies but that counterexamples can frequently be found. In chapter 7 we will discuss in more detail how to deal with this rather complex situation, which poses a serious challenge to morphological theory.

We are now in a position to turn to the description of individual affixes. Due to the methodological and practical problems involved in discerning affixed words and the pertinent affixes, it is impossible to say exactly how many affixes English has, but it is clear that there are dozens. For example, in their analysis of the Cobuild corpus, Hay and Baayen (2002) arrive at 54 suffixes and 26 prefixes, Stockwell and Minkova (2001), drawing on various sources, list 129 affixes. In section 4.4 below, I will deal with 41 suffixes and 8 prefixes in more detail.

There are different ways of classifying these affixes. The most obvious way is according to their position with regard to the base, i.e. whether they are prefixes, suffixes, or infixes, and we will follow this practice here, too. More fine-grained classifications run into numerous problems. Thus, affixes are often classified according to the syntactic category of their base words, but, as we have already seen in chapter 2, this does not always work properly because affixes may take more than one type of base. Another possible basis of classification could be the affixes' semantic properties, but this has the disadvantage that many affixes can express a whole range of meanings, so it would often not be clear under which category an affix should be listed. Yet another criterion could be whether an affix changes the syntactic category of its base word. Again, this is problematic because certain suffixes sometimes do change the category of the base and sometimes do not. Consider, for example, *-ee*, which is category-changing in *employee*, but not so in *festschriftee*.

There is, however, one criterion that is relatively unproblematic, at least with suffixes, namely the syntactic category of the derived form. Any given English suffix derives words of only one category (the only exception to this generalization seems to be *-ish*, see below). For example, *-ness* only derives nouns, *-able* only adjectives, *-ize* only verbs. Prefixes are more problematic in this respect, because they not only attach to bases of different categories, but also often derive different categories (cf. the discussion of *un-* in chapter 2). We will therefore group suffixes according to the output category and discuss prefixes in strictly alphabetical order.

In the following sections, only a selection of affixes are described, and even these descriptions will be rather brief and sketchy. The purpose of this overview is to illustrate the variety of affixational processes available in English giving basic information on their semantics, phonology, and structural restrictions. For more detailed information, the reader is referred to standard sources like Marchand (1969) or Adams (2001), and of course to discussions of individual affixes in the pertinent literature, as mentioned in the further reading section at the end of this chapter. Although English is probably the best-described language in the world, the exact properties of many affixes are still not sufficiently well determined and there is certainly a need for more and more detailed investigations.

Note that sections 4.4 and 4.5 differ markedly from the rest of the book in the style of presentation. The reader will not find the usual problem-oriented didactic approach, but rather the enumeration of what could be called 'facts.' This gives this part of the book the character of a reference text (instead of an instructive one).

4.4   Suffixes

4.4.1   *Nominal suffixes*

Nominal suffixes are often employed to derive abstract nouns from verbs, adjectives, and nouns. Such abstract nouns can denote actions, results of actions, or other related concepts, but also properties, qualities, and the like. Another large group of nominal suffixes derives person nouns of various sorts. Very often, these meanings are extended to other, related senses so that practically every suffix can be shown to be able to express more than one meaning, with the semantic domains of different suffixes often overlapping.

-age

This suffix derives nouns that express an activity (or its result) as in *coverage*, *leakage*, *spillage*, and nouns denoting a collective entity or quantity, as in *acreage*, *voltage*, *yardage*. Due to inherent ambiguities of certain coinages, the meaning can be extended to include locations, as in *orphanage*. Base words may be verbal or nominal and are often monosyllabic.

-al

A number of verbs take *-al* to form abstract nouns denoting an action or the result of an action, such as *arrival*, *overthrowal*, *recital*, *referral*, *renewal*. Base words for nominal *-al* all have their main stress on the last syllable.

-ance *(with its variants* -ence/-ancy/-ency*)*

Attaching mostly to verbs, *-ance* creates action nouns such as *absorbance*, *riddance*, *retardance*. The suffix is closely related to *-ce/-cy*, which attaches productively to adjectives ending in the suffix *-ant/-ent*. Thus, a derivative like *dependency* could be analyzed as having two suffixes (*depend-ent-cy*) or only one (*depend-ency*). The question then is to determine whether *-ance* (and its variants) always contain two suffixes, to the effect that all action nominals would in fact be derived from adjectives that in turn would be derived from verbs. Such an analysis would predict that we would find *-ance* nominals only if there are corresponding *-ant* adjectives. This is surely not the case, as evidenced by *riddance* (**riddant*), *furtherance* (**furtherant*), and we can therefore assume the existence of an independent suffix *-ance*, in addition to a suffix combination *-ant-ce*.

The distribution of the different variants is not entirely clear; several doublets are attested, such as *dependence*, *dependency*, or *expectance*, *expectancy*. Sometimes the doublets seem to have identical meanings, sometimes slightly different ones. It appears, however, that forms in *-ance/-ence* have all been in existence (sic!) for a very long time, and that *-ance/-ence* formations are interpreted as deverbal, *-ancy/-ency* formations as de-adjectival.

-ant

This suffix forms count nouns referring to persons (often in technical or legal discourse, cf. *applicant*, *defendant*, *disclaimant*) or to substances involved in biological, chemical, or physical processes (*attractant*, *dispersant*, *etchant*, *suppressant*). Most bases are verbs of Latinate origin.

-ce/-cy

As already mentioned in connection with the suffix *-ance*, this suffix attaches productively to adjectives in *-ant/-ent* (e.g. *convergence, efficiency, emergence*), but also to nouns ending in this string, as is the case with *agency, presidency, regency*. Furthermore, adjectives in *-ate* are eligible bases (*adequacy, animacy, intimacy*). The resulting derivatives can denote states, properties, qualities or facts (*convergence* can, for example, be paraphrased as 'the fact that something converges'), or, by way of metaphorical extension, can refer to an office or institution (e.g. *presidency*). Again the distribution of the two variants is not entirely clear, although there is a tendency for nominal bases to take the syllabic variant *-cy*.

-dom

The native suffix *-dom* is semantically closely related to *-hood* and *-ship*, which express similar concepts. *-dom* attaches to nouns to form nominals which can be paraphrased as 'state of being X' as in *apedom, clerkdom, slumdom, yuppiedom*, or which refer to collective entities, such as *professordom, studentdom*, or denote domains, realms or territories as in *kingdom, cameldom, maoridom*.

-ee

The meaning of this suffix can be rather clearly discerned. It derives nouns denoting sentient entities that are involved in an event as non-volitional participants (so-called 'episodic *-ee*'). Thus, *employee* denotes someone who is employed, a *biographee* is someone who is the subject of a biography, and a *standee* is someone who is forced to stand (on a bus, for example). Due to the constraint that the referents of *-ee* derivatives must be sentient, an *amputee* can only be someone who has lost a limb, and not the limb that is amputated. As a consequence of the event-related, episodic semantics, verbal bases are most frequent, but nominal bases are not uncommon (e.g. *festschriftee*). Phonologically, *-ee* can be described as an autostressed suffix, i.e. it belongs to the small class of suffixes that attract the main stress of the derivative. If base words end in the verbal suffix *-ate* the base words are frequently truncated and lose their final rime. This happens systematically in those cases where *-ee* attachment would create identical onsets in the final syllables, as in, for example, **ampu.ta.tee* (cf. truncated *amputee*), **rehabili.ta.tee* (cf. *rehabilitee*).

-eer

This is another person-noun-forming suffix, whose meaning can be paraphrased as 'person who deals in, is concerned with, or has to do with X,' as evidenced in forms such as *auctioneer, budgeteer, cameleer, mountaineer, pamphleteer*. Many words have a depreciative tinge. The suffix *-eer* is autostressed and attaches almost exclusively to bases ending in a stressed syllable followed by an unstressed syllable.

-er *(and its orthographic variant -or)*

The suffix *-er* can be seen as closely related to *-ee*, as its derivatives frequently signify entities that are active or volitional participants in an event (e.g. *teacher, singer, writer*, etc.). This is, however, only a subclass of *-er* derivatives, and there is a wide range of forms with quite heterogeneous meanings. Apart from performers of actions we find instrument nouns such as *blender, mixer, steamer, toaster*, and nouns denoting entities associated with an activity such as *diner, lounger, trainer, winner* (in the sense 'winning shot'). Furthermore, *-er* is used to create person nouns indicating place of origin or residence (e.g. *Londoner, New Yorker, Highlander, New Englander*). This heterogeneity suggests that the semantics of *-er* should be described as rather underspecified, simply meaning something like 'person or thing having to do with X.' The more specific interpretations of individual formations would then follow from an interaction of the meanings of base and suffix and further inferences on the basis of world knowledge.

-er is often described as a deverbal suffix, but there are numerous forms (not only inhabitant names) that are derived on the basis of nouns (e.g. *sealer, whaler, noser, souther*), numerals (e.g. *fiver, tenner*), or even phrases (*four-wheeler, fourth-grader*).

The orthographic variant *-or* occurs mainly with Latinate bases ending in /s/ or /t/, such as *conductor, oscillator, compressor*.

-(e)ry

Formations in *-(e)ry* refer to locations which stand in some kind of connection to what is denoted by the base. More specific meanings such as 'place where a specific activity is carried out' or 'place where a specific article or service is available' could be postulated (cf., for example, *bakery, brewery, fishery, pottery* or *cakery, carwashery, eatery*), but examples such as *mousery, cannery, rabbitry* speak for an underspecified meaning, which is then fleshed out for each derivative on the basis of the meaning of the base.

In addition to the locations, *-(e)ry* derivatives can also denote collectivities (as in *confectionery, cutlery, machinery, pottery*), or activities (as in *summitry* 'having many political summits,' *crookery* 'foul deeds').

-ess

This suffix derives a comparatively small number of mostly established nouns referring exclusively to female humans and animals (*princess, stewardess, lioness, tigress, waitress*). The *OED* lists only three twentieth-century coinages (*hostess, burgheress, clerkess*).

-ful

The nominal suffix *-ful* derives measure partitive nouns (similar to expressions such as *a lot of, a bunch of*) from nominal base words that can be construed as containers: *bootful, cupful, handful, tumblerful, stickful*. As seen in section 3.4, there is also an adjectival suffix *-ful*. This will be treated in section 4.4.3 below.

-hood

Similar in meaning to *-dom*, *-hood* derivatives express concepts such as state (as in *adulthood, childhood, farmerhood*) and collectivity (as in *beggarhood, Christianhood, companionhood*). As with other suffixes, metaphorical extensions can create new meanings, for example the sense 'area' in the highly frequent *neighborhood*, which originates in the collectivity sense of the suffix.

-(i)an *(and its variant -ean)*

Nouns denoting persons and places can take the suffix *-(i)an*. Derivatives seem to have the general meaning 'person having to do with X' (as in *technician, historian, Utopian*), which, where appropriate, can be more specifically interpreted as 'being from X' or 'being of X origin' (e.g. *Bostonian, Lancastrian, Mongolian, Scandinavian*), or 'being the follower or supporter of X': *Anglican, Chomskyan, Smithsonian*. Many *-(i)an* derivatives are also used as adjectives.

Most words belonging to this category are stressed on the syllable immediately preceding the suffix, exhibiting stress shifts where necessary (e.g. *Húngary–Hungárian, Égypt–Egýptian*).

-ing

Derivatives with this deverbal suffix denote processes (*begging, running, sleeping*) or results (*building, wrapping, stuffing*). The suffix is somewhat peculiar among derivational suffixes in that it is primarily used as a verbal inflectional suffix forming present participles. Examples of pertinent derivatives are abundant since *-ing* can attach to practically any verb. See also adjectival *-ing* below.

-ion

This Latinate suffix has three allomorphs: when attached to a verb in *-ify*, the verbal suffix and *-ion* surface together as *-ification* (*personification*). When attached to a verb ending in *-ate*, we find *-ion* (accompanied by a change of the base-final consonant from [t] to [ʃ], *hyphenation*), and we find the allomorph *-ation* in all other cases (*starvation, colonization*). Phonologically, all *-ion* derivatives are characterized by having their primary stress on the last-but-one syllable (the so-called **penult**), which means that *-ion* belongs to the class of suffixes that can cause a stress shift.

Derivatives in *-ion* denote events or results of processes. As such, verbal bases are by far the most frequent, but there is also a comparatively large number of forms where *-ation* is directly attached to nouns without any intervening verb in *-ate*. These forms are found primarily in scientific discourse with words denoting chemical or other substances as bases (e.g. *epoxide–epoxidation, sediment–sedimentation*).

-ism

Forming abstract nouns from other nouns and adjectives, derivatives belonging to this category denote the related concepts state, condition, attitude, system of beliefs or theory, as in *blondism, Parkinsonism, conservatism, racism, revisionism, Marxism*, respectively.

-ist

This suffix derives nouns denoting persons, mostly from nominal and adjectival bases (*balloonist, careerist, fantasist, minimalist*). All nouns in *-ism* which denote attitudes, beliefs or theories have potential counterparts in *-ist*. The semantics of *-ist* can be considered underspecified 'person having to do with X,' with the exact meaning of the derivative being a function of the meaning of the base and further inferencing. Thus, a balloonist is someone who ascends in a balloon, a careerist is someone who is chiefly interested in her/his career, while a fundamentalist is a supporter or follower of fundamentalism.

-ity

Words belonging to this morphological category are nouns denoting qualities, states or properties usually derived from Latinate adjectives (e.g. *curiosity, productivity, profundity, solidity*). Apart from the compositional meaning just described, many *-ity* derivatives are **lexicalized**, i.e. they have become permanently incorporated into the mental lexicons of speakers, thereby often adopting idiosyncratic meanings, such as *antiquity* 'state of being antique' or 'ancient time,' *curiosity* 'quality of being curious' and 'curious thing.' All adjectives ending in the suffixes *-able, -al* and *-ic* or in the phonetic string [ɪd] can take *-ity* as a nominalizing suffix (*readability, formality, erraticity, solidity*).

The suffix is capable of changing the stress pattern of the base, to the effect that all *-ity* derivatives are stressed on the last-but-two syllable (the so-called **antepenult**). Furthermore, many of the polysyllabic base words undergo an alternation known as **trisyllabic shortening** (or trisyllabic laxing), whereby the stressed vowel or diphthong of the base word, and thus the last-but-two syllable, becomes destressed and shortened, as in *obsc*[i]*ne–obsc*[ɛ]*nity*, *prof*[aʊ]*nd–profu*[ʌ]*ndity*, *verb*[ðʊ]*se* – *verb*[ɒ]*sity*). Another phonological peculiarity of this suffix is that there are systematic lexical gaps whenever *-ity* attachment would create identical onsets in adjacent syllables, as evidenced by the impossible formations *acutity*, *completity*, *obsoletity* or *candidity*, *sordidity*.

-ment

This suffix derives action nouns denoting processes or results from (mainly) verbs, with a strong preference for monosyllables or disyllabic base words with stress on the last syllable (e.g. *assessment, endorsement, involvement, treatment*). See also the remarks on *-ment* in section 4.2 above, and in section 3.5.2.

-ness

Quality noun forming *-ness* is perhaps the most productive suffix of English. With regard to potential base words, *-ness* is much less restrictive than its close semantic relative *-ity*. The suffix can attach to practically any adjective, and apart from adjectival base words we find nouns as in *thingness*, pronouns as in *us-ness*, and frequently phrases as in *over-the-top-ness*, *all-or-nothing-ness*. For a discussion of the semantic differences between *-ness* and *-ity* derivatives see section 3.5.3.

-ship

The suffix *-ship* forms nouns denoting state or condition, similar in meaning to derivatives in *-age, -hood* and *-dom*. Base words are mostly person nouns as in *apprenticeship, clerkship, friendship, membership, statesmanship, vicarship*. Extensions of the basic senses occur, for example 'office,' as in *postmastership*, or 'activity,' as in *courtship* 'courting' or *censorship* 'censoring.'

4.4.2   Verbal suffixes

There are four suffixes which derive verbs from other categories (mostly adjectives and nouns), *-ate, -en, -ify*, and *-ize*.

-ate

Forms ending in this suffix represent a rather heterogeneous group. There is a class of derivatives with chemical substances as bases, which systematically exhibit so-called ornative and resultative meanings. These can be paraphrased as 'provide with X' (ornative), as in *fluorinate*, or 'make into X' (resultative), as in *methanate*. However, a large proportion of forms in *-ate* do not conform to this pattern, but show various kinds of idiosyncrasies, with *-ate* being apparently no more than an indicator of verbal status. Examples of such non-canonical formations are back-formations (*formate* ←*formation*), local analogies (*stereoregular: stereoregulate :: regular: regulate*, see section 2.3), conversion (*citrate*), and completely idiosyncratic formations such as *dissonate* or *fidate*.

Phonologically, *-ate* is largely restricted to attachment to words that end in one or two unstressed syllables. If the base ends in two unstressed syllables, the last syllable is truncated: *nitrosyl–nitrosate, mercury–mercurate*. In other words, the rime of the last syllable is deleted to avoid stress lapses (i.e. two adjacent unstressed syllables, as in **ní.tro.sy.làte* or **mér.cu.ry.àte*) and achieve a strictly alternating stress pattern.

-en

The Germanic suffix *-en* attaches to monosyllables that end in a plosive, fricative or affricate. Most bases are adjectives (e.g. *blacken, broaden, quicken, ripen*), but a few nouns can also be found (e.g. *strengthen, lengthen*). The meaning of *-en* formations can be described as causative 'make (more) X.'

-ify

This suffix attaches to three kinds of base word: to monosyllabic words, to words stressed on the final syllable, and to words stressed on the penult followed by a final syllable ending in unstressed /ɪ/. Neologisms usually do not show stress shift, but some older forms do (*húmid–humídify, sólid–solídify*). These restrictions have the effect that *-ify* is in (almost) complementary distribution with the suffix *-ize* (see the answer key, exercise 3.5, for details). The only, but systematic, exception to the complementarity of *-ize/-ify* can be observed with the said base words ending in /ɪ/, which take *-ify* under loss of that segment (as in *nazify*), or take *-ize* (with no accompanying segmental changes apart from optional glide insertion, as in *toddy*[j]*ize*). Semantically, *-ify* shows the same range of meanings as *-ize* and the two suffixes could therefore be considered phonologically conditioned allomorphs.

-ize

Both *-ize* and *-ify* are polysemous suffixes, which can express a whole range of related concepts such as locative, ornative, causative/factitive, resultative, inchoative, performative, similative. Locatives can be paraphrased as 'put into X,' as in *computerize, hospitalize, tubify*. *Patinatize, fluoridize, youthify* are ornative examples ('provide with X'), *randomize, functionalize, humidify* are causative ('make (more) X'), *carbonize, itemize, trustify* and *nazify* are resultative ('make into X'), *aerosolize* and *mucify* are inchoative ('become X'), *anthropologize* and *speechify* are performative ('perform X'), *cannibalize, vampirize* can be analyzed as similative ('act like X').

The suffix *-ize* attaches primarily to bases ending in an unstressed syllable and the resulting derivatives show rather complex patterns of base allomorphy. For example, bases are systematically truncated (i.e. they lose the rime of the final syllable) if they are vowel-final and end in two unstressed syllables (cf. truncated vowel-final *mémory–mémorize*, vs. non-truncated consonant-final *hóspital–hóspitalize*). Furthermore, polysyllabic derivatives in *-ize* are not allowed to have identical onsets in the two last syllables, if these are unstressed. In the pertinent cases truncation is used as a repair strategy, as in *feminine–feminize* and *emphasis–emphasize*.

4.4.3   Adjectival suffixes

The adjectival suffixes of English can be subdivided into two major groups. A large proportion of derived adjectives are **relational adjectives**, whose role is simply to relate the noun the adjective qualifies to the base word of the derived adjective. For example, *algebraic mind* means 'a mind having to do with algebra, referring to algebra, characterized by algebra,' *colonial officer* means 'officer having to do with the colonies,' and so on. On the other hand, there is a large group of derived adjectives that express more specific concepts, and which are often called **qualitative adjectives**. Sometimes, relational adjectives can adopt qualitative meanings, as can be seen with the derivative *grammatical*, which has a relational meaning 'having to do with grammar' in the sentence *she is a grammatical genius*, but which also has a qualitative sense 'conforming to the rules of grammar,' as in *This is a grammatical sentence*. Note that relational adjectives usually occur only in attributive position, i.e. as prenominal modifiers (as in *a lexical problem*). If we find them in predicative position in a clause (as in *This sentence is grammatical*), they usually have adopted a qualitative sense.

-able/-ible

This suffix chiefly combines with transitive and intransitive verbal bases, as in *deterrable* and *perishable*, respectively, as well as with nouns, as in *serviceable, fashionable*. The semantics of deverbal *-able* forms seem to involve two different cases, which have been described as 'capable of being Xed' (cf. *breakable, deterrable, readable*), and 'liable or disposed to X' (cf. *agreeable, perishable, variable*; *changeable* can have both meanings). What unites the two patterns is that in both cases the referent of the noun modified by the *-able* adjective is described as a potential non-volitional participant in an event. In this respect, *-able* closely resembles episodic *-ee*. Denominal forms can convey the same meaning, as e.g. *marriageable, jeepable, kitchenable, roadable*. There are also some lexicalized denominal forms with the meaning 'characterized by X,' as in *fashionable* (but cf. the concurrent compositional meaning 'that can be fashioned'), *knowledgeable, reasonable.*

Phonologically, *-able* exhibits diverse properties. Only some lexicalized derivatives exhibit stress shift (e.g. *cómparable*), and base verbs in *-ate* are often, but not systematically, truncated, as in *allocable, irritable, navigable, permeable, operable* vs. *cultivatable, emancipatable, operatable.*

In established loan words we also find the orthographic variant *-ible*: *comprehensible, discernible, flexible, reversible.*

-al

This relational suffix attaches almost exclusively to Latinate bases (*accidental, colonial, cultural, federal, institutional, modal*). All derivatives have stress either on their penultimate or antepenultimate syllable. If the base does not have its stress on one of the two syllables preceding the suffix, stress is shifted to the antepenultimate syllable of the derivative (e.g. *cólony–colónial*).

Apart from the allomorphy already discussed in section 2.2 (*-ar* after bases ending in [l], *-al* elsewhere), there are the two variants *-ial* (as in *confidential, labial, racial, substantial*) and *-ual* (as in *contextual, gradual, spiritual, visual*). With bases ending in [s] or [t], *-ial* triggers assimilation of the base-final sound to [ʃ] (e.g. *facial, presidential*). The distribution of *-ial* and *-ual* is not entirely clear, but it seems that bases ending in *-ant/ance* (and their variants) and *-or* obligatorily take *-ial* (e.g. *circumstantial, professorial*).

-ary

Again a relational adjective-forming suffix, *-ary* usually attaches to nouns, as in *complementary, evolutionary, fragmentary, legendary, precautionary.* We find stress-shifts only with polysyllabic base nouns ending in *-ment* (cf. *compliméntary* vs. *mómentary*).

-ed

This suffix derives adjectives with the general meaning 'having X, being provided with X,' as in *broad-minded, pig-headed, wooded.* The majority of derivatives are based on compounds or phrases (*empty-headed, pig-headed, air-minded, fair-minded*).

-esque

The suffix *-esque* is attached to both common and proper nouns to convey the notion of 'in the manner or style of X': *Chaplinesque, Hemingwayesque, picturesque, Kafkaesque.* There is a strong preference for polysyllabic base words.

-ful

Adjectival *-ful* has the general meaning 'having X, being characterized by X' and is typically attached to abstract nouns, as in *beautiful, insightful, purposeful, tactful*, but verbal bases are not uncommon (e.g. *forgetful, mournful, resentful*). See section 3.4 for the productivity of adjectival *-ful*, and section 4.4.1 above for nominal *-ful*.

-ic/-ical

Being another relational suffix, *-ic* also attaches to foreign bases (nouns and bound roots). Quite a number of *-ic* derivatives have variant forms in *-ical* (*electric–electrical, economic–economical, historic–historical, magic–magical*, etc.). Sometimes these forms are clearly distinguished in meaning (e.g. *economic* 'profitable' vs. *economical* 'money-saving'), in other cases it remains to be determined what governs the choice of one form over the other.

Derivatives in *-ic* are stressed on the penultimate syllable, with stress being shifted there, if necessary (e.g. *héro–heróic, párasite–parasític*).

-ing

This verbal inflectional suffix primarily forms present participles, which can in general also be used as adjectives in attributive positions (and as nouns, see above). The grammatical status of a verb suffixed by *-ing* in predicative position is not always clear. In *the changing weather* the *-ing* form can be analyzed as an adjective, but in *the weather is changing* we should classify it as a verb (in particular as a progressive form). In *the film was boring*, however, we would probably want to argue that *boring* is an adjective, because the relation to the event denoted by the verb is much less prominent than in the case of *changing*.

-ish

This suffix can attach to adjectives (e.g. *clearish, freeish, sharpish*), numerals (*fourteenish, threehundredfortyish*), adverbs (*soonish, uppish*), and syntactic phrases (e.g. *stick-in-the-muddish, out-of-the-wayish, silly-little-me-late-again-ish*) to convey the concept of 'somewhat X, vaguely X.' When attached to nouns referring to human beings the derivatives can be paraphrased as 'of the character of X, like X,' which is obviously closely related to the meaning of the non-denominal derivatives. Examples of the latter kind are *James-Deanish, monsterish, summerish, townish, vampirish*. Some forms have a pejorative meaning, e.g. *childish*.

-ive

This suffix forms adjectives mostly from Latinate verbs and bound roots that end in [t] or [s]: *connective, explosive, fricative, offensive, passive, preventive, primitive, receptive, speculative*. Some nominal bases are also attested, as in *instinctive, massive*.

Apart from some exceptions (e.g. *álternate–altérnative*), there is no stress shift, but a number of fairly systematic base alternations can be observed: [d] → [s] (e.g. *conclude–conclusive*), [iv] → [εpt] (e.g. *receive–receptive*), [djus] → [dʌkt] (e.g. *produce–productive*). Probably modeled on the highly frequent derivatives with verbs in *-ate*, some forms feature the variant *-ative* without an existing verb in *-ate*: *argumentative, quantitative, representative*.

-less

Semantically, denominal *-less* can be seen as antonymic to *-ful*, with the meaning being paraphrasable as 'without X': *expressionless, hopeless, speechless, thankless*.

-ly

This suffix is appended to nouns and adjectives. With base nouns denoting persons, *-ly* usually conveys the notion of 'in the manner of X' or 'like an X,' as in *brotherly, daughterly, fatherly, womanly*. Other common types of derivative have bases denoting temporal concepts (e.g. *half-hourly, daily, monthly*) or directions (*easterly, southwesterly*).

-ous

This suffix derives adjectives from nouns and bound roots, the vast majority being of Latinate origin (*curious, barbarous, famous, synonymous, tremendous*). Like derivatives in *-al*, *-ous* formations are stressed either on the penultimate or the antepenultimate syllable with stress being shifted there, if necessary (e.g. *plátitude–platitúdinous*). There are further variants of the suffix, *-eous* (e.g. *erroneous, homogeneous*), *-ious* (e.g. *gracious, prestigious*), and *-uous* (e.g. *ambiguous, continuous*).

4.4.4 Adverbial suffixes

-ly

The presence of this exclusively de-adjectival suffix is for the most part syntactically triggered and obligatory, and it can therefore be considered inflectional. However, in some formations there is a difference in meaning between the adjective and the adverb derived by *-ly* attachment: *shortly, hardly*, and *dryly* are semantically distinct from their base words and *hotly, coldly*, and *darkly* can only have metaphorical senses. Such changes of meaning are unexpected for an inflectional suffix, which speaks against the classification of adverbial *-ly* as inflectional. See also the model answer to exercise 1.6. for a discussion of this question.

-wise

This suffix derives adverbs from nouns, with two distinguishable subgroups: manner/dimension adverbs, and so-called viewpoint adverbs. The former adverb type has the meaning 'in the manner of X, like X' as in *The towel wound sarongwise about his middle*, or indicates a spatial arrangement or movement, as in *The cone can be sliced lengthwise*. It is, however, not always possible to distinguish clearly between the 'manner' and 'dimension' readings (e.g. is '*cut X crosswise*' an instance of one or the other?). The smaller and much more recent group of viewpoint adverbs is made up of adverbs whose meaning can be rendered as 'with respect to, in regard to, concerning X.' The scope of the viewpoint adverbs is not the verb phrase, but the whole clause or sentence, a fact which is visible in the surface word order in *They make no special demands food-wise* and *Statuswise, you are at a disadvantage*.

4.5   Prefixes

The prefixes of English can be classified semantically into the following groups. First, there is a large group that quantify over their base words' meaning, for example, 'one' (*uni-, unilateral, unification*), 'twice or two' (*bi-, bilateral, bifurcation* and *di-, disyllabic, ditransitive*), 'many' (*multi-, multi-purpose, multilateral* and *poly-, polysyllabic, polyclinic*), 'half' (*semi-, semi-conscious, semi-desert*), 'all' (*omni-, omnipotent, omnipresent*), 'small' (*micro-, micro-surgical, microwave*), 'large' (*macro-, macro-economics, macro-biotic*), 'to excess' (*hyper-, hyperactive, hypermarket* and *over-, overestimate, overtax*), 'not sufficiently' (*undernourish, underpay*).

Second, there are numerous locative prefixes such as *circum-* 'around' (*circumnavigate, circumscribe*), *counter-*'against' (*counterbalance, counterexample*), *endo-* 'internal to X' (*endocentric, endocrinology*), *epi-* 'on, over' (*epiglottis, epicentral*), *inter-*'between' (*interbreed, intergalactic*), *intra-* 'inside' (*intramuscular, intravenous*), *para-* 'along with' (*paramedic, paranormal*), *retro-*'back, backwards' (*retroflex, retrospection*), *trans-* 'across' (*transcontinental, transmigrate*).

Third, there are temporal prefixes expressing notions like 'before' (*ante-, pre-*, and *fore-*, as in *antechamber, antedate, preconcert, predetermine, premedical*, *forefather, foresee*), 'after' (*post-, poststructuralism, postmodify, postmodern*), or 'new' (*neo-, neoclassical, Neo-Latin*). A fourth group consists of prefixes expressing negation (*a(n)-, de-, dis-, in-, non-, un-*; see below for examples).

Numerous prefixes do not fit into any of the four groups, however, and express diverse notions, such as 'wrong, evil' (*mal-, malfunction, malnutrition*), 'badly, wrongly' (*mis-, misinterpret, mistrial*), 'false, deceptive' (*pseudo-*), 'together, jointly' (*co-*), 'in place of' (*vice-*), etc. The vast majority of prefixes do not change the syntactic category of their base words; they merely act as modifiers. Furthermore, it can be observed that they generally attach to more than one kind of syntactic category (verb, adjective, or noun) and do not influence the stress pattern of their bases.

In the following we look in more detail at the negative prefixes and two of their close relatives, *mis-* and *anti-*. The negative prefixes appear to be more complex in their distribution and behavior than most of the other prefixes and their domains overlap considerably.

a(n)-

This prefix only occurs in Latinate adjectives. With denominal adjectives, the meaning can either be paraphrased as 'without what is referred to by the nominal base,' cf. for example *achromatic* 'without color,' *asexual* 'without sex,' or as 'not X,' as in *ahistorical, asymmetrical*. Opposites formed by *a(n)-* are mostly contraries (see section 2.3 for a discussion of the notion of contraries).

anti-

This polysemous prefix can express two different but related notions. In words like *anti-war, anti-abortion, anti-capitalistic, anti-scientific, anti-freeze, anti-glare* it can be paraphrased as 'against, opposing,' with denominal, de-adjectival and deverbal derivatives behaving like adjectives (cf. *anti-war movement, Are you pro-abortion or anti-abortion?, an anti-freeze liquid*). Another type of denominal *anti-* derivatives are nouns denoting something like 'the opposite of an X' or 'not having the proper characteristics of an X,' as in *anti-hero, anti-particle, anti-professor*.

de-

This prefix attaches to verbs and nouns to form reversative or privative verbs: *decolonize, decaffeinate, deflea, depollute, dethrone, deselect*. Very often, *de-* verbs are parasynthetic formations, as evidenced by, for example, *decaffeinate*, for which no verb **caffeinate* is attested.

dis-

Closely related semantically to *un-* and *de-*, the prefix *dis-* forms reversative verbs from foreign verbal bases: *disassemble, disassociate, discharge, disconnect, disproof, disqualify*. Apart from deriving reversative verbs, this suffix uniquely offers the possibility to negate the base verb in much the same way as clausal negation does: *disagree* 'not agree,' *disobey* 'not obey,' *dislike* 'not like.'

Dis- is also found inside nouns and nominalizations, but it is often unclear whether *dis-* is prefixed to the nominalization (cf. [*dis-*[*organization*]]) or to the verb before the nominalizing suffix was attached (cf. [[*disorganiz*]-*ation*]; see section 2.4 for a general discussion of such bracketing problems). There are, however, a few forms that suggest that prefixation to nouns is possible, conveying the meaning 'absence of X' or 'faulty X': *disanalogy, disfluency, disinformation*.

Finally, *dis-* also occurs in lexicalized adjectives with the meaning 'not X': *dishonest, dispassionate, disproportional*.

in-

This negative prefix is exclusively found with Latinate adjectives and the general negative meaning 'not': *incomprehensible, inactive, intolerable, implausible, illegal, irregular*. It assimilates to the first sound of the base in the manner described in the answer key to exercise 2.5.

mis-

Modifying verbs and nouns (with similar bracketing problems as those mentioned above for *dis-*), *mis-* conveys the meaning 'inaccurate(ly), wrong(ly)': *misalign, mispronounce, misreport, misstate, misjoinder, misdemeanor, mistrial*. The prefix is usually either unstressed or secondarily stressed. Exceptions with primary stress on the prefix are either lexicalizations (e.g. *míschief*) or some nouns that are segmentally homophonous with verbs: *míscount* (noun) vs. *miscóunt* (verb), *mísmatch* vs. *mismátch, mísprint* vs. *misprínt*.

non-

When attached to adjectives this prefix has the general meaning of 'not X': *non-biological, non-commercial, non-returnable*. In contrast to *un-* and *in-*, negation with *non-* does not carry evaluative force, as can be seen from the pairs *unscientific* vs. *non-scientific, irrational* vs. *non-rational*. Furthermore, *non-* primarily forms contradictory and complementary opposites (see section 2.3 for a discussion of the different concepts of oppositeness).

Nouns prefixed with *non-* can either mean 'absence of X' or 'not having the character of X': *non-delivery, non-member, non-profit, non-stop*. The latter meaning has been extended to 'being X, but not having the proper characteristics of an X': *non-issue, non-answer*.

un-

As already discussed in chapter 2, *un-* can attach to verbs and sometimes nouns (mostly of native stock) to yield a reversative or privative ('remove X') meaning: *unbind, uncork, unleash, unsaddle, unwind, unwrap*. The prefix is also used to negate simple and derived adjectives: *uncomplicated, unhappy, unsuccessful, unreadable*. Adjectival *un-* derivatives usually express contraries, especially with simplex bases (see section 2.3 for a more detailed discussion).

Nouns are also attested with *un-*, usually expressing 'absence of X' (e.g. *unease, unbelief, uneducation, unrepair*). Such nouns are often the result of analogy or back-formation (e.g. *educated : uneducated :: education : **uneducation***). We also find a meaning extension similar to the one observed with *anti-* and *non-*, namely 'not having the proper characteristics of X': *uncelebrate, unevent, un-Hollywood* (all attested in the BNC).

The prefix shows optional place assimilation: before labials, the variant [ʌm] can occur, and before velar consonants [ʌŋ] is a free variant. In all other cases we find only [ʌn].

4.6   Infixation

Morphologists usually agree that English has no infixes. However, there is the possibility of inserting expletives in the middle of words to create new words expressing the strongly negative attitude of the speaker (e.g. *kanga-bloody-roo, abso-blooming-lutely*). Thus we could say that English has a process of infixation of (certain) words, but there are no bound morphemes that qualify for infix status. Such forms raise two questions. The first is what structural properties these infixed derivatives have, and the second is whether we should consider this type of infixation as part of the English word-formation component or not. We will deal with each question in turn.

From a phonological point of view these forms are completely regular. Hammond (1999: 161–164) shows that the expletive is always inserted in the same prosodic position. Consider the following data and try to determine the pertinent generalization before reading on. The expletive is represented by 'ᴇxᴘʟ,' and primary and secondary stresses are marked as usual by acute and grave accents, respectively:

(19)   Possible and impossible infixations
        fròn-E X P L-tíer   *tí-E X P L-ger
        sàr-E X P L-díne   *se-E X P L-réne
        bì-E X P L-chlórìde   *Cá-E X P L-nada
        bàn-E X P L-dánna   *ba-E X P L-nána
        ámper-E X P L-sànd   *ám-E X P L-persànd
        cárni-E X P L-vóre   *cár-E X P L-nivòre

The data show that infixation is obviously sensitive to the stress pattern of the base words. There must be a stressed syllable to the left and one to the right of the expletive (hence the impossibility of *tí-EXPL-ger*, *Cá-EXPL-nada*, or *ba-EXPL-nána*). But why then are *ám-EXPL-persànd* and *cár-EXPL-nivòre* impossible? In order to arrive at the correct (and more elegant) generalization we need to be aware of a prosodic unit called a **foot**, which is of crucial importance here. A foot is a metrical unit consisting of either one stressed syllable, or one stressed syllable and one or more unstressed syllables. It is usually assumed that English is a primarily trochaic language, which means that there is a strong tendency to form disyllabic feet that have their stress on the left (so-called **trochees**, as in *bóttle*, *héaven*, *strúcture*, *wáter*). Other languages, such as French, only have feet with stress on the right, so-called **iambs**, as in *París*, *egále*, *traváil*, *travaillér*. Each word of English can be assigned a metrical structure in terms of feet, with each stressed syllable heading one foot. A word like *ámpersànd* would then be analyzed as having two feet: (*ám.per*)(*sànd*), with foot boundaries indicated by parentheses.

Returning to expletive infixation, the foot structure of the words in (19) can be represented as in (20). Parentheses indicate feet:

(20)   **Possible foot structures**   **Impossible foot structure**
        (fròn)-E X P L-(tíer)   *(tí-E X P L-ger)
        (sár)-E X P L-(dìne)   *se-E X P L-(réne) or *(se-E X P L-réne)
        (bì)-E X P L-(chlór)(ìde)   *(Cá-E X P L-nada) or *(Cá-E X P L-na)da
        (bàn)-E X P L-(dánna)   *ba-E X P L-(nána) or *(ba-E X P L-ná)na
        (ámper)-E X P L-(sànd)   *(ám-E X P L-per)(sànd)
        (cárni)-E X P L-(vòre)   *(cár-E X P L-ni)(vòre)

We are now in a position to establish the pertinent generalization: the expletive must be inserted between two feet. It is not allowed to interrupt a foot, as in *(tí-EXPL-ger), *(ám-EXPL-per)(sànd), and *(cár-EXPL-ni) (vòre), nor may it appear between an unstressed syllable not belonging to a foot and a foot, as in *se-EXPL-(réne) or *ba-EXPL-(nána).

In sum, we have seen that infixation in English is determined by the metrical structure of the base, or, more specifically, by its foot structure. Expletive infixation can be regarded as a case of **prosodic morphology**, i.e. a kind of morphology where prosodic units and prosodic restrictions are chiefly responsible for the shape of complex words. More examples of prosodic morphology will be discussed in the next chapter.

We may now turn to the question of whether expletive infixation should be considered part of word-formation. Some scholars hold that "morphological operations that produce outputs that are not classifiable as either distinct words or inflectional word forms are not part of morphological grammar" and exclude expletive infixation from word-formation "because neither new words nor inflectional word forms are formed" (Dressler and Merlini Barbaresi 1994: 41). One might ask, however, what is meant by "new word"? From a semantic point of view, one could perhaps argue that expletive infixation does not create a new lexeme because the core meaning of the base word is not affected. However, the derived word tells us something about the speaker's attitude (see Aronoff 1976: 69), which is an additional, new meaning.

Treating expletive infixation as regular word-formation is also in line with the idea (to which the aforementioned authors subscribe) that diminutives (like *doggy*) and augmentatives (like *super-cool*) are instances of word-formation. Even big dogs are called *doggy* by their loving owners, which shows that diminutives do not generally add the meaning 'small' (cf. Schneider 2003), but often merely express the speaker's emotional attitude. This would force us to say that in many cases, diminutives and augmentatives would not form 'new words' in the sense of Dressler and Merlini Barbaresi (1994) either.

Another argument that could be raised against expletive infixation as word-formation concerns lexicalization. Thus it could be argued that diminutives may be listed as new words in the lexicon, which is not the case with infixed forms such as the ones cited above. A first objection against this argument is that a claim is made about listedness which would have to be backed up by empirical evidence, for example through psycholinguistic evidence. A second objection is that, as we have seen in the discussion of psycholinguistic aspects of word-formation in section 3.3, lexicalization is chiefly a matter of frequency. Hence, the alleged lack of lexicalization of infixed forms may simply be due to the comparatively low token frequencies of the individual formations.

A final argument for the inclusion of expletive infixation into our morphological grammar is that structurally it is a completely regular process and as such must be part of our linguistic competence.

4.7   Summary

In this chapter we have looked at numerous affixational processes in English. We saw that it is not always easy to differentiate affixes from other morphological entities. We then explored different ways to obtain large amounts of data, introducing reverse dictionaries, the *OED*, and electronic text corpora. It turned out that in spite of the advantages of the available electronic media it still takes a well-educated morphologist to conscientiously process the raw data and turn them into potentially interesting data sets.

We then investigated some general characteristics of English affixation, showing that important generalizations can be stated on the basis of the phonological make-up of affixes. Finally, a survey of affixes was provided that exemplified the wide range of derivational patterns available in the language. We saw that suffixation and prefixation are very common, whereas infixation is a marginal and extremely restricted phenomenon in English word-formation. In the next chapter we will have a closer look at the characteristics of some non-affixational processes by which new words can be derived.

Further reading

A recent investigation into the demarcation between affixation and compounding is Dalton-Puffer and Plag (2001). Neoclassical word-formation is discussed in Bauer (1998a) and Lüdeling et al. (2002). Methodological questions with regard to the use of dictionaries and text corpora are laid out in considerable detail in Plag (1999). For more detailed surveys of English affixes, see Jespersen (1942), Marchand (1969), Adams (2001), and Bauer and Huddleston (2002). Raffelsiefen (1999) is an excellent overview of general phonological restrictions holding in English suffixation. More detailed investigations of specific affixes are numerous, and only a few can be mentioned here: Aronoff (1976) on *-able, -ity, -ous*, and some other suffixes, Barker (1998) on *-ee*, Ryder (1999) on *-er*, Dalton-Puffer and Plag (2001) on *-ful* and *-wise*, Kaunisto (1999) on *-ic* and *-ical*, Borer (1990) on *-ing*, Malkiel (1977) on *-ish* and *-y*, Riddle (1985) on *-ness* and *-ity*, Ljung (1970) on denominal adjectives, Zimmer (1964) on negative prefixes, Plag (1999) on verbal suffixes, and Baeskow (2002) on derived nouns denoting persons.

Exercises

Basic level

Exercise 4.1

This exercise is designed to train your methodological skills. The aim is to extract data from the *OED* for the suffix *-able*. Do so separately for the seventeenth century, the eighteenth century, and for the second half of the twentieth century. Choose the file with the smallest amount of words and clean the raw data. Take note of those forms where it was problematic to decide whether to include or exclude the form in question. On which basis did you include or exclude items? Try to formulate your methodology and justify your decisions as accurately as possible.

Exercise 4.2

Part 1: What do the suffixes *-ion* and *-ure* have in common, apart from their being nominalizing suffixes? Examine the following data and state your generalization as accurately as possible. Focus on the morpho-phonological side of the matter. You may formulate your generalizations in the form of a morpho-phonological rule similar to the one for *-al/-ar* discussed in section 2.2.

a.						
erode	→	*erosion*		*compose*	→	*composure*
conclude	→	*conclusion*		*erase*	→	*erasure*
confuse	→	*confusion*		*close*	→	*closure*
persuade	→	*persuasion*		*dispose*	→	*disposure*

Part 2: Do the same for the suffixes *-ity*, *-ize*, *-ify*, and *-ism* on the bases of the following data:

b.						
atomic	→	*atomicity*		*classic*	→	*classicize*
iambic	→	*iambicity*		*erotic*	→	*eroticize*
historic	→	*historicity*		*opaque*	→	*opacify*
opaque	→	*opacity*		*classic*	→	*classicism*
historic	→	*historicize*		*romantic*	→	*romanticism*

Advanced level

Exercise 4.3

Now consider the following forms and relate their behavior to the behavior of the words in the previous exercise. Reconsider the accurateness of the rule stated in exercise 4.2.

anarchy	*anarchism*
monarch	*monarchism*
masochist	*masochism*

Exercise 4.4

We saw in this chapter that there is a rivalry among the negative prefixes *un-*, *in-*, *dis*, *de-*, *non-*, and *anti-*. It seems that certain words can take more than one of these prefixes and the question arises whether there are any restrictions governing the distribution of the negative prefixes. This exercise is an attempt to answer this question.

To do so, set up a table that lists the combinatorial and semantic properties of each prefix as they are discussed in section 4.5 above. On the basis of this overview it should be possible to state – at least roughly – where the domains of certain prefixes overlap and where they can be clearly separated. Formulate the pertinent generalizations.

5

Derivation without affixation

Outline

This chapter deals with non-affixational word-formation processes. First, three major problems of conversion are discussed. This is followed by an introduction to prosodic morphology with a detailed analysis of some morphological categories that are expressed by chiefly prosodic means, such as truncated names, -*y* diminutives, clippings, and blends. Finally, abbreviations and acronyms are investigated.

5.1   Conversion

Apart from the perhaps more obvious possibility of deriving words with the help of affixes, there are a number of other ways to create new words on the basis of already existing ones. We have already illustrated these in the first chapter of this book, when we briefly introduced the notions of conversion, truncations, clippings, blends, and abbreviations. In this chapter we will have a closer look at these non-concatenative processes. We will begin with conversion.

Conversion can be defined as the derivation of a new word without any overt marking. In order to find cases of conversion we have to look for pairs of words that are derivationally related and are completely identical in their phonetic realization. Such cases are not hard to find, and some are listed in (1):

(1)   a. the bottle   to bottle
            the hammer   to hammer
            the file   to file
            the skin   to skin
            the water   to water
         b. to call   a call
            to dump   a dump
            to guess   a guess
            to jump   a jump
            to spy   a spy

c.	better	to better
	empty	to empty
	hip	to hip
	open	to open
	rustproof	to rustproof
d.	poor	the poor
	rich	the rich
	well-fed	the well-fed
	blind	the blind
	sublime	the sublime

As can be seen from the organization of the data, different types of conversion can be distinguished, in particular noun to verb (1a), verb to noun (1b), adjective to verb (1c), and adjective to noun (1d). Other types can also be found, but seem to be more marginal (e.g. the use of prepositions as verbs, as in *to down the can*). Conversion raises three major theoretical problems that we will discuss in the following sections: the problem of directionality, the problem of zero-morphs, and the problem of the morphology-syntax boundary.

5.1.1   The directionality of conversion

The first problem is the directionality of conversion. We have simply assumed, but not shown, that in (1a) it is the verb that is derived from the noun and not the noun that is derived from the verb. For the data in (1b) we have assumed the opposite, namely that the verb is basic and the noun derived. Similar assumptions have been made for the data in (1c) and (1d). But how can these assumptions be justified or substantiated? There are four possible ways of determining the directionality of conversion.

The first would be to look at the history of the language and see which word was first. While this may work nicely with many words, there are other word pairs where the historical relationship would go against our present-day intuition. For example, most speakers would probably say that the verb *to crowd* seems to be derived from the noun *crowd*. However, according to the *OED*, historically the verb was first. In Old English, the verb *crūdan* meant 'to press, hasten, drive,' with its first attestation in AD 937. The then primary meaning 'to press' was later specialized to refer to the compression of multitudes. Only after this specialization of meaning was the verb (in the sixteenth century) converted into a noun denoting a compressed mass of people or things, a meaning that was later broadened to denote any mass of people. This example shows that simply looking at earliest attestations does not solve the directionality problem, because complex semantic changes may overwrite the original direction of conversion. Similar arguments hold for *moan*, which was first attested in 1225 as a noun, and not until later, in the sixteenth century, was this noun converted into a verb (see *OED*, s.v. *moan*). Today's meaning of *moan* is perhaps best described as 'the act of moaning,' which shows that for present-day speakers the noun depends on the verb for its interpretation and not vice versa.

The example of *moan* already indicates a more promising way of determining the direction of conversion, namely investigating the semantic complexity of the two words in question. In general, derived words are semantically more complex than their bases, since affixes normally add a certain meaning to the meaning of the base. A parallel reasoning can be applied to conversion: the derived (i.e. converted) word should be semantically more complex than the base word from which it is derived. Thus, if one member of the pair can be analyzed as being semantically more complex than or as being semantically dependent on the other member, we have good evidence that the dependent member is derived from the other form. Consider four of the examples in (1): the meaning of the verb *bottle* is 'to put into a bottle,' the meaning of the noun *call* is 'the act of calling,' the meaning of the verb *to better* is 'to make or become better,' and the meaning of the noun *poor* is 'poor people (as a class).' In all four cases the second member of the pair is semantically more complex than the first member and depends in its interpretation on the latter. Speaking in terms of concepts, the verb *to bottle* requires the existence of the concept of a bottle. Without a bottle there is no bottling.

The semantic dependency between base and derived word is chiefly responsible for the intuitive feeling that the words on the right in (1) are derived on the basis of the words on the left, and not vice versa.

But historical and semantic information alone will not solve the directionality problem. Base form and derived form also often differ in formal properties. Consider, for example, the data in (2):

(2)	**present tense**	**past tense**	**meaning**
	ring	ringed	'provide with a ring'
	ring	rang	*'provide with a ring'
	wing	winged/*wang/*wung	'provide with wings'
	grandstand	grandstanded/*grandstood	'to act to impress spectators'

The past-tense forms of the converted verbs are all regular, although there is in principle the possibility of irregular inflection. The past-tense form *rang* cannot mean 'provide with a ring,' the past-tense form of *to wing* cannot be formed in analogy to similar-sounding verbs like *sing, ring,* or *sting,* and the past-tense form of *to grandstand* must also be regular. Why should this be so? The reason for this state of affairs lies in the nature of irregular inflection. Irregularly inflected words like *went, took,* or *brought* must be learned by children (and second language learners) item by item, i.e. by storing every irregular form in the lexicon. If for a given word there is no irregular form stored in the lexicon, this form will be inflected according to the regular inflectional patterns. This is the reason why small children may say things like *bringed* or *taked*, and why newly created words, which do not yet have a stored entry in the mental lexicon, are inflected regularly.

Now, if we can state that converted verbs in general must be regularly inflected, we can make an argument concerning the directionality of conversion based on the inflectional behavior: if we find a homonymous verb-noun pair which is a potential case of conversion, and one of the words is irregularly inflected, this is a strong indication that the regularly inflecting word is derived from the irregularly inflecting word. For instance, the irregular inflectional behavior of verbs like *to drink, to hit, to shake*, or *to sleep* is a strong argument for the deverbal nature of the nouns *drink, hit, shake*, and *sleep*. In sum, the inflectional behavior of forms can give evidence for a particular direction of conversion.

Another formal property that comes to mind when thinking about conversion is stress. Take a look at (3):

(3)   a. to tormént – a tórment
            to permít – a pérmit
            to constrúct – a cónstruct
            to extráct – an éxtract
            to abstráct – an ábstract
        b. to gèt awáy – a gét-awày
            to lèt dówn – a lét-dòwn
            to pùll dówn – a púll-dòwn
            to pùsh úp – a púsh-up
            to wàlk òver – a wálk-òver

The data in (3) show pairs of verbs (on the left) and nouns (on the right) which can be analyzed as standing in a derivational relationship. Based on semantic considerations, we can state that these are all cases of deverbal nouns. From a formal perspective these pairs are also interesting because the two members differ in one formal property, their stress pattern. When spelled without the accents indicating stresses, there is no *visible* marking, but when pronounced, there is a clear difference between the verbs and the nouns: the verbs in (3a) have primary stress on their last syllable, while the related nouns have stress on the first syllable. Similarly, the phrasal verbs in (3b) have primary stress on the preposition, while the related nouns have primary stress on the first element. Thus, in all those cases where we observe a stress-shift, we have a good argument to say that we are dealing with derived nouns. Note, however, that the above examples are not clear cases of conversion, because the relationship between the pairs is marked overtly, even though this marking is done not by an affix, but by a prosodic property. But even if we do not regard pairs such as those in (3) as instances of conversion, we would still have to account for the derivational relationship and find out which member of the pair is basic and which one is derived. What these examples show independently of their being classified as instances of conversion or not is that formal properties can be adduced to substantiate other, in this case semantic, criteria for the directionality of derivation, even in the absence of affixes.

The last property relevant for the determination of directionality is frequency of occurrence. In general, there is a strong tendency for derived words being less frequently used than their base words. For example, it has been shown in Plag (2002) that in a random sample of 92 -*able* derivatives taken from the BNC, only 7 derivatives were more frequent than their base words, whereas all other -*able* derivatives in the sample were less frequent than their bases. The same was shown for a sample of -*ize* derivatives, where only 11 out of 102 derivatives were more frequent than their base words. The simple reason for these facts is again semantics. Being semantically more complex, derived words tend to have a narrower range of meaning, to the effect that they cannot be used in as many contexts as their base words. With regard to conversion, we would therefore expect that by and large the derived word is the less frequent one. For the directionality question this means that, for example, if the noun *water* is more frequent than the verb *to water* (which indeed is the case), this is an indication that the verb is derived from the noun. In the case of *drink*, the verb is more frequent, which supports our above arguments that the verb is basic and the noun derived.

In sum, we have seen that there is a whole range of criteria by which the directionality of conversion can be established. Nevertheless, one may occasionally end up with difficult cases. For example, forms such as *love* (the noun) and *love* (the verb) are hard to decide upon. Both are current since Old English times, and neither of them seems to be semantically primary. Thus *to love* could be paraphrased as 'being in a state of love,' indicating that it may be a denominal derivative. However, the opposite direction can also be argued for, since the noun could be paraphrased as 'state of loving,' which would make the verb primary. The non-semantic criteria discussed above do not lead to a clear result either. Although such equivocal cases do occur, it seems that for the vast majority of cases it is possible to establish the direction of conversion.

Let us turn to the second theoretical problem raised by conversion, the problem of zero.

5.1.2   Conversion or zero-affixation?

Although we have argued in section 2.1.2 that in principle the existence of zero-forms should not be rejected entirely, the question remains in which particular cases it is justified to postulate a zero-form. Most morphologists think that a zero-form is justified only in those cases where there is also an overt (i.e. non-zero) form that expresses exactly the same meaning or function (cf. e.g. Sanders 1988:

160–161). This constraint has also been called the **overt analogue criterion**. The obvious question now is whether there is such an overt analogue in the cases of conversion introduced above.

This means that for each type of conversion (noun to verb, verb to noun, adjective to verb, adjective to noun) we would have to find at least one affix that expresses exactly the same range of meanings as conversion. If so, we can safely assume the existence of a zero-affix, if not, we have to reject it. You might wonder why such a decision is necessary in the first place. After all, in both cases, both conversion and zero-affixation would fulfill the same function, i.e. do their job properly. That is of course true, but if we extend our – so far – narrow descriptive perspective beyond the phenomenon of conversion into the realm of general morphological theory, this question becomes an important one. Thus, there are theories that claim that all derivational processes, i.e. overt affixation, conversion, truncation, ablaut, and all other kinds of formal morphological marking, are in fact affixational (e.g. Lieber 1992). Such an assumption has the advantage that the morphological apparatus is reduced to one central mechanism (i.e. affixation) and all other seemingly different mechanisms have no theoretical status and are pure surface phenomena. This kind of theory is very elegant, but together with this elegance we buy the necessity to provide an affixational analysis for all processes that – at least on the surface – do not have an affix. And if we failed in doing so, the theory that all morphology is essentially and exclusively affixational would have to be rejected. Thus, showing that there is in fact no zero-affix would seriously challenge this kind of theory.

Let us return to the facts to see whether the overt analogue criterion holds, starting with conversion into verbs. The crucial question is whether there is a verb-deriving affix that has precisely the same meaning as our putative zero-affix. In Plag (1999) I have argued that this is not the case and that the overt suffixes *-ate, -ify,* and *-ize* express much more restricted ranges of meanings than conversion. For example, in twentieth-century neologisms, the following types of meaning of converted verbs can be discerned:

(4)

type of meaning	paraphrase	example
locative	'put (in)to X'	*jail*
ornative	'provide with X'	*staff*
causative	'make (more) X'	*yellow*
resultative	'make into X'	*bundle*
inchoative	'become X'	*cool*
performative	'perform X'	*counterattack*
similative	'act like X'	*chauffeur, pelican*
instrumental	'use X'	*hammer*
privative	'remove X'	*bark*
stative	'be X'	*hostess*

In addition to the meanings in (4), more idiosyncratic meanings can also be observed, such as *to eel*, which can mean 'fish for eel' or 'to move . . . like an eel,' or *to premature*, which is recorded as having the meaning 'Of a shell or other projectile: to explode prematurely,' or *to crew* can mean 'act as a (member of a) crew' or 'assign to a crew.' None of the overt verb-deriving affixes of English can express such a wide range of meanings (see again the discussion of the verb-deriving suffixes in section 4.4.2 of the preceding chapter), so that on the basis of this analysis we have to conclude that the overt analogue criterion is not met. Hence there is no basis for the assumption of a zero-affix.

To test the overt analogue criterion with verb-to-noun conversion, we have to compare the meaning of overt suffixes like *-ation, -al, -ing, -ment*, etc. with converted nouns. This is not an easy task at all because action nouns tend to be polysemous. Although in many cases there seems to be no clear semantic difference between overtly suffixed nouns and converted nouns, Cetnarowska (1993: 113) has shown that there are at least two remarkable systematic differences between nouns referring to actions derived by *-ing* and converted nouns (e.g. *drawing* vs. *draw*, *beating* vs. *beat*). First, when the base word is a transitive verb, the suffixed noun can be related to all senses of the verb, while the converted noun relates only to one sense of the base word. Thus *drawing* refers to any activity of drawing, whereas *draw* is restricted in its reference to the drawing of cards or lots. Secondly, verbs that can be used both transitively and intransitively exhibit different effects under nominalization by suffixation or conversion. The suffixed nominalization will be related to the transitive usage of the verb, while the conversion will be related to the intransitive usage. Thus, we say *the beating of the prisoners* but *the beat of my heart*. These systematic differences suggest that verb-to-noun conversion and overt nominal suffixation are not semantically identical and that one can therefore not be regarded as an overt analogue of the other.

With regard to adjective-to-noun conversion we can observe that there is no overt analogue in sight. There are suffixes that derive nouns denoting collectivities similar to the nouns in (1d) (*-dom*, and *-hood* in particular, e.g. *martyrdom*, see section 4.4.1), but these suffixes are strictly denominal and are therefore not possible analogues. And de-adjectival suffixes such as *-ness* or *-ity* do not produce the same semantic effect as conversion, because they derive nouns denoting states or properties, but not collective entities (see section 4.4.1 for details).

Finally, adjective-to-verb conversion equally does not present a clear case of zero-derivation. Derivatives like *to young* ('to present the apparently younger side,' *OED*) show that the range of meaning of de-adjectival converted verbs is larger than the strictly and exclusively causative or inchoative interpretations ('make (more) X' or 'become X') of overtly suffixed de-adjectival verbs (see again section 4.4.2 for more details on verbal suffixes).

In sum, the application of the overt analogue criterion seems to give evidence against the assumption of zero-derivation and in favor of non-affixational conversion.

We may now turn to the third major theoretical problem involved in the analysis of conversion, that of the boundary between syntax and morphology.

5.1.3   Conversion: syntactic or morphological?

So far, we have tacitly assumed that conversion is a morphological, i.e. lexical, process. However, one could also argue that conversion is a purely syntactic mechanism. In other words, conversion could be defined as the use of a word with a given syntactic category in a syntactic position that it normally does not occupy. And if it appears in such a position, it takes on the properties of those items that usually occupy this position. Consider, for example, the following sentences:

(5)   a. James *watered* the plants every other day.
         b. Jenny *wintered* in Spain.

We could argue that the verbs *water* and *winter* are not derived by a morphological process, but simply by putting them into a verbal slot in the sentences (5a) and (5b), which would be a syntactic, not a morphological operation.

However, such a view creates new problems. Usually it is assumed that words must have a clear category specification because such information is necessary for the application of syntactic rules. For example, in order to construct a well-formed English sentence we must know which word is an article, a noun, an auxiliary, a verb etc., so that we can place them in the right order. Thus *the lion will sleep in a cage* is a grammatical sentence, whereas *sleep cage the in will lion a* is ungrammatical, because articles must precede their nouns, the auxiliary *will* must precede the verb *sleep*, etc. Such rules make crucial reference to the part-of-speech of words and if this category information did not exist or could be easily ignored in the application of syntactic rules, we would end up with ill-formed sentences, in which verbs occur in the positions of nouns, articles in the position of verbs, etc.

Some proponents of a syntactic view of conversion (e.g. Farrell 2001) have argued that lexical category information may be underspecified, so that full specification is achieved only when the word appears in a specific syntactic context. For example, one might argue that the word *hammer* could be claimed to be semantically determined only in such a way that it can refer to anything in connection with such a tool. In a nominal position, as in *the hammer*, the word *hammer* receives a nominal interpretation ('a tool for hammering'), while in a verbal slot (as in *She hammered the metal flat*), the word *hammer* receives a verbal interpretation ('action of hammering').

How can this issue be decided? The best way to solve this problem is to see what distinguishes syntactic processes from morphological ones in general, and then look again at conversion and see which properties (syntactic or lexical-morphological) hold. Such an approach is confronted with the problem of determining the general properties of syntactic rules or processes. This is a serious problem because there are many different syntactic theories which have very different views on this. For example, many people will say that syntactic rules in general do not change the syntactic category of a word, but need to know the category of a word in order to be able to treat it accordingly. Thus, in English there is the syntactic rule that articles precede adjectives, which in turn precede nouns (as in *the clever student*), so that, in order to serialize the words correctly, the rule must have access to the category information of the words, but cannot change this information. In this sense, we would have a seemingly clear criterion that would tell us that conversion is non-syntactic. However, in a different theory of syntax, we would probably say that there is a syntactic rule which says that adjectives can generally be used in syntactic positions reserved for nouns, if they are preceded by the definite article *the*, as for example in *the rich*, or *the obvious*. This would have the effect that a syntactic rule practically changes the syntactic category of these adjectives. We do not want to argue in this book for or against certain theories of syntax, but there is one (more or less) theory-independent argument that can help to solve the problem of syntax-morphology boundary raised by conversion.

The most important property that distinguishes morphological rules and entities from syntactic ones is the idiosyncrasies of morphological formations. Complex words can display all kinds of exceptional properties, whereas syntactic patterns and their interpretations tend to be rather exceptionless. This is especially evident with regard to the usually compositional meaning of syntactic phrases as against the often non-compositional, lexicalized meaning of complex morphological structures. Applying this idea to conversion, it seems that with regard to converted verbs, idiosyncratic meanings and lexical gaps are rather common, which indicates their lexical, non-syntactic, nature. Coming back to example (5b), we can observe that *to winter* is possible, but that the analogous forms *to spring* or *to autumn* seem to be utterly strange. Furthermore, many unclear restrictions hold as to which kinds of nouns can be converted into verbs. Many nouns can only take overt suffixes, and the reason seems to be often a morphological one. For example, most complex nouns (e.g. derivatives in *-ness*, *-ity*, *-ation*, *-ment*, etc.) cannot occur in syntactic positions normally reserved for verbs (cf. e.g. *Jane curiousnesses every day*). Such restrictions are extremely uncommon (to put it mildly) in syntax. Syntactic rules usually check the syntactic category of a word, but not its internal derivational morphology, i.e. what kinds of derivational affixes the word has. In view of these arguments it makes sense to conceive of conversion in general as a lexical, i.e. morphological, process, and not as a syntactic one.

However, the non-idiosyncratic behavior of adjectives used to refer to collective entities (e.g. *the poor, the blind*) can be taken as evidence for the syntactic nature of this special type of conversion.

To summarize our discussion of the three major problems of conversion, we have seen that the directionality problem can be solved by combining historical, semantic, formal, and frequential evidence, the problem of zero can be solved by strictly applying the overt analogue criterion, and the morphology-syntax boundary problem can be solved by adducing considerations on the nature of lexical rules.

5.2   Prosodic morphology

As already introduced in chapter 4, prosodic morphology deals with the interaction of morphological and prosodic information in determining the structure of complex words. In section 4.3, we discussed cases of phonology-morphology interaction that involved suffixation. We saw, among other things, that the attachment of a certain suffix can be responsible for a specific stress pattern that holds for all members of the pertinent morphological category. For instance, all nouns in *-ity* carry primary stress on the antepenultimate syllable, all *-ic* adjectives have stress on the penult, and all nouns in *-ee* have stress on the suffix. In other words, even in suffixation we find that the structure of derivatives is determined by an interaction of morphology and prosody. The term 'prosodic morphology' is, however, usually reserved for those cases where the relevant category is expressed predominantly or exclusively through prosody, which is certainly not the case with the suffixes just mentioned (but with the pairs of words introduced in (3)). We will discuss two kinds of word-formation processes in English where prosody plays a prominent role, truncations and blends.

5.2.1   *Truncations: truncated names, -y diminutives, and clippings*

Truncation is a process in which the relationship between a derived word and its base is expressed by the lack of phonetic material in the derived word. Examples were already given in chapter 1 and are repeated here for convenience:

(6)   a. Ron (← Aaron)   b. condo (← condominium)
          Liz (← Elizabeth)   demo (← demonstration)
          Mike (← Michael)   disco (← discotheque)
          Trish (← Patricia)   lab (← laboratory)

The examples in (7) below involve suffixation by -*y* (orthographic variants of which are -*ie* and sometimes -*ee*), but their form seems also to be heavily influenced by truncation, which is the reason why we treat them in this chapter and not in the section on suffixation in the previous chapter.

(7)   Mandy (←Amanda)
        Andy (← Andrew)
        Charlie (← Charles)
        Patty (← Patricia)
        Robbie (← Roberta)

Given that all three types of formation are rather common and comparatively productive, the obvious question is how such words are formed, and what kinds of rules or restrictions are at work.

In previous work on these categories such forms have usually been regarded as highly idiosyncratic, and name truncations, -*y* diminutives, and clippings have been argued to be outside grammatical morphology (see, for example, Dressler and Merlini Barbaresi 1994, Dressler 2000). However, we will shortly see that such claims are not really justified. Truncations in English are highly systematic, and their systematicity indicates that the knowledge about the structural properties of these categories should be treated as part of the morphological competence of the speakers.

Truncated names can be distinguished from -*y* diminutives both semantically and formally. Truncated names (and clippings like *lab*) are used to express familiarity. Thus, truncated names are normally used by people who feel familiar with the person referred to and who want to express this familiarity overtly. Diminutives such as *sweety* or *Frannie* express not only familiarity, but also a (usually) positive attitude towards the person or thing referred to (see Schneider 2003 for discussion). The nature of the semantic or pragmatic modulation caused by name truncations, -*y* diminutives, and clippings has been taken by some researchers (e.g. Dressler 2000) as evidence against the status of truncation as a word-formation process proper. The problem is essentially the same as the one we have already discussed in our treatment of infixation in the previous chapter and boils down to the question of what exactly we mean when we say that a word-formation process should add 'new meaning' to a base, thereby creating a new lexeme. Do we consider the expression of attitude a 'new meaning'? Or only as a minor modulation in usage? This question can only be answered properly if we make explicit assumptions about the nature of meaning and its relation to language use. The development of such a theory of semantics and pragmatics is beyond the scope of this introduction to word-formation, and we will therefore assume a notion of word-formation wide enough to accommodate name truncations, clippings, and diminutives as products of word-formation.

Let us move on from these theoretical problems to the formal properties of name truncations. Consider the following data and take a moment to think about their prosodic properties, both in terms of their own structure, but also in terms of how this structure is related to that of their respective base words. The data and analysis are taken from Lappe (2003):

(8)	base		truncated name	base		truncated name
	Aaron	→	Ron	Alonzo	→	Al
	Abigail	→	Gail	Alonzo	→	Lon
	Abraham	→	Abe	Amelia	→	Mel
	Adelbert	→	Bert	Antoinette	→	Net
	Adolphus	→	Dolph	Arabella	→	Belle
	Agatha	→	Ag	Augustus	→	Guss
	Albert	→	Al	Barbara	→	Barb
	Alexandra	→	Xan	Bartholomew	→	Bart
	Alfred	→	Al	Belinda	→	Belle
	Alfred	→	Alf	Bertram	→	Bert

Taking only the truncated form into consideration, we see that all truncations are monosyllabic, no matter how long the base word is. Even a four-syllable name is truncated to form a monosyllabic truncated name. Furthermore, we can state that truncated names have a very strong tendency to begin and end in a consonant, even though the bases may start or end in a vowel. Thus, only four truncations (*Abe, Ag, Al,* and *Alf*) start with a vowel and none ends in a vowel, although there are 16 bases with various initial vowels (all spelled <A>) and 8 bases with final vowels (/ə/, ⌣/uː/, or /oʊ/, *Agatha, Alexandra, Alonzo, Amelia, Arabella, Barbara, Bartholomew, Belinda*). Additional data like *Lou, Ray, Sue* (← *Louis, Raymond, Suzanne*) show that occasionally it is possible to have truncated names ending in a vowel. However, in these cases a long vowel or diphthong is obligatory (cf. [luː] vs. *[lʊ], or [reɪ] vs. *[rɛ]). Interestingly, there are no truncated names attested that consist solely of vowels. Forms such as *[eɪ] (← *Abraham*) or *[oʊ] (← *Otis*) are impossible and unattested, whereas *Abe* and *Ote* are attested. Overall, we can make the generalization that name truncations have a strong tendency to conform to a rather fixed prosodic structure, a so-called **template**, which can be characterized as in (9). 'C' stands for 'consonant,' 'V' for 'vowel.'

(9)   a. CVC
        b. CVV
        c. VC

The templates in (9) are still somewhat simplistic because they ignore the possibility of consonant clusters (as in *Steve, Dolph,* or *Bart*) or, in (9a) and (9c), the possibility of long vowels or diphthongs (as in *Gail* or *Abe*). We can thus complement the templates in (9) by introducing these optional additional elements in small capitals, as in (10):

(10)   a. Cc VvCc
        b. CcVV
        c. VvCc

Having clarified the possible prosodic structure of truncated names, we should now turn to the question of how the derived word is related to the base word. With affixed words, this question is usually straightforward because the base is an integral part of the derivative (sometimes somewhat modified by base allomorphy). With truncations, however, only parts of the base survive derivation, and the speakers should have knowledge about which parts can survive.

What part of the name makes it into the truncation is often variable, but nevertheless predictable. For example, *Evelyn* can end up as *Eve* or *Lyn*, while *Florence* becomes *Flo* or *Floss*, and *Patricia* is truncated to *Pat* or *Trish*. Returning to our data set in (8), we can make the following generalizations. First, there are forms where the material to fill the template is taken from the very first syllable (and sometimes some subsequent segments), as in *Alonzo → Al*. Second, there is a group of forms where a primarily stressed syllable provides the material for the truncation (e.g. *Adolphus → Dolph*), and third, there is a group of words where a secondarily stressed syllable survives truncation (*Abigail → Gail*). In cases where the first syllable is also stressed (e.g. as in *Barbara*) the choice seems especially straightforward. The three groups are given in (11):

(11)

First syllable survives	Primarily stressed syllable survives	Secondarily stressed syllable survives
Albert – Al	Abraham – Abe	Abigail – Gail
Alonzo – Al	Adolphus – Dolph	Adelbert – Bert
Alfred – Alf	Agatha – Ag	
Barbara – Barb	Alonzo – Lon	
Bartholomew – Bart	Albert – Al	
	Alexandra – Xan	
	Amelia – Mel	
	Antoinette – Net	
	Augustus – Guss	
	Alfred – Alf	
	Arabella – Belle	

These observations, based here only on our comparatively small data set, prove to be quite robust over larger sets of truncated names, as shown in detail in Lappe (2003). In our data set, only one form (*Aaron → Ron*) does not behave in the predicted fashion and takes a non-initial, unstressed syllable.

There is one more characteristic of name truncations that we have not yet discussed, namely their segmental make-up. In some of the above names, as well as in quite a number of other forms, we find also a number of segmental changes on the way from the base to the truncation. For example, /r/ is replaced by /l/ if it is the single coda consonant (as in *Harry → Hal*, *Sarah → Sal*). /r/ survives, however, if it occurs in the onset of a truncation (as in *Ron, Rob, Rick*), and if it occurs as the first member of a coda cluster (as in *Barb, Bert, Bart*). The behavior of /θ/ is also remarkable in that it is generally avoided and replaced by /t/. There are a number of other things peculiar to truncated names, such as the occasional change in vowels (e.g. in *Am*[i]*lia → M*[ɛ]*l*), or the selection of non-adjacent sounds from the base (e.g. in *Florence → Floss*), which, for reasons of space, will not be discussed here.

To summarize, we have seen that the formation of truncated names is highly systematic and that it is subject to strong prosodic restrictions. This also holds for -*y* diminutives to which we now turn.

As usual, we start with some pertinent data:

(12)   -*y* diminutives

Albert	→	Bertie	Barbara	→	Barbie
alright	→	alrightie	beast	→	beastie
Andrew	→	Andy	bed	→	beddie
Angela	→	Angie	Bernard	→	Bernie
Anna	→	Annie	Chevrolet	→	Chevvie
Archibald	→	Archie	Chris	→	Chrissie
aunt	→	auntie	cigarette	→	ciggie
Australian	→	Aussie	comfortable	→	comfy

First of all, we find two orthographic variants -*y* and -*ie* in (12), which, however, are pronounced identically (occasionally even a third spelling can be encountered, -*ee*). If we look at the base words we find adjectives (*alright, comfortable*) and, predominantly, proper and common nouns. What are the properties of the diminutives, apart from ending in -*y*? Again we can analyze two aspects, the prosodic structure itself and the diminutive's relation to the base word.

Apart from *alrightie*, all diminutives are disyllabic with stress on the first syllable. Furthermore, the second syllable never shows a complex onset, even if the base has a complex onset in its second syllable (e.g. *Andrew → Andy*, not *Andry*). Thus the following templatic restrictions hold: -*y* diminutives are trochaic disyllables, with the second syllable consisting of a single consonant and the suffix. To satisfy the templatic restrictions, longer base words are severely truncated. As evidenced in our small data set above, it is the first syllable that usually survives truncation, irrespective of its being stressed or unstressed (cf. *Australian → Aussie*), but occasionally a stressed syllable can also serve as an anchor (*umbrella* → *brollie*, *tobacco* → *baccie*). On the segmental level, we find alternations similar to those we observed for truncated names (e.g. *Nathaniel* → *Natty*, *Martha* → *Marty*), which suggests that truncations may be the input to diminutive formation.

   To finish our discussion of truncations, let us turn to a class of forms that seem to be less coherent than truncated names or *-y* diminutives. For convenience I label this subclass of truncations **clippings**, a term that in other publications is often used as an equivalent to 'truncations.' Clippings appear as a rather mixed bag of forms abbreviated from larger words, which, however, share a common function, namely to express familiarity with the denotation of the derivative (see above for discussion). Thus, *lab* is used by people who work in laboratories, *demo* is part of the vocabulary of people who attend demonstrations, and so on. Some clippings find their way into larger communities of speakers, in which case they lose their in-group flavor, as for example *ad* (for *advertisement*). Consider some data:

(13)   ad   ←   advertisement
         condo   ←   condominium
         demo   ←   demonstration
         disco   ←   discotheque
         fax   ←   telefax
         lab   ←   laboratory
         phone   ←   telephone
         photo   ←   photography
         porn   ←   pornography
         prof   ←   professor

The restrictions on clippings may not be as tight as those on name truncations or *-y* diminutives, but some strong tendencies, resembling those on name truncations, are still observable. For example, most clippings are monosyllabic or disyllabic, and are usually based on the first part of the base word, or, much less frequently, on material from a stressed syllable (*télephòne, télefàx*). Without going into further details, we see that it is restrictions on prosodic categories that constrain both the structure of clippings and their relation to their base words.

5.2.2   Blends

   Another large class of complex words whose formation is best described in terms of prosodic categories is blends. Blending differs from the processes discussed in the previous section in that it involves two or (rarely) more base words (instead of only one), but shares with truncations a massive loss of phonetic (or orthographic) material. Blending has often been described as a rather irregular phenomenon (e.g. Dressler 2000), but, as we will shortly see, we find a surprising degree of regularity.

Definitions of blends in the morphological literature differ a great deal, but most treatments converge on a definition of blends as words that combine two (rarely three or more) words into one, deleting material from one or both of the source words. Examples of blends can be assigned to two different classes, illustrated in (14) and (15). Have a look at the two sets of forms and try to find out what characterizes the two types:

(14)   Blends, type 1
         breath + analyzer   →   breathalyzer
         motor + camp   →   mocamp
         motor + hotel   →   motel
         science + fiction   →   sci-fi

(15)   Blends, type 2
         boat + hotel   →   boatel
         boom + hoist   →   boost
         breakfast + lunch   →   brunch
         channel + tunnel   →   chunnel
         compressor + expander   →   compander
         goat + sheep   →   geep
         guess + estimate   →   guesstimate
         modulator + demodulator   →   modem
         sheep + goat   →   shoat
         smoke + fog   →   smog
         Spanish + English   →   Spanglish
         stagnation + inflation   →   stagflation

In (14) we are dealing with existing compounds that are shortened to form a new word. The meaning of these forms is one where the first element modifies the second element. Thus, a *breath analyzer* is a kind of analyzer (not a kind of breath), a *motor camp* is a kind of camp (not a kind of motor), etc. As we will shortly see, there are good reasons not to treat shortened compounds as proper blends (e.g. Kubozono 1991).

In contrast to the abbreviated compounds in (14), the base words of the blends in (15) are typically not attested as compounds in their full form. Furthermore, the semantics of the proper blends differs systematically from the abbreviated compounds in (14). The blends in (15) denote entities that share properties of the referents of both elements. For example, a *boatel* is both a boat and a hotel, a *brunch* is both breakfast and lunch, a *chunnel* is a tunnel which is under a channel, but it could also refer to a tunnel which is in some respects a channel, and so on.

In this semantic respect, proper blends resemble **copulative compounds** (such as *actor-director, writer-journalist*), to be discussed in the next chapter. Another semantic property that follows from what was just said is that both base words of a blend must be somehow semantically related (otherwise a combination of properties would be impossible). Furthermore, the two words are of the same syntactic category, mostly nouns.

In spite of their resemblance to copulative compounds we deal with blends in this chapter because their formal properties make them belong to the realm of prosodic morphology, as we will shortly see. The first important formal generalization that can be drawn on the basis of the data in (15) is that it is always the first part of the first element that is combined with the second part of the second element (see also Bauer 1983). This can be formulated as a rule, with A, B, C, and D, referring to the respective parts of the elements involved:

(16)   Blending rule
       A B + C D   →   A D

As evidenced by *guesstimate*, B or C can be null, i.e. one of the two forms may appear in its full form. If we take the orthographic representation, *guesstimate* does not truncate the first element (B is null), if we take the phonological representation, we could also argue that *estimate* is not truncated, hence C is null. Similar examples can be found. There is only one veritable exception to this pattern in the above data, namely *modem*, where the blend has the structure AC instead of AD (*modulator-demodulator*). In general, blends that do not correspond to the structure AD are in a clear minority (only 4 to 6 percent of all blends, Kubozono 1991: 4).

The interesting question is, of course, where speakers set their cuts on the base words. As we will shortly see, this is not arbitrary but constrained by prosodic categories. Taking again our sample data from above, two types of restrictions emerge. The first has to do with syllable structure, the second with size. We will start with syllable structure. Recall that in the previous chapter the notion of syllable structure was introduced. The structure of a syllable was described as having four constituents, onset, nucleus, and coda, with nucleus and coda forming the so-called rime. If we apply this structural model to the data above, we see that in the truncation process the constituents of syllables are left intact. Only syllabic constituents as a whole can be deleted. Taking first only the monosyllabic blends into consideration, we see that they take either the onset of the first element and the rime of the second element, or onset and nucleus of the first element and the coda of the second. See (17) for illustration:

(17)   Combinations of syllabic constituents in monosyllabic blends, applying the blend-ing rule A B + C D → A D

a. goat + sheep → geep

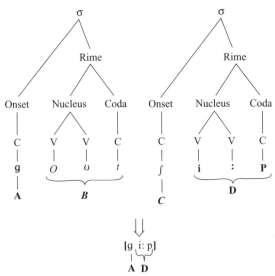

b. **A** (= onset) + **D** (= rime)   **A** (= onset + nucleus) + **D** (= coda)

goat + sheep → geep   **boom** + hoi̶s̶t̶ →   boost

sheep + goat → shoat

smoke + **fog** → smog (*sog)

breakfast + **lunch** → brunch

Turning to polysyllabic blends, we see that they conform to the same constraints, the difference is only that there are more constituents that can be combined, which leads to a rather large set of possibilities, as illustrated only on the basis of our sample data in (18):

(18)   Combinations of syllabic constituents in polysyllabic blends (AB + CD → AD)

A	D	A + D, examples
onset	penultimate rime and ultimate syllable	b + oatel
		ch + unnel
onset and nucleus	ultimate syllable	boa + tel
onset and nucleus	coda and ultimate syllable	Spa + nglish
onset	syllables	g + estimate
syllable	ultimate rime	boat + el
syllable	syllables	com + pander
		guess + timate
		stag + flation

Having shown that prosodic constituents, in this case syllabic constituents, play an important role in constraining the type of material to be deleted or combined, we can move on to the second type of restriction, already mentioned above, i.e. size. Let us first simply count the number of syllables of the base words and that of the blends. This is done in (19):

(19)   The size of blends, measured in number of syllables

base words	blend	AB	CD	AD
boat + hotel	boatel	1	2	2
boot + hoist	boost	1	1	1
breakfast + lunch	brunch	2	1	1
channel + tunnel	chunnel	2	2	2
compressor + expander	compander	3	3	3
goat + sheep	geep	1	1	1
guess + estimate	guesstimate	1	3	3
sheep + goat	shoat	1	1	1
smoke + fog	smog	1	1	1
Spanish + English	Spanglish	2	2	2
stagnation + inflation	stagflation	3	3	3

With most of the blends we see that two words are combined that have the same size (measured in number of syllables). In these cases the blend is of the same size as the constituents. If there is a discrepancy between the two base words, we find a clear pattern: the blend has the size of the second element, as can be seen with *brunch*, *boatel*, and *guesstimate*.

Overall, our analysis of blends has shown that the structure of blends is constrained by semantic, syntactic, and prosodic restrictions. In particular, blends behave semantically and syntactically like copulative compounds and their phonological make-up is characterized by three restrictions. The first is that the initial part of the first word is combined with the final part of the second word. Secondly, blends only combine syllable constituents (onsets, nuclei, codas, rimes, or complete syllables), and thirdly, the size of blends (measured in terms of syllables) is determined by the second element.

To summarize our discussion of prosodic morphology, we can state that English has a number of derivational processes that are best described in terms of prosodic categories. Name truncations and -*y* diminutives can be characterized by templatic restrictions that determine both the structure of the derived word and its relation to its base. With clippings such restrictions are perhaps less severe, but nevertheless present. Finally, blends were shown to be restricted not only in their prosody, but also semantically and syntactically. Overall, it was shown that these seemingly irregular processes are highly systematic in nature and should therefore not be excluded from what has been called 'grammatical morphology.'

5.3   Abbreviations and acronyms

Apart from the prosodically determined processes discussed in the previous section, there is one other popular way of forming words, namely abbreviation. Abbreviations are similar in nature to blends, because both blends and abbreviations are amalgamations of parts of different words. Like truncation and blending, abbreviation involves loss of material (not addition of material, as with affixation). Abbreviation differs, however, from truncation and blending in that prosodic categories do not play a prominent role. Rather, orthography is of central importance.

Abbreviations are most commonly formed by taking initial letters of multi-word sequences to make up a new word, as shown in (20):

(20)   BA   Bachelor of Arts
        DC   District of Columbia
        EC   European Community
        FAQ   frequently asked question

Apart from words composed of initial letters, one can also find abbreviations that incorporate non-initial letters:

(21)   BSc   Bachelor of Science
        Inc.   Incorporated
        Norf.   Norfolk
        Ont.   Ontario
        kHz   kilohertz

Formally, some abbreviations may come to resemble blends by combining larger sets of initial and non-initial letters (e.g. *kHz*). However, such forms still differ crucially from proper blends in that they neither obey the three pertinent prosodic constraints, nor do they necessarily show the semantic property of blends described above.

The spelling and pronunciation of abbreviations offer interesting perspectives on the formal properties of these words. Consider the following abbreviations with regard to their spelling and pronunciation differences:

(22)   ASAP, a.s.a.p.   as soon as possible
        CARE   Cooperative for Assistance and Relief Everywhere
        CIA   Central Intelligence Agency
        e.g.   for example
        etc.   et cetera
        FBI   Federal Bureau of Investigation

NATO   North Atlantic Treaty Organization
VAT, vat   value added tax
radar   radio detecting and ranging
START   Strategic Arms Reduction Talks
USA   United States of America

The orthographic and phonetic properties of the abbreviations are indicated in (23). For some abbreviations there is more than one possibility:

(23)   Spelling and pronunciation of abbreviations

spelling	pronunciation	example
in capitals	as individual letters	ASAP, CIA, FBI, VAT
in capitals	as a regular word	ASAP, CARE, NATO, START
in lower-case letters	as a regular word	asap, radar, vat
in lower-case letters with dots	as individual letters	a.s.a.p., e.g., etc.
in lower-case letters with dots	the abbreviated words are individually pronounced	a.s.a.p., etc.

Disregarding the cases where the abbreviation can trigger the regular pronunciation of the abbreviated words (*a.s.a.p., e.g., etc.*) and ignoring the use or non-use of dots, abbreviations can be grouped according to two orthographic and phonological properties. They can be spelled with either capital or lower-case letters, and they can be pronounced either by naming each individual letter (so-called **initialisms**, as in *USA* [ju.ɛs.eɪ]) or by applying regular reading rules (e.g. NATO [neɪ.toʊ]). In the latter case the abbreviation is called an **acronym**. The table in (24) systematizes this observation:

(24)   Spelling and pronunciation of abbreviations

spelling	pronunciation	example
in capitals	as initialism	CIA
in capitals	as acronym	NATO
in lower-case letters	as initialism	e.g.
in lower-case letters	as acronym	radar

The spelling of acronyms may differ with regard to the use of capital letters. Usually capital letters are used, which can be interpreted as a formal device that clearly links the acronym to its base word. Some words that historically originated as acronyms are nowadays no longer spelled with capital letters, and for the majority of speakers these forms are no longer related to the words they originally abbreviated (e.g. radar).

Acronyms, being pronounced like regular words, must conform to the phonological patterns of English, which can create problems in applying regular reading rules if the reading out would result in illegal phonological words. For example, an abbreviation like *BBC* is an unlikely candidate for an acronym, because [bbk] or [bbs] feature an illegal word-internal combination of sounds in English. Sometimes, however, speakers make abbreviations pronounceable, i.e. create acronyms. This seems to be especially popular in the naming of linguistics conferences:

(25)   NWAVE   [ɛnweɪv]   New Ways of Analyzing Variation in English
        SLRF   [slərf]   Second Language Research Forum

Sometimes abbreviations are formed in such a way as to yield not only pronounceable words (i.e. acronyms), but also words that are homophonous to existing words. This is often done for marketing or publicity reasons, especially in those cases where the homonymous word carries a meaning that is intended to be associated with the referent of the acronym. Consider the following examples:

(26)   CARE   Cooperative for Assistance and Relief Everywhere
        START   Strategic Arms Reduction Talks

The word START in particular is interesting because it was coined not only as a word to refer to an envisioned disarmament treaty between the US and the Soviet Union, but presumably also to evoke the idea that the American side had the intention to make a new, serious effort in disarmament talks with the Soviet Union at a time when many people doubted the willingness of the US government to seriously pursue disarmament. Incidentally, the START program replaced an earlier, unsuccessful disarmament effort named SALT (*Strategic Arms Limitation Talks*). Such data show that in political discourse, the participants consider it important to name a phenomenon in a particular way in order to win a political argument. The assumption underlying such a strategy is that the name used for a given phenomenon will influence the language user's concept of and attitude towards that phenomenon.

The examples of START and SALT also raise the question of whether abbreviations are new lexemes or simply new surface forms, i.e. allomorphs, of the same lexeme. In the case of START and SALT we could argue that the abbreviation is not completely identical in meaning to the base word because the abbreviation carries a different connotation, hence a new lexeme has been created by abbreviating the base word. Similar arguments could be invoked in those cases where the use of the abbreviation indicates a social meaning, similar to that of clippings. Thus, within certain groups of speakers, the use of an abbreviation can be taken as a marker of social identity: speaker and listener(s), but not outsiders, know what the speaker is talking about. Certainly, many abbreviations do not show a meaning difference with regard to their base words and would therefore best be analyzed as variant realizations, i.e. allomorphs, of their base lexemes.

5.4   Summary

In this chapter we have looked at a number of word-formation processes that do not involve affixes as their primary or only means of deriving words from other words or morphemes. We have seen that English has a rich inventory of such non-concatenative processes, including conversion, truncation, blending, and abbreviation. Each of these mechanisms was investigated in some detail and it turned out that, in spite of the initial impression of irregularity, a whole range of systematic structural restrictions can be determined. As with affixation, these restrictions can make reference to the semantic, syntactic, and phonological properties of the words involved and are highly regular in nature.

Further reading

For a more detailed treatment of conversion see, for example, Aronoff (1980) and Clark and Clark (1979). A more recent approach is Don (1993). A thorough discussion of underspecification as a way to deal with conversion is presented in Farrell (2001). Work on the prosodic morphology of English is rather scarce. A detailed investigation of the formal properties of name truncations and -*y* diminutives can be found in Lappe (2003), the semantic and pragmatic aspects of English diminutives are discussed in Schneider (2003), blends are investigated by Kubozono (1991). A detailed investigation of different types of acronyms and abbreviations is Rúa (2002).

For different views of extra-grammatical morphology see the articles in Doleschal and Thornton (2000), in particular Dressler (2000) and Fradin (2000).

Exercises

Basic level

Exercise 5.1

The following words are the products of non-affixational derivation. Find the base words from which they are derived and name the type of non-affixational process by which the derivative was formed. Consult a dictionary or other sources, if necessary.

Greg	UFO	boycott	deli	*OED*
Caltech	Amerindian	frogurt	laser	intro

Exercise 5.2

What are the three main theoretical problems concerning conversion? Illustrate each problem with an example.

Exercise 5.3

What is 'prosodic' in prosodic morphology? What distinguishes prosodic morphology from other types of morphology? Choose name truncations versus -*ness* suffixation for illustration.

Advanced level

Exercise 5.4

Discuss the directionality of conversion in the following pairs of words, using the criteria of frequency, stress pattern, and semantic complexity as diagnostics. The frequencies are taken from the BNC lemmatized word list.

verb	frequency	noun/adjective	frequency
to release	7822	release	5029
to name	6284	name	32309
to clear	8302	clear	21260
to smoke	3516	smoke	2823
to jail	949	jail	1178

Exercise 5.5

We have seen in this chapter that English truncated names show very specific prosodic patterns. Below you will find another set of such derivatives and their base forms, which show another peculiar type of pattern. We have said that name truncations can be formed on the basis of the first syllable or of a stressed syllable of the base. This is illustrated by *Pat* or *Trish*, formed on the basis of *Patricia*. However, there is a set of words that systematically does not allow the survival of the first syllable. They are given in (c):

a.	Patrícia	✓ Pat
	Cassándra	✓ Cass
	Delílah	✓ Del

b.   Ábigàil   ✓ Ab
      Èbenézer   ✓ Eb
      Émma   ✓ Em
c.   Octávia   *Oc
      Elízabeth   *El
      Amélia   *Am

What exactly makes the words in (c) behave differently from the words in (a) and (b)? Which new generalization emerges from the data?

Exercise 5.6

There is a marginal class of diminutives that are derived by partial repetition of a base word, a formal process also known as partial **reduplication**. Consider the following examples:

Andy-Wandy   Annie-Pannie piggie-wiggie Roddy-Doddy Stevie-Weavy
Brinnie-Winnie lovey-dovey   Charlie-Parlie boatie-woatie housey-wousey

The interesting question is of course what determines the shape of the second element, the so-called **reduplicant**. In particular, one would like to know which part of the base is reduplicated and in which way this part is then further manipulated to arrive at an acceptable reduplicated diminutive. Try to determine the pertinent generalizations.

6

Compounding

Outline

This chapter is concerned with compounds. Section 6.1 focuses on the basic characteristics of compounds, investigating the kinds of element compounds are made of, their internal structure, headedness, and stress patterns. This is followed by descriptions of individual compounding patterns and the discussion of the specific empirical and theoretical problems these patterns pose. In particular, nominal, adjectival, verbal, and neoclassical compounds are examined, followed by an exploration of the syntax–morphology boundary.

6.1   Recognizing compounds

Compounding was mentioned in passing in the preceding chapters and some of its characteristics have already been discussed. For example, in chapter 1 we briefly commented on the orthography and stress pattern of compounds, and in chapter 4 we investigated the boundary between affixation and compounding and introduced the notion of neoclassical compounds. In this chapter we will take a closer look at compounding and the intricate problems involved in this phenomenon. Although compounding is the most productive type of word-formation process in English, it is perhaps also the most controversial one in terms of its linguistic analysis and I must forewarn readers seeking clear answers to their questions that compounding is a field of study where intricate problems abound, numerous issues remain unresolved, and convincing solutions are generally not so easy to find.

Let us start with the problem of definition: what exactly do we mean when we say that a given form is a compound? To answer that question we first examine the internal structure of compounds.

6.1.1   What are compounds made of?

In the very first chapter, we defined **compounding** (sometimes also called **composition**) rather loosely as the combination of two words to form a new word. This definition contains two crucial assumptions, the first being that compounds consist of two (and not more) elements, the second being that these elements are words. As we will shortly see, both assumptions are in need of justification. We will discuss each in turn.

There are, for example, compounds such as those in (1), which question the idea that compounding involves only two elements. The data are taken from a user's manual for a computer printer:

(1)   power source requirement
         engine communication error
         communication technology equipment

The data in (1) seem to suggest that a definition saying that compounding involves always two (and not more) words is overly restrictive. This impression is further enhanced by the fact that there are compounds with four, five, or even more members, e.g. *university teaching award committee member*. However, as we have seen with multiply affixed words in chapter 2, it seems generally possible to analyze polymorphemic words as hierarchical structures involving binary (i.e. two-member) subelements. The above-mentioned five-member compound *university teaching award committee member* could thus be analyzed as in (2), using the bracketing and tree representations as merely notational variants (alternative analyses are also conceivable; see further below):

(2)   a.   [[[university [teaching award]] committee] member].
         b.

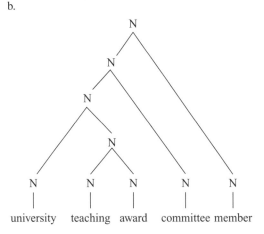

According to (2) the five-member compound can be divided into strictly binary compounds as its constituents. The innermost constituent [*teaching award*] 'an award for teaching' is made up of [*teaching*] and [*award*], the next largest constituent [*university teaching award*] 'the teaching award of the university' is made up of [*university*] and [*teaching award*], the constituent [*university teaching award committee*] 'the committee responsible for the university teaching award' is made up of [*university teaching award*] and [*committee*], and so on. Under the assumption that such an analysis is possible for all compounds, our definition can be formulated in such a way that compounds are binary structures.

What is also important to note is that – at least with noun-noun compounds – new words can be repeatedly stacked on an existing compound to form a new compound. If, for instance, there was a special training for members of the university teaching award committee, we could refer to that training as the *university teaching award committee member training*. Thus the rules of compound formation are able to repeatedly create the same kind of structure. This property is called **recursivity**, and it is a property that is chiefly known from the analysis of sentence structure. For example, the grammar of English allows us to use subordinate clauses recursively by putting a new clause inside each new clause, as in *John said that Betty knew that Harry thought that Janet believed . . .* and so on. Recursivity seems to be absent from derivation, but some marginal cases such as *great-great-great-grandfather* are attested in prefixation. There is no structural limitation on the recursivity of compounding, but the longer a compound becomes the more difficult it is for the speakers/listeners to process, i.e. produce and understand correctly. Extremely long compounds are therefore disfavored not for structural but for processing reasons.

Having clarified that even longer compounds can be analyzed as essentially binary structures, we can turn to the question of what kinds of unit can be used to form compounds. Consider the following forms and try to determine which types of unit can occur as elements in compounds:

(3)   a. astrophysics
          biochemistry
          photoionize
       b. parks commissioner
          teeth marks
          systems analyst
       c. pipe-and-slipper husband
          off-the-rack dress
          over-the-fence gossip
       d. *husband pipe-and-slipper
          *dress off-the-rack
          gossip over the fence

In (3a) we find compounds involving elements (*astro-*, *bio-*, *photo-*) which are not attested as independent words (note that *photo-* in *photoionize* means 'light' and is not the same lexeme as *photo* 'picture taken with a camera'). In our discussion of neoclassical formations in chapter 4 we saw that bound elements like *astro-*, *bio-*, *photo-*, etc. behave like words (and not like affixes), except that they are bound. Hence they are best classified as (bound) roots. We could thus redefine compounding as the combination of roots, and not of words. Such a move has, however, the unfortunate consequence that we would have to rule out formations such as those in (3b), where the first element is a plural form, hence not a root but a (grammatical) word. To make matters worse for our definition, the data in (3c) show that even larger units, i.e. syntactic phrases, can occur as elements in compounds, even if only as left-hand members. Phrases in the right-hand position of compounds are either impossible (e.g. *husband pipe-and-slipper*) or are crucially not interpreted as compounds but – together with the then left-hand element – as phrases (e.g. *gossip over the fence*).

Given the empirical data, we are well advised to slightly modify our above definition and say that a compound is a word that consists of two elements, the first of which is either a root, a word or a phrase, the second of which is either a root or a word.

6.1.2   More on the structure of compounds: the notion of head

The vast majority of compounds in English are interpreted in such a way that the left-hand member somehow modifies the right-hand member. Thus, a *film society* is a kind of society (namely one concerned with films), a *parks commissioner* is a commissioner occupied with parks, *to deep-fry* is a verb designating a kind of frying, *knee-deep* in *She waded in knee-deep water* tells us something about how deep the water is, and so on. We can thus say that such compounds exhibit what is called a **modifier–head structure**. The term **head** is generally used to refer to the most important unit in complex linguistic structures. In compounds it is the head which is modified by the other member of the compound. Semantically, this means that the set of entities possibly denoted by the compound (i.e. all film societies) is a subset of the entities denoted by the head (i.e. all societies).

With regard to their head, compounds have a very important systematic property: their head usually occurs on the right-hand side (the so-called **right-hand head rule**, Williams 1981a: 248). The compound as a whole inherits most of its semantic and syntactic information from its head. Thus, if the head is a verb, the compound will be a verb (e.g. *deep-fry*), if the head is a count noun, the compound will be a count noun (e.g. *beer bottle*), if the head has feminine gender, the compound will have feminine gender (e.g. *head waitress*). Another property of the compound head is that if the compound is pluralized the plural marking occurs on the head, not on the non-head. Thus, *parks commissioner* is not the plural of *park commissioner*; only *park commissioners* can be the plural form of *park commissioner*. In the existing compound *parks commissioner*, the plural interpretation is restricted to the non-head and not inherited by the whole compound. This is shown schematically in (4), with the arrow indicating the inheritance of the grammatical features from the head. The inheritance of features from the head is also (somewhat counter-intuitively) referred to as **feature percolation**:

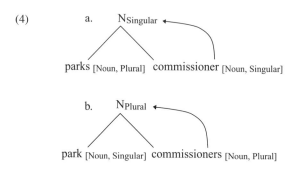

(4)   a.   N$_{Singular}$

parks [Noun, Plural]   commissioner [Noun, Singular]

b.   N$_{Plural}$

park [Noun, Singular]   commissioners [Noun, Plural]

The definition developed at the end of section 6.1.1 and the notion of head allow us to deal consistently with words such as *jack-in-the-box, good-for-nothing*, and the like, which one might be tempted to analyze as compounds, since they are words that internally consist of more than one word. Such multi-word sequences are certainly words in the sense of the definition of word developed in chapter 1 (e.g. they are uninterruptable lexical items that have a syntactic category specification). And syntactically they behave like other words, be they complex or simplex. For example, *jack-in-the-box* (being a count noun) can take an article, can be modified by an adjective, and can be pluralized, hence it behaves syntactically like any other noun with similar properties. However, and crucially, such multi-word words do not have the usual internal structure of compounds, but have the internal structure of syntactic phrases. Thus, they lack a right-hand head, and they do not consist of two elements that meet the criteria of our above definition of compound. For example, under a compound analysis *jack-in-the-box* is headless, since a *jack-in-the-box* is neither a kind of box, nor a kind of *jack*. Furthermore, *jack-in-the-box* has a phrase (the so-called prepositional phrase [*in the box*]) as its *right*-hand member, and not as its *left*-hand member, as required for compounds involving syntactic phrases as one member (see above). In addition, *jack-in-the-box* fits perfectly the structure of English noun phrases (cf. *(the) fool on the hill*). In sum, words like *jack-in-the-box* are best regarded as lexicalized phrases, i.e. they are memorized holistically by the speakers.

Our considerations concerning the constituency and headedness of compounds allow us to formalize the structure of compounds as in (5):

(5)   The structure of English compounds
       a. [X Y]$_Y$
       b. X = {root, word, phrase}
          Y = {root, word}
          $_Y$ = grammatical properties inherited from Y

(5) is a template for compounds which shows us that they are binary, and which kinds of element may occupy which positions. Furthermore, it tells us that the right-hand member is the head, since this is the member from which the grammatical properties percolate to the compound as a whole.

We may now turn to another important characteristic of English compounds, their stress pattern.

6.1.3   Stress in compounds

As already said in chapter 2, compounds tend to have a stress pattern that is different from that of phrases. This is especially true for nominal compounds, and the following discussion of compound stress is restricted to this class of compounds. For comments on the stress patterns of adjectival and verbal compounds see sections 6.4 and 6.5 below.

While phrases tend to be stressed phrase-finally, i.e. on the last word, compounds tend to be stressed on the first element. This systematic difference is captured in the so-called **nuclear stress rule** ('phrasal stress is on the last word of the phrase') and the so-called **compound stress rule** ('stress is on the left-hand member of a compound'), formalized in Chomsky and Halle (1968: 17). Consider the data in (6) for illustration, in which the most prominent syllable of the phrase is marked by an acute accent:

(6)   a. *noun phrases:*
          [the green cárpet], [this new hóuse], [such a good jób]
       b. *nominal compounds:*
          [páyment problems], [installátion guide], [spáce requirement]

This systematic difference between the stress assignment in noun phrases and in noun compounds can even lead to minimal pairs where it seems to be only the stress pattern that distinguishes between the compound and the phrase (and their respective interpretations). Some phonetic studies (e.g. Farnetani et al. 1988, Ingram et al. in press) have shown, however, that segmentally identical phrases and compounds such as those in (7) below differ not only significantly in their stress pattern, but also in length, with phrases being generally shorter than the corresponding compounds.

(7)

noun compound	noun phrase
a. bláckboard	a black bóard
'a board to write on'	'a board that is black'
b. gréenhouse	a green hóuse
'a glass building for growing plants'	'a house that is green'
c. óperating instructions	operating instrúctions
'instructions for operating something'	'instructions that are operating'
d. instálling options	installing óptions
'options for installing something'	'the installing of options,' or
	'options that install something'

While the compound stress rule makes correct predictions for the vast majority of nominal compounds, it has been pointed out (e.g. by Liberman and Sproat 1992, Bauer 1998b, Olsen 2000b) that there are also numerous exceptions to the rule. Some of these exceptions are listed in (8). The most prominent syllable is again marked by an acute accent on the vowel.

(8)

geologist-astrónomer	apple píe
scholar-áctivist	apricot crúmble
Michigan hóspital	Madison Ávenue
Boston márathon	Penny Láne
summer níght	aluminum fóil
may flówers	silk tíe

How can we account for such data? One obvious hypothesis would be to say that the compound stress rule holds for all compounds, so that, consequently, the above word combinations cannot be compounds. But what are they, if not compounds? Before we start reflecting upon this difficult question, we should first try an alternative approach.

Proceeding from our usual assumption that most phenomena are at least to some extent regular, we could try to show that the words in (8) are not really idiosyncratic but that they are more or less systematic exceptions of the compound stress rule. This hypothesis has been entertained by a number of scholars (e.g. Fudge 1984, Ladd 1984, Liberman and Sproat 1992, Olsen 2000b, 2001).

Although these authors differ slightly in details of their respective approaches, they all argue that rightward prominence is restricted to only a severely limited number of more or less well-defined types of meaning relationships. For example, compounds like *geologist-astronomer* and *scholar-activist* differ from other compounds in that both elements refer to the same entity. A *geologist-astronomer*, for example, is a single person who is an astronomer and at the same time a geologist. Such compounds are called **copulative compounds** and will be discussed in more detail below. For the moment it is important to note that this clearly definable subclass of compounds consistently has rightward stress (*geologist-astrónomer*), and is therefore a systematic exception to the compound stress rule. Other meaning relationships typically accompanied by rightward stress are temporal or locative (e.g. *a summer níght, the Boston márathon*), or causative, usually paraphrased as 'made of' (as in *aluminum fóil, silk tíe*), or 'created by' (as in *a Shakespeare sónnet, a Mahler sýmphony*). It is, however, not quite clear how many semantic classes should be set up to account for all the putative exceptions to the compound stress rule. This remains a problem for proponents of this hypothesis. It also seems that certain types of combination choose their stress pattern in analogy to combinations having the same rightward constituents. Thus, for example, all street names involving *street* as their right-hand member pattern alike in having leftward stress (e.g. *Óxford Street, Máin Street, Fóurth Street*), while all combinations with, for example, *avenue* as right-hand member pattern alike in having rightward stress.

To summarize this brief investigation of the hypothesis that stress assignment in compounds is systematic, we can say that there are good arguments to treat compounds with rightward stress indeed as systematic exceptions to the otherwise prevailing compound stress rule.

Let us, however, also briefly explore the other hypothesis, which is that word combinations with rightward stress cannot be compounds, which raises the question of what else such structures could be. One natural possibility is to consider such forms as phrases. However, this creates new serious problems. First, such an approach would face the problem of explaining why not all forms that have the same superficial structure, for example [noun-noun], are phrases. Second, one would like to have independent criteria coinciding with stress in order to say whether something is a compound or a phrase. This is, however, impossible: apart from stress itself, there seems to be no independent argument for claiming that *Mádison Street* should be a compound, whereas *Madison Ávenue* should be a phrase. Both have the same internal structure (noun-noun), both show the same meaning relationship between their respective constituents, both are right-headed, and it is only in their stress patterns that they differ. A final problem for the phrasal analysis is the above-mentioned fact that the rightward stress pattern is often triggered by analogy to other combinations with the same rightward element. This can only happen if the forms on which the analogy is based are stored in the mental lexicon. And storage in the mental lexicon is something we would typically expect from words (i.e. compounds), and only exceptionally from phrases (as in the case of *jack-in-the-box* discussed above).

To summarize our discussion of compound stress, we can say that in English, compounds generally have leftward stress. Counterexamples to this generalization exist, but in their majority seem to be systematic exceptions that correlate with certain types of semantic interpretation or that are based on the analogy to existing compounds.

Given the correctness of the compound stress rule, another interesting problem arises: how are compounds stressed that have more than two members? Consider the following compounds, their possible stress patterns, and their interpretations.

(9)   máil delivery service   mail delívery service
        stúdent feedback system   student féedback system
        góvernment revenue policy   government révenue policy

The data show that a certain stress pattern seems to be indicative of a certain kind of interpretation. A *máil delivery service* is a *service* concerned with *máil delivery* (i.e. the delivery of mail), whereas a *mail delívery service* is a *delívery service* concerned with mail. This is a small semantic difference indeed, but still one worth taking note of. A *stúdent feedback system* is a *system* concerned with *stúdent feedback*, whereas a *student féedback system* may be a *féedback system* that has something to do with students (e.g. was designed by students or is maintained by students). And while the *góvernment revenue policy* is a *policy* concerned with the *góvernment revenue*, the *government révenue policy* is a certain *révenue policy* as implemented by the government. The two different interpretations correlating with the different stress patterns are indicated by the brackets in (10):

(10)   [[máil delivery] service]   [mail [delívery service]]
        [[stúdent feedback] system]   [student [féedback system]]
        [[góvernment revenue] policy]   [government [révenue policy]]

Note that the semantic difference between the two interpretations is sometimes so small (e.g. in the case of *mail delivery service*) that the stress pattern appears easily variable. Pairs with more severe semantic differences (e.g. *góvernment revenue policy* vs. *government révenue policy*) show, however, that certain interpretations consistently go together with certain stress patterns. The obvious question now is how the mapping of a particular structure with a particular stress pattern proceeds.

Let us look again at the structures in (10). The generalization that emerges from the three pairs is that the most prominent stress is always placed on the left-hand member of the compound inside the compound and never on the member of the compound that is not a compound itself. Paraphrasing the rule put forward by Liberman and Prince (1977), we could thus say that in a compound of the structure [XY], Y will receive strongest stress, if, and only if, it is a compound itself. This means that a compound [XY] will have left-hand stress if Y is not a compound itself. If Y is a compound, the rule is applied again to Y. This stress-assigning algorithm is given in plain language in (11):

(11)   Stress assignment algorithm for English compounds
       Is the right-hand member a compound?
       If yes, the right-hand member must be more prominent than the left-hand
       member.
       If no, the left-hand member must be more prominent than the right-hand
       member.

Let us see how the algorithm works with the following example, whose internal
structure is given in (12b):

(12)   a. bathroom towel designer
           'designer of towels for the bathroom'
        b. [[[bathroom] towel] designer]

Following our algorithm, we start with the right-hand member and ask whether it is
a compound itself. The right-hand member of the compound is [*designer*], i.e. not
a compound, hence the other member, [*bathroom towel*], must be more prominent,
so that [*designer*] is left unstressed. Applying the algorithm again on [[*bathroom*]
towel] yields the same result: its right-hand member is not a compound either,
hence is unstressed. The next left-hand member is [*bathroom*], where the right-
hand member is equally not a compound, hence unstressed. The most prominent
element is therefore the remaining word [*bath*], which must receive the primary
stress of the compound. The result of the algorithm is shown in (13), where 'w' (for
'weak') is assigned to less prominent constituents and 's' (for 'strong') is assigned
to more prominent constituents. The most prominent constituent is the one which
is only dominated by s's:

(13)   [[[bathroom] towel] designer]

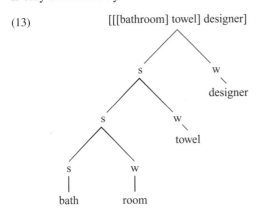

6.1.4 Summary

   In the preceding sections we have explored the basic general characteristics of compounds. We have found that compounds can be analyzed as words

with binary structure, in which roots, words, and even phrases (the latter only as left-hand members) are possible elements. We also saw that compounds are right-headed and that the compound inherits its major properties from its head. Furthermore, compounds exhibit a regular compound-specific stress pattern that differs systematically from that of phrases.

While this section was concerned with the question of what all compounds have in common, the following section will focus on the question of what kinds of systematic differences can be observed between different compounding patterns.

6.2   An inventory of compounding patterns

In English, as in many other languages, a number of different compounding patterns are attested. Not all words from all word classes can combine freely with other words to form compounds. In this section we will try to determine the inventory of possible compounding patterns and see how these patterns are generally restricted.

One possible way of establishing compound patterns is to classify compounds according to the nature of their heads. Thus there are compounds involving nominal heads, verbal heads, and adjectival heads. Classifications based on syntactic category are of course somewhat problematic because many words of English belong to more than one category (e.g. *walk* can be a noun and a verb, *blind* can be an adjective, a verb, and a noun, *green* can be an adjective, a verb, and a noun, etc.), but we will nevertheless use this type of classification because it gives us a clear set of form classes, whereas other possible classifications, based on, for example, semantics, appear to involve an even greater degree of arbitrariness. For example, Brekle (1970) sets up about one hundred different semantic classes, while Hatcher (1960) has only four.

In the following, we will ignore compounds with more than two members, and we can do so because we have argued above that more complex compounds can be broken down into binary substructures, which means that the properties of larger compounds can be predicted on the basis of their binary constituents. Hence, larger compounds follow the same structural and semantic patterns as two-member compounds.

In order to devise an inventory of compounding patterns I have tentatively schematized the possible combinations of words from different parts of speech in (14) below. The table includes the four major categories noun, verb, adjective, and preposition. Prepositions (especially those in compound-like structures) are also referred to in the literature as **particles**. Potentially problematic forms are accompanied by a question mark.

(14)   Inventory of compound types, first try

	noun (N)	verb (V)	adjective (A)	preposition (P)
N	*film society*	*brainwash*	*knee-deep*	–
V	*pickpocket*	*stir-fry*	–	*breakdown* (?)
A	*greenhouse*	*blackmail*	*light-green*	–
P	*afterbirth*	*downgrade* (?)	*inbuilt* (?)	*into* (?)

There are some gaps in the table. Apart from extremely rare exceptions, such as the oft-cited *fail-safe*, verb-adjective or adjective-preposition compounds are simply not attested in English and seem to be ruled out on a principled basis. The number of gaps increases if we look at the four cells that contain question marks, all of which involve prepositions. As we will see, it can be shown that these combinations, in spite of their first appearance, should not be analyzed as compounds.

Let us first examine the combinations PV, PA, and VP, further illustrated in (15):

(15)   a. PV: *to download, to outsource, to upgrade,*
              the backswing, the input, the upshift
        b. PA: *inbuilt, incoming, outgoing*
        c. VP: *breakdown, push-up, rip-off*

Prepositions and verbs can combine to form verbs, but sometimes this results in a noun, which is unexpected given the headedness of English compounds. However, it could be argued that *backswing* or *upshift* are not PV compounds but PN compounds (after all, *swing* and *shift* are also attested as nouns). Unfortunately such an argument does not hold for *input*, which first occurred as a noun, although *put* is not attested as a noun. Thus it seems that such would-be compounds are perhaps the result of some other mechanism. And, indeed, Berg (1998) has shown that forms like those in (15a) and (15b) are mostly derived by inversion from phrasal combinations in which the particle follows the base word:

(16)   load down   →   download NOUN/VERB
        come in   →   income NOUN/VERB
        put in   →   input NOUN/VERB
        built in   →   inbuilt ADJECTIVE

For this reason, such complex words should not be considered compounds, but the result of an inversion process.

Similarly, the words in (15c) can be argued to be the result of the conversion of a phrasal verb into a noun (accompanied by a stress shift):

(17)   to break dówn $_{VERB}$ →   a bréakdown $_{NOUN}$

          to push úp $_{VERB}$ →   a púsh-up $_{NOUN}$

          to rip óff $_{VERB}$ →   a ríp-off $_{NOUN}$

In sum, the alleged compound types PV, PA, and VP are not the result of a regular compounding process involving these parts of speech, but are complex words arising from other word-formation mechanisms, i.e. inversion and conversion.

The final question mark in table (14) concerns complex prepositions like *into* or *onto*. Such sequences of two prepositions are extremely rare, apart from *into* and *onto* only very few other examples come to mind (e.g. *upon, without, within*). New words of this type cannot be freely formed, as evidenced by the scarcity of existing examples and the impossibility of new formations (**fromunder,* upin, *onby*, etc.). It seems that *into* and *onto* do not constitute cases of compounding but are lexicalizations of two frequently co-occurring prepositions, which, historically, may develop a unitary semantic interpretation which leads speakers to perceive and treat them as one word.

The elimination of forms involving prepositions from the classes of productive compounding patterns leaves us then with the following patterns:

(18)   Inventory of compound types, revised

	noun (N)	verb (V)	adjective (A)
noun	*film society*	*brainwash*	*stone-deaf*
verb	*pickpocket*	*stir-fry*	–
adjective	*greenhouse*	*blindfold*	*light-green*
preposition	*afterbirth*	–	–

The table gives the impression that nouns, verbs, and adjectives can combine quite freely in compounding. However, as we will see in the following section, not all of these patterns are equally productive and there are severe restrictions on some of the patterns in (18). The properties and restrictions of the individual types of compound will be the topic of the following sections.

6.3   Nominal compounds

In terms of part of speech, nominal compounds, i.e. compounds with nouns as heads, fall into the three subclasses mentioned above, involving nouns, verbs, and adjectives as non-heads.

Noun-noun compounds are the most common type of compound in English. The vast majority of noun-noun compounds are right-headed, i.e. they have a head and this head is the right-hand member of the compound. There are, however, also a number of compounds which do not lend themselves easily to an analysis in terms of headedness. We will therefore turn to this problem first.

6.3.1   Headedness

Consider the difference between the forms in (19a) on the one hand, and (19b) and (19c) on the other:

(19)   a. laser printer
book cover
letter head
b. redneck
loudmouth
greybeard
c. pickpocket
cut-throat
spoilsport

The forms in (19a) all have in common that they are noun-noun compounds and that they denote a subclass of the referents of the head: a *laser printer* is a kind of printer, a *book cover* is a kind of cover, a *letter head* is the head of a letter. We could say that the semantic head of these compounds is inside the compound, which is the reason why these compounds are called **endocentric** compounds (cf. the neoclassical element *endo-* 'inside'). With the forms in (19b) and (19c) things are different. First, they are not noun-noun compounds but contain either an adjective (19b) or a verb (19c) as first element. Second, their semantics is strikingly deviant: a *redneck* is not a kind of neck but a kind of person, *loudmouth* does not denote a kind of mouth but again a kind of person, and the same holds for *greybeard*. Similarly, in (19c), a *pickpocket* is not a kind of pocket, but someone who picks pockets, a *cut-throat* is someone who cuts throats, and a *spoilsport* is someone who spoils enjoyable pastimes of other people.

The compounds in (19b) and (19c) thus all refer to persons, which means that their semantic head is outside the compound, and they are therefore traditionally called **exocentric compounds.** Another term for this class of compounds is **bahu-vrihi,** a term originating from the tradition of the ancient Sanskrit grammarians, who already dealt with problems of compounding. It is striking, however, that the exocentric compounds in (19b) and (19c) can only be said to be semantically exocentric. If we look at other properties of these compounds, we observe that at least the part of speech is inherited from the right-hand member, as is generally the case with right-headed compounds: *redneck* is a noun (and not an adjective), *loudmouth* is a noun (and not an adjective), and *pickpocket* is also a noun (and not a verb). One could therefore state that these compounds do have a head and that, at least in terms of their grammatical properties, these seemingly exocentric compounds are in fact endocentric.

Semantic exocentricity with English compounds seems to be restricted to forms denoting human beings (or higher animals, but see also *greenback* for a US dollar note). Furthermore, of the semantically exocentric compounds, only the class exemplified in (19b) is (moderately) productive, whereas those of the type (19c) are extremely rare (e.g. Bauer and Renouf 2001). The compounds in (19b) are also sometimes called **possessive compounds**, because they denote an entity that is characterized (sometimes metaphorically) by the property expressed by the compound. A *loudmouth* is a person that possesses 'a loud mouth,' a *greybeard* is a person or animal with a grey beard, and so on. Possessive exocentric compounds usually have an adjective as their left-hand element.

Apart from endocentric, exocentric, and possessive compounds there is another type of compound which requires an interpretation different from the ones introduced so far. Consider the hyphenated words in the examples in (20):

(20)   a. singer-songwriter
            scientist-explorer
            poet-translator
            hero-martyr
        b. the doctor-patient gap
            the nature-nurture debate
            a modifier-head structure
            the mind-body problem

Both sets of words are characterized by the fact that neither of the two members of the compound seems in any sense more important than the other. They could be said to have two semantic heads, neither of them being subordinate to the other. Given that no member is semantically prominent, but both members equally contribute to the meaning of the compound, these compounds have been labeled **copulative compounds** (or **dvandva compounds** in Sanskrit grammarian terms).

Why are the copulative compounds in (20) divided into two different sets (20a) and (20b)? The idea behind this differentiation is that copulatives fall into two classes, depending on their interpretation. Each form in (20a) refers to one entity that is characterized by both members of the compound. A *poet-translator*, for example, is a person who is both a poet and a translator. This type of copulative compound is sometimes called an **appositional compound**. By contrast, the dvandvas in (20b) denote two entities that stand in a particular relationship with regard to the following noun. The particular type of relationship is determined by the following noun. The *doctor-patient gap* is thus a gap between doctor and patient, the *nature-nurture debate* is a debate on the relationship between nature and nurture, and so on. This second type of copulative compound is also known as a **coordinative compound**. If the noun following the compound allows both readings, the compound is in principle ambiguous. Thus a *scientist-philosopher crew* could be a crew made up of scientist-philosophers, or a crew made up of scientists and philosophers. It is often stated that dvandva compounds are not very common in English (e.g. Bauer 1983: 203), but in a more recent study by Olsen (2001) hundreds of attested forms are listed, which shows that such compounds are far from marginal.

Copulative compounds in particular raise two questions that have to do with the question of headedness. The first is whether they are, in spite of the first impression that they have two heads, perhaps equally right-headed as the other compounds discussed above. The second is whether the existence of copulative compounds is an argument against the view adopted above that all compounding is binary (see the discussion above).

We have already seen that compounds that have traditionally been labeled exocentric pattern like endocentric compounds with regard to their grammatical properties (e.g. *pickpocket* is a noun, not a verb). The same reasoning could be applied to copulative compounds, which show at least one property expected from right-headed compounds: plural marking occurs only on the right-hand member, as illustrated in (21):

(21)   There are many *poet-translators/*poets-translator/*poets-translators* in this country.

Admittedly, this is only a small piece of evidence for the headedness of copulative compounds, but it supports the theory that English compounds are generally headed, and that the head is always the right-hand member.

Turning to the question of hierarchical organization and binarity, it may look as if copulative compounds could serve as a prime case for non-hierarchical structures in compounding, because both members seem to be of equal prominence. However, there are also arguments in favor of a non-flat structure. Under the assumption that copulative compounds are headed, we would automatically arrive at a hierarchical morphological structure (head vs. non-head), even though the semantics may not suggest this in the first place. In essence, we would arrive at a more elegant theory of compounding, because only one type of structure for all kinds of compounds would have to be assumed, and not different ones for different types of compound. Whether this is indeed the best solution is still under debate (see Olsen 2001 for the most recent contribution to this debate).

Having discussed the problems raised by exocentric and copulative compounds, we may now turn to the interpretation of the more canonical endocentric noun-noun compounds.

6.3.2   Interpreting nominal compounds

As should be evident from all the examples discussed so far, these compounds show a wide range of meanings, and there have been many attempts at classifying these meanings (e.g. Hatcher 1960, Lees 1960, Brekle 1970, Downing 1977, Levi 1978). Given the proliferation and arbitrariness of possible semantic categories (e.g. 'location,' 'cause,' 'manner,' 'possessor,' 'material,' 'content,' 'source,' 'instrument,' 'have,' 'from,' 'about,' 'be'; see Adams 2001: 83ff for a synopsis) such semantically based taxonomies appear somewhat futile. What is more promising is to ask what kinds of interpretations are in principle possible, given a certain compound. Studies investigating this question (e.g. Meyer 1993 or Ryder 1994) have shown that a given noun-noun compound is in principle ambiguous and can receive very different interpretations depending on, among other things, the context in which it occurs. This does not of course preclude the fact that for many lexicalized compounds the interpretation is more or less fixed. I write 'more or less' because even in cases of would-be fixed meanings, alternative meanings are conceivable and do occur. For example, a *chainsaw* has the lexicalized meaning of 'saw with a chain,' but given the right context and circumstances, we can imagine the word *chainsaw* referring to a saw that is used to cut chains (and not, say, wood).

In isolation, i.e. without preceding or following discourse, a given compound is interpreted chiefly by relating the two members of the compound to each other in terms of the typical relationship between the entities referred to by the two nouns. What is construed as 'the typical relationship' depends partly on the semantics of the noun. We have to distinguish at least two different classes of nouns, **sortal** nouns and **relational** nouns. Sortal nouns are used for classifying entities. A given object might for example be called either *chair*, *stool*, or *table*. In contrast, relational nouns denote relations between a specific entity and a second one. For example, one cannot be called a *father* without being the father of someone (or, metaphorically, of something). Similarly, one cannot do *surgery* without performing surgery on something. The second, conceptually necessary, entity (e.g. the child in the case of *father*) to which the relational noun relates is called an **argument**. Note that a similar analysis can be applied to the relations between the participants of an action as expressed by a verb. The necessary participants in the event denoted by the verb are also called arguments, to the effect that a verb has at least one argument. With intransitive verbs the only argument of the verb is the subject, for example *I* in *I* *am sleeping*. With transitive verbs there are either two arguments, i.e. the subject and object, as in *I* love *morphology*, or three arguments, as in *She* gave *me the ticket* (arguments are underlined).

Coming back to our problem of interpretation, we can now say that if the right-hand member of a compound is a relational noun, the left-hand member of the compound will normally be interpreted as an argument of the relational noun. For example, the left-hand member of a compound with the relational noun *surgery* as head will be interpreted as an argument of *surgery*, i.e. as the entity which is necessarily affected by the action of surgery. Thus *brain surgery* is interpreted as surgery performed on the brain, *finger surgery* is interpreted as surgery performed on fingers. This process, by which a phrase or word in the neighborhood of a head word is assigned the status of the head word's argument, is called **argument-linking**. The idea behind this term is that relational nouns and verbs have empty slots in their semantic representation (the so-called **argument structure**), which need to be filled by arguments. These empty slots in the argument structure are filled by linking the slots with arguments that are available in the neighborhood of the noun or verb in question.

Argument linking is also important for compounds whose right-hand member is a noun that is derived from a verb, and whose left-hand member serves as an argument of the verb. Such compounds, which are often referred to as **synthetic compounds**, are illustrated in (22):

(22)   beer drinker   pasta-eating
        car driver   window-cleaning
        bookseller   shop clearance
        church-goer   soccer-playing

In principle, there are two possibilities for analyzing synthetic compounds structurally. Either the suffix is attached to a compound consisting of the two words, or the suffix is attached to the right-hand word and the derived word then forms a compound together with the non-head. In the first case, we would be dealing with compounding inside derivation, in the second with derivation inside compounding. The two possibilities are exemplified for *bookseller*:

(23)   a. [[book sell] -er]
        b. [book [sell-er]

Given that *booksell* and similar noun-verb compounds (such as *car-drive, *beer-drink, *church-go*) are not possible formations, it seems that (23b) provides the better analysis. After all, a *bookseller* is a seller of books, which means that the derivative *seller* inherits an empty argument slot from the verb *sell*, and this argument slot can be filled either by an *of*-phrase (*a seller of books*) or by the first member of a compound.

Sometimes, however, argument linking in compounds fails. Thus, if the first element of the compound is semantically not compatible with its possible status as argument, an alternative relationship is construed. For example, a *Sunday driver* is not someone who drives a Sunday, but who drives on a Sunday, and a *street seller* usually does not sell streets, but sells things on the street. Similarly, *computer surgery* is normally not interpreted as surgery performed on computers, because computers are usually not treated by surgeons in the way human organs are. If this interpretation is ruled out, a new interpretation can arise that relies on other possible links between the referents of the two nouns. In the case of *computer surgery* the following inferencing procedure is likely to happen. Given that computers are used in all kinds of medical instruments, and complex medical instruments are used by surgeons, another possible interpretation of *computer surgery* would be 'surgery with the help of a computer, computer-assisted surgery.'

Similar inferencing procedures are applied by default whenever non-relational nouns occur in a compound. For example, in isolation *stone wall* will be interpreted preferably as a wall made out of stone, because it is a typical relationship between stones and walls that the latter are built with the former. However, and crucially, such an interpretation is not compulsory. Given the right context, we could interpret *stone wall* quite differently, for example as a wall against which a stone was flung, a wall that is painted with a graffiti showing a stone, etc. Or take another example, *marble museum*. Two interpretations come to mind, depending on which aspects of the two nouns are highlighted. The first interpretation is based on the concept of a museum as a building. Given that buildings are made of stone, and marble is a kind of stone used for constructing buildings, a *marble museum* might be a museum built with marble. Another interpretation could be based on the concept of a museum as a place where precious objects are displayed. Given that marble is an expensive type of stone that is also used to make cultural artefacts (e.g. sculptures), a *marble museum* could be a museum in which marble objects are exhibited. These examples show how the interpretation of compounds depends on the possible conceptual and semantic properties of the nouns involved and how these properties can be related to create compositional meaning in compounds.

The last example, *marble museum*, brings us to the second major factor involved in compound interpretation, the surrounding discourse. Which interpretation of *marble museum* will finally be evoked may largely depend on the preceding discourse. If the word occurs, for example, in an article about an exhibition of marble sculptures, the interpretation of *marble museum* as a museum where marble objects are on display will automatically surface. In a context where the building material of public buildings is the topic, the interpretation 'museum building made of marble' will be favored. To further illustrate the discourse dependency of compound interpretation, have a look at the following example. While in isolation you might want to interpret *snake girl* as a girl that has extremely flexible limbs, Adams (2001: 88) cites the following headline from the *Guardian*, which shows that the context provides for a very different reading:

(24)   *Snake girls' record*
        Two Chinese girls set record living for 12 days in a room with 888 snakes.

After having read the sub-headline, the reader will interpret *snake girls* as 'girls living with snakes.' This example also highlights the general discourse function of compounding, namely, loosely speaking, to squeeze complex concepts into very short expressions, which is particularly important for writing headlines or advertisement texts.

In sum, the interpretation of noun-noun compounds is highly variable and depends on the argument structure of the head, the semantics of the two nouns, the possible conceptual relationship between the two nouns, and on the surrounding discourse.

Let us now turn to the interpretation of adjective-noun and verb-noun compounds, where the picture does not look very different. We saw that words like *loudmouth* or *greybeard* form a productive pattern of semantically exocentric compounds referring to human beings or higher animals. It would be wrong, however, to assume that all A-N compounds are exocentric. In (25) I have listed some examples that show that there are also semantically headed compounds of the A-N type:

(25)   greenhouse   High Court
        blackbird   hothouse
        blackberry   smallpox
        blueprint   soft-ball
        White House   easy chair

What is striking about most of the above compounds is that their meaning is not fully compositional. Thus a *blackbird* is a black bird (an indication of the semantic right-headedness of *blackbird*), but being a *blackbird* involves more than being a black bird. Similarly an *easy chair* is a kind of chair, but what kind of chair it really is, is not predictable on the basis of the first element *easy*.

The high proportion of lexicalized A-N compounds is an indication of the fact that this type of compounding is not nearly as productive as noun-noun compounding. However, we can still see that the interpretation of these compounds largely follows the modifier-head pattern we have encountered with noun-noun compounds.

Verb-noun compounds follow the same interpretative mechanisms as noun-noun and adjective-noun compounds. Apart from the few semantically exocentric compounds such as *pickpocket* or *spoilsport*, there are also a small number of endocentric verb-noun compounds, examples of which are *swearword, think tank, playground*. Unlike in the exocentric compounds mentioned, the right-hand member in endocentric verb-noun compounds such as *swearword, think tank, playground* is not an argument of the verb, but acts as a head which is modified by the initial verbal element.

Preposition-noun compounds are again of the modifier-head structure and mostly involve the prepositions *after* (e.g. *afterbirth, afterbrain, afterlife*), *out* (e.g. *outbuilding, outpost, outroom*), and *under* (e.g. *underarm, underbrush, underhair*). For some further discussion of this type of compound see exercise 6.5.

6.4   Adjectival compounds

Adjectival compounds can have nouns or other adjectives as non-heads. The interpretation of noun-adjective compounds basically follows the same principles as that of noun-noun compounds. The non-head element can serve either as a modifier or, given the appropriate adjectival head, as an argument of the head. Consider the examples in (26):

(26)   capital-intensive   sugar-free
        knee-deep   structure-dependent
        dog-lean   girl-crazy
        blood-red   class-conscious

Depending on the semantics of the compound members and on likely semantic relationships between them, the compounds in the left-hand column receive various kinds of interpretations ('intensive with regard to capital,' 'deep to the height of one's knee,' 'lean as a dog,' 'red like blood'). The most common type of interpretation is the one involving a comparison ('lean as a dog,' 'red like blood'), and very often the first element of such compounds assumes the role of an intensifier, so that *dog-lean, dog-tired* etc. may be paraphrased as 'very lean,' 'very tired.'

The items in the right-hand column of (26) can be analyzed in such a way that the first element of the compound satisfies an argument position of the adjective. In syntactic constructions this argument would appear next to a preposition: *free of sugar, dependent on structure, crazy for girls, conscious of class (differences)*.

Adjective-adjective compounds with the first adjective as modifier (as in *icy-cold, blueish-green*) do not seem to be as numerous as noun-adjective compounds.

Among the adjective-adjective type we also find copulative compounds similar to the nominal ones discussed in section 6.3.1 above. On the one hand, there are appositional compounds such as *sweet-sour* and *bitter-sweet*, which refer to entities (in this case tastes or emotions) that are at the same time *sweet* and *sour*, or *bitter* and *sweet*. On the other hand, there are coordinative compounds that are, like their noun-noun counterparts, exclusively used attributively: *a French-German cooperation, the high-low alternation, a public-private partnership*.

Finally, there are adjectival compounds that involve derived adjectives as heads and that behave in a similar fashion as deverbal synthetic compounds. Examples are given in (27):

(27)   blue-eyed   university-controlled   hair-raising
        clear-sighted   Washington-based   awe-inspiring

Again there are two possibilities for the structural analysis, exemplified for *blue-eyed, university-controlled*, and *hair-raising* in (28):

(28)   a. [[blue eye] -ed]
        b. [blue [eye-ed]]
        c. [[university control] -ed]
        d. [university [control-ed]]
        e. [[hair raise] -ing]
        f. [hair [raise-ing]]

The meaning of *blue-eyed* as 'having a blue eye/blue eyes' strongly suggests that (28a) is the best analysis for these words. We are dealing with the derivational suffix *-ed*, whose derivatives can be paraphrased as 'having X, provided with X' (cf. *binoculared, blazered, gifted*, see section 4.4.3), and this suffix can be attached to phrases such as [*blue eye*]. What appears to be slightly problematic with such an analysis is that it entails that phrases (such as [*blue eye*] or [*clear sight*]) may serve as input to a derivational rule. This is an unusual state of affairs, since most suffixes do not attach freely to phrases, but only to roots or words. However, we have seen in chapter 4 that the possibility of phrases and compounds feeding derivation is needed anyway to account for the behavior of the suffixes *-er* (e.g. *fourth-grader*), *-ish* (e.g. *stick-in-the-muddish*), and *-ness* (e.g. *over-the-top-ness*), which all readily attach to phrases.

Although involving the same surface form *-ed*, the case of *university-controlled* is different from the case of *blue-eyed* in that we are dealing not with the ornative suffix *-ed*, but with the adjectivally used past participle *controlled*, which is modified by *university*. Compounds with adjectival heads that are based on past participles often receive a passive interpretation ('controlled by the university'), with the non-head expressing the agent argument of the verb. Hence, structure (28d) seems to be the best analysis.

The same analysis holds for *hair-raising* (see (28f)) and similar compounds, in which the non-head is usually interpreted as the object of the verbal base of the head (e.g. a hair-raising experience is an experience that raises one's hair, and an awe-inspiring person is a person that inspires awe).

With regard to their stress pattern, adjectival compounds show both leftward and rightward stress. For example, all copulative adjectival compounds, and compounds like *knee-déep, bone-drý, dog-tíred, top-héavy* are all stressed on the final element, but other formations have initial stress: *fóotloose, thréadbare.* The source of this variability is unclear, but the stress criterion is not as important for determining the status of adjectival compounds as compounds as it is for nominal compounds.

6.5   Verbal compounds

In our table of possible and impossible compound patterns in (18) we saw that compounds with a verbal head may have nouns, adjectives, and verbs as their non-head, as exemplified in (29):

(29)

noun as non-head	adjective as non-head	verb as non-head
proof-read	deep-fry	stir-fry
talent-spot	shortcut	dry-clean
ghost-write	blindfold	freeze-dry
chain-smoke	broadcast	drink-drive

Upon closer inspection we notice, however, that the majority of compounds involving a verbal head are best analyzed as the result of a back-formation (see section 2.3) or conversion process (see section 5.1). Thus, the items in the leftmost column are all back-formations from noun-noun compounds with either a verbal noun in *-ing* or a person noun in *-er* in head position (e.g. *proof-reading, talent-spotter, ghost-writer, chain-smoker*). With regard to adjective-verb compounds, conversion is involved with *to shortcut* ('to take a shortcut'), and *to blindfold* ('to use a blindfold'), while *to deep-fry* and *to broadcast* seem to be rather idiosyncratic instances of this type, whose semantics is not transparent.

That the back-formation and conversion analyses make sense is supported by the above-mentioned fact that verbal compounds with nouns as non-heads are impossible in English, and by the fact that verbs cannot incorporate adjectival/adverbial non-heads. For instance, neither *read a book, steal a car* nor *drive fast, move slowly* can be readily turned into compounds (**bookread, *carsteal, *fastdrive, *slow(ly)-move*), whereas nominalized verbs and their arguments (as in *the reading of books, a driver of trains*) and deverbal adjectives and their adverbial/adjectival modifiers are happily condensed to compounds (*book-reading, train-driver, a fast-driving chauffeur, a slow-moving animal*).

In contrast to noun-verb and adjective-verb combinations, verb-verb compounds are not so readily explained as the product of back-formation or conversion. They seem to be regular copulative compounds referring to events that involve the conceptual integration of two events into one (e.g. *to stir-fry* 'to fry and stir simultaneously'). This interpretation parallels that of appositional nominal and adjectival compounds. Appositional verbal compounds are much less frequent, however.

With regard to stress assignment, verbal compounds show no uniform behavior. While variable stress assignment can be observed, *freeze-dry* and most of the other compounds in (29) have initial stress. As with adjectival compounds, the reasons for this variability are not clear, but, again, stress is not a crucial criterion for determining the compound status of these formations.

6.6   Neoclassical compounds

In chapter 4 we defined neoclassical formations as forms in which lexemes of Latin or Greek origin are combined to form new combinations that are not attested in the original languages (hence the term NEO classical). I repeat here the examples from chapter 4:

(30)   *bio*chemistry   *photo*graph   geo*logy*
       *bio*rhythm   *photo*ionize   bio*logy*
       *bio*warfare   *photo*analysis   neuro*logy*
       *bio*graphy   *photo*voltaic   philo*logy*

We have already argued briefly in section 4.1 why such formations are best described not as the result of affixation. In this section we will examine in more detail the properties of neoclassical forms, focusing on three phenomena that deserve special attention: first, the position and combinatorial properties of neoclassical elements; second, the phonological properties of the resulting compounds; and third, the status and behavior of medial *-o-* that often appears in such forms.

Let us start our analysis by looking at a larger number of pertinent forms. The list of forms that can be argued to belong to the class of neoclassical forms is rather long. For illustration I have compiled the collection in (31):

(31)

form	meaning	example
a. astro-	'space'	astro-physics, astrology
bio-	'life'	biodegradable, biocracy
biblio-	'book'	bibliography, bibliotherapy
electro-	'electricity'	electro-cardiograph, electrography
geo-	'earth'	geographic, geology
hydro-	'water'	hydro-electric, hydrology
morpho-	'figure'	morphology, morpho-genesis
philo-	'love'	philotheist, philo-gastric
retro-	'backwards'	retroflex, retro-design
tele-	'distant'	television, telepathy
theo-	'god'	theocratic, theology
b. -cide	'murder'	suicide, genocide
-cracy	'rule'	bureaucracy, democracy
-graphy	'write'	sonography, bibliography
-itis	'disease'	laryngitis, lazyitis
-logy	'science of'	astrology, neurology
-morph	'figure'	anthropomorph, polymorph
-phile	'love'	anglophile, bibliophile
-phobe	'fear'	anglophobe, bibliophobe
-scope	'look at'	laryngoscope, telescope

Let us first consider the position and combinatorial properties of the elements in question. As indicated by the hyphens, none of these forms can usually occur as a free form. With the exception of *morph-/-morph* and *phil-/-phile*, which can occur both in initial or in final position, the elements in (31) occur either initially or finally. Hence a distinction is often made between **initial combining forms** and **final combining forms**. The difference between affixes and combining forms is that neither affixes nor bound roots can combine with each other to form a new word: an affix can combine with a bound root (cf. e.g. *bapt-ism, prob-able*), but cannot combine with another affix to form a new word (**re-ism, *dis-ism, *ism-able*). And a bound root can take an affix (cf. again *bapt-ism, prob-able*), but cannot combine exclusively with another bound root (e.g. **bapt-prob*). Combining forms, however, can combine either with bound roots (e.g. *glaciology, scientology*), with words (*lazyitis, hydro-electric, morpho-syntax*), or with another combining form (*hydrology, morphology*) to make up a new word.

With regard to the phonological properties of neoclassical elements we see that their behavior is not unitary. Initial combining forms seem to vary in their segmental structure and in their stress contour, depending on whether they combine with free forms or certain other combining forms. Consider, for example, the pronunciations of the following pairs (acute accents indicate primary stresses):

(32)   a. astro-phýsics   b. astrólogy
           biodegrádable   biócracy
           biblio-thérapy   bibliógraphy

As we can see in (32), the stress behavior of neoclassical compounds differs considerably from that of other compounds. First, the data in (32a) do not show the usual leftward stress pattern, but have their main stress on the right-hand member of the compound. This stress pattern holds for most neoclassical compounds that involve initial combining forms as first members and words as second members.

With regard to the formations in (32b), it can be observed that the combining forms *-graphy*, *-cracy*, and *-logy* all impose a certain stress contour on the compounds: they all carry antepenultimate stress. In this respect, *-graphy*, *-cracy*, and *-logy* behave like stress-influencing suffixes (such as *-ity*), discussed in sections 4.3 and 4.4, and unlike the elements in non-neoclassical compounds.

Finally, we turn to the status of *-o-* in neoclassical formations. In the above tables, I represented all of the initial combining forms (but one, *tele-*) with the final letter <o> (e.g. *hydro-, morpho-*, etc.), and all final combining forms without this letter (cf. e.g. *-logy, -morph, -phile*). This is, however, a controversial thing to do.

First, it could be argued that, if all (or most) of the initial combining forms end in *-o*, we should treat *-o* as a kind of suffix. Or, alternatively, we could venture the hypothesis that *-o* is not a suffix attached to the initial combining form, but a prefix attached to the final combining form. Obviously, what is needed here is a systematic analysis of the behavior of *-o-*. Let us therefore look at the data in more detail, starting with the general question of when *-o-* appears and when not. Given the (as yet) uncertainty of its status, and in order not to prejudge the issue, we will call this *-o-* a 'linking element' (instead of a prefix or a suffix or a root-final <o>).

In the vast majority of cases we find the linking element *-o-* in the above compounds, but there are a number of interesting exceptions, listed in (33):

(33)

	combining form	examples lacking *-o-*	examples with *-o-*
a.	tele-	television, telepathy	–
b.	-cide	suicide	genocide
	-itis	laryngitis, lazyitis	–
	-morph	polymorph	anthropomorph
	-scope	telescope	laryngoscope
c.	-cracy	bureaucracy	democracy

Tele- is the only initial combining form that never allows the linking element, while there are four final combining forms allowing vowels other than *-o-* preceding them. Finally, in (33c) we have *bureaucracy*, which may seem like an exception, but only in orthography: phonologically, the form has the same linking element as we find it in *dem*[ɒ]*cracy*. This suggests that the phenomenon is not orthographic, but phonological in nature, since the orthography obviously tolerates the use of other letters as long as they represent the required sound.

Probing further in the phonological direction, we can make an interesting generalization on the basis of the forms in (33): if there is already a vowel in the final position of the initial combining form or in the initial position of the final combining form, -*o*- does not show up. Thus, *tele-scope* has no -*o*-, but *laryng-o-scope* has it, *poly-morph* has no -*o*-, but *anthrop-o-morph* has it, *suicide* has no -*o*-, but *gen-o-cide* has it. And -*itis* does not take -*o*- as a linking element either, because it starts in a vowel.

If this account of the facts is correct, we can make the prediction that there should be initial combining forms ending in a consonant that do not take -*o*- when combined with a vowel-initial final combining form, but that do take -*o*- when combined with a consonant-initial final combining form. And indeed, such data exist: the initial combining form *gastr*- 'stomach' alternates with the form *gastro*-, and the alternation depends on the following sound: if it is a vowel, the consonant-final form surfaces (as in *gastr-itis*), whereas if the following sound is a consonant, the linking element surfaces (*gastr-o-graphy*). Hence, we can conclude that the occurrence of -*o*- is, at least with some formations, phonologically determined.

However, such an account does not work for all combining forms. Consider the data in (34) and try to find the problem these forms create for the hypothesis that -*o*- is a thematic vowel whose occurrence and non-occurrence is phonologically governed:

(34)   a. biology   bio-acoustic   *bi-acoustic
           biophysical   bio-energy   *bi-energy
           biotechnology   bio-implanted   *bi-implanted
        b. geocentric   geoarchaeological   *ge-archaeological
           geology   geoelectric   *ge-electrical
           geography   geoenvironmental   *ge-environmental

The forms in (34) show that *bio*- and *geo*- do not have alternant forms (**bi-/bio-*, **ge-/geo-*), which means that with these initial combining forms, -*o*- does not have the status of a thematic vowel, but is part of the phonological representation of the initial combining form. From this we can conclude that the status of -*o*- is not the same in all neoclassical formations, but should be decided on for each combining form separately on the basis of distributional evidence.

To summarize our discussion of neoclassical compounds, we have seen that these formations possess a number of interesting formal properties that distinguish them from the other types of compound discussed in the previous sections.

6.7   Compounding: syntax or morphology?

In the preceding subsections we have alluded to the possibility that compounding may not be regarded as a word-formation process, but rather as a syntactic process, hence outside the realm of morphology. This line of argument has been taken by a number of scholars and in this section we will have a closer look at the merits and problems of such approaches.

Proponents of a syntactic view of compounding put forward the idea that the very productive class of noun-noun compounds in particular results from a syntactic rule which states that in a **noun phrase** (abbreviated as 'NP') not only adjectives, but also nouns can modify the following noun. This rule is schematized in (35a) and illustrated with the examples in (35b) and (35c):

(35)   a. NP → article {adjective, noun} noun
         b. the long marathon
         c. the Boston marathon

The curly brackets in (35a) indicate that either an adjective or a noun may occur in this position. The rule reads like this: 'a noun phrase may consist of an article, an adjective, and a noun, or of an article, a noun, and a noun.' The element immediately preceding the rightmost noun of the phrase (i.e. the head of the phrase) modifies the phrasal head. In (35b) the modifier is an adjective, in (35c) it is a noun. Although rule (35a) looks like a wonderful way to get rid of the category of compounds (thus streamlining our theory of language), it has the considerable disadvantage that it does not explain why the majority of adjective-noun combinations are usually stressed on the noun and have the flavor of phrases, while noun-noun combinations are usually stressed on the first noun and have the flavor of words, i.e. of being compounds.

On the basis of these last considerations we are tempted to say that there is no syntactic rule such as (35a). This would be, however, somewhat premature, because there is a set of constructions where nouns should indeed be analyzed as phrasal premodifiers of other nouns. Consider the data in (36):

(36)   the New York markets
         a three-syllable word
         the two-year period

One would perhaps want to argue that *New York markets*, *three-syllable word*, and *two-year period* are compounds. However, such an analysis creates problems with regard to the insertion of adjectives, which, surprisingly, is possible:

(37)   the New York financial markets
        a three-syllable prosodic word
        the two-year probationary period

If *New York markets*, *three-syllable word*, and *two-year period* were really compounds, it would be impossible to insert an adjective between the two nouns. This can be seen with structures that are uncontroversially regarded as compounds:

(38)   waterbird   *water wild bird
        jellyfish   *jelly floating fish
        rain forest *rain tropical forest

How can this puzzle be solved? One way out is to look again at our stress criterion. The structures in (36) have in common the fact that they are stressed on the rightmost element of the phrase, while the data in (38) have leftward stress. This may be taken as an indication (though not proof, see our discussion in section 6.1.3) of the phrasal status of the entities in (36) and (37). Now, if we assume that these structures are indeed phrases, then it does not come as a surprise that we can insert an adjective between the two nouns in (37). In sum, the syntactic behavior and the stress pattern *together* strongly argue in favor of a phrasal analysis of these specific constructions.

But does that mean that all compounds are phrasal, or that all compounds with final stress are phrasal? I don't think so. We could also argue that there are only some restricted classes of nouns whose members are allowed to act as syntactic modifiers of nouns. Two of these classes are exemplified above (i.e. nouns indicating a location and nouns incorporating a numeral), and it remains to be shown which other classes can be established.

In their textbook on English words, Stockwell and Minkova (2001) seem to adopt a compromise position with regard to the question of whether compounds are syntactic or morphological objects. They restrict the notion of compounding to composite words that have taken on a unique new meaning that is not completely inferable on the basis of the two elements involved (Stockwell and Minkova 2001: 13). In doing so, they distinguish between what they call lexical and syntactic compounds. While lexical compounds are non-transparent, syntactic compounds are always transparent and are "formed by regular rules of grammar" (*ibid.*). According to this view, everything that is regular is conceived as syntactic and everything that is lexicalized and idiosyncratic is morphological. Such a view is, however, highly problematic, since, as we have seen in the previous chapters, morphological processes are often quite regular and regularity alone is not a sufficient criterion to distinguish between word-formation rules and syntactic rules.

But which criteria could help us to solve this problem? The question of whether a process that combines words into larger entities is morphological or syntactic in nature has already been in focus when we discussed conversion. There, we have argued that syntactic and morphological processes can be distinguished by a range of properties, some of which we discussed in chapter 5, for example that complex words can display all kinds of exceptional properties, whereas syntactic patterns and their interpretations tend to be rather exceptionless. Below I summarize some differences between sentence-structure rules and word-structure rules (see Katamba 1993: 217 for a similar list):

(39)

word-structure rules	sentence-structure rules
a. may change word classes (as in conversion)	do not change word classes
b. may be sensitive to the morphological make-up of bases	are not sensitive to the internal structure of words
c. often have arbitrary exceptions and their output is often lexicalized	their output is normally not lexicalized and there are usually no arbitrary exceptions
d. are rarely recursive (only some prefixes)	are highly recursive

The criteria (39a) and (39b) have already been discussed in the preceding chapter in the context of conversion. Their relevance with regard to compounding is, however, very limited since compounding in English is not word-class-changing and there are no restrictions observable as to the morphological structure of the elements involved. With regard to the criterion (39c) we could state that the different systematic and not so systematic stress patterns observable with certain sets of compounds are the kind of arbitrary exceptions characteristic of word-structure rules. Furthermore, as correctly pointed out by Stockwell and Minkova (2001), compounds are often lexicalized, a property not typical of syntactic phrases. Criterion (39d) is again not easy to interpret for compounds. We have said above that recursion is a well-known property of noun-noun compounds, which rather points towards their syntactic status. However, some prefixes are also recursive, which shows that the avoidance of recursion in suffixation may be an artefact of the selectional properties of most affixes and not a sign of a deeper structural difference between syntax and morphology. For example, the verbal suffixes *-ify*, *-ize*, or *-ate* never attach to any type of verb, not only not to verbs that already have the same suffix. Hence, the combinations *-ify-ize* and *-ate-ize* are just as impossible as the recursive combination *-ize-ize*.

Applying the criteria listed in (39) therefore does not conclusively solve the problem of the syntactic or morphological nature of compounding, although they may speak slightly in favor of a morphological view of compounding.

What would be needed to really decide on this issue is a well-defined theory of syntax, which makes clear statements about the nature of the mechanisms it employs. Currently, there are many syntactic theories on the market whose underlying assumptions concerning the role of morphology in grammar differ greatly, which makes it virtually impossible to solve the problem of compounding without reference to a particular theory of grammar. Given the nature of this book as an introduction to word-formation that does not assume prior training in syntactic theory, we may leave this theoretical issue unresolved. Chapter 7 will take up the question of the syntax-morphology connection again from a more general perspective.

6.8   Summary

In this chapter we have looked at the most productive means to create new words in English, namely compounding. We have seen that there are numerous different patterns of compound formation which can be distinguished on the basis of formal and semantic criteria. Compounds systematically combine words of certain categories, they display certain predictable stress patterns, and they are interpreted in principled ways.

We have also seen that compounds raise a host of theoretical issues (some of them still not satisfactorily resolved), such as the internal structure of compounds, the notion of head, the mapping of stress patterns onto semantic and structural interpretations, and the boundary between morphology and syntax.

Having gained some experience in dealing with theoretical problems emerging from empirical investigations, we are now in a position to probe deeper and at a more general level into theory, in particular the relationship between morphology and phonology and between morphology and syntax. This will be done in the following, theoretically oriented chapter, where I present some theories that have explicitly aimed at modeling these relationships.

Further reading

The literature on the different phonological, semantic, and syntactic aspects of compounds is vast. Marchand (1969), Adams (2001), Bauer and Renouf

(2001), and Bauer and Huddleston (2002) provide descriptive overviews of a wide range of common and less common compounding patterns. Olsen (2000a) and Fabb (1998) are useful state-of-the-art articles on cross-linguistic properties of compounds, summarizing the different strands of research. For views on compound stress the reader should consult, for example, Fudge (1984), Liberman and Sproat (1992), Ladd (1984), and Olsen (2000b). Meyer (1993) and Ryder (1994) are book-length treatments of the interpretations of compounds, Spencer (1991) contains a useful overview of the literature on synthetic compounds. Williams (1981a) and Di Sciullo and Williams (1987) are the classic references for the notion of head, Bauer (1990) contains a critical discussion thereof. Neoclassical word-formation is discussed in Bauer (1998a) and Lüdeling et al. (2002), and Bauer (1998b) deals with the notoriously difficult distinction between phrases and compounds. Phonetic correlates of this distinction are investigated in Farnetani et al. (1988) and Ingram et al. (in press).

Exercises

Basic level

Exercise 6.1

Classify the following words as being products of either inflection, derivation, or compounding. Justify your analysis in the potentially problematic cases.

blackboard eraser	*unacceptability*	*flowerpots*	*movie monster*
broad-shouldered	*hard-working*	*speaking*	*developmental*

Exercise 6.2

Name three general characteristics of English compounds. Use the data below for illustration.

oak-tree   drawbridge   sky-blue   mind-boggling

Exercise 6.3

Classify the following compounds as exocentric, endocentric, possessive, appositional, or coordinative.

frying pan	*redhead*	*maidservant*	*author-reader (exchange)*
Austria-Hungary	*hardtop*	*silkworm*	*man-machine (interaction)*
bootblack	*German-English*	*actor-manager*	*gas-light*

Advanced level

Exercise 6.4

In section 6.7 we discussed the idea that compounds may not be words but phrases, and we investigated several criteria to distinguish between the two types of entity, i.e. words vs. phrases. In particular, stress pattern and interruptability were mentioned as possible tests.

Now, it could be argued that coordinative compounds in particular are phrases, and should not be considered words. Discuss this idea, taking the data from (20b), and using the stress pattern and the interruptability tests as diagnostic criteria. Further arguments for or against the compound status of coordinative compounds may also arise from a systematic comparison of coordinative compounds with their corresponding phrases (e.g. *doctor-patient gap* vs. *the gap between doctor(s) and patient(s)*). Is the evidence entirely conclusive?

Exercise 6.5

Are *underdog, undercoat* and *overtax, overripe* compounds or prefixed derivatives? Go back to the discussion of affixes and prefixes in sections 4.1 and 4.5. Which arguments can be adduced for the status of *under-* and *over-* in the above forms?

7

Theoretical issues: modeling
word-formation

Outline

In this chapter theories are introduced that try to find principled answers
to two central problems of morphology. We will first examine the theory of Lexical
Phonology as a theory that tries to model the interaction of phonology and morphology. In the second part of the chapter we discuss how different morphological
theories conceptualize the form and nature of word-formation rules.

7.1   Introduction: why theory?

This chapter is devoted to theory and the obvious question is 'why?'.
Haven't we so far rather successfully dealt with numerous phenomena without
making use of morphological theory? The answer is clearly 'no.' Whenever we had
to solve an empirical problem, i.e. to explain an observation with regard to complex
words, we had to make recourse to theoretical notions such as 'word,' 'affix,' 'rule,'
'alternation,' 'prosody,' 'head,' etc. In other words, during our journey through the
realm of complex words, we tacitly developed a theory of word-formation without
ever addressing explicitly the question of how our theoretical bits and pieces may
fit together to form an overall theory of word-formation.

But what is a theory? *Webster's Third* defines the term 'theory' as "a coherent set
of hypothetical, conceptual and pragmatic principles forming the general frame of
reference for a particular field of inquiry (as for deducing principles, formulating
hypotheses for testing, undertaking actions)" (*Webster's Third*, s. v. *theory*). In
a more restricted sense a certain theory is a "hypothetical entity or structure explaining or relating an observed set of facts" (*Webster's Third*, s. v. *theory*). Thus,
a morphological theory would help us not only to understand observed (and yet
unobserved) facts concerning complex words, but would also help us to develop
hypotheses in order to arrive at general principles of word-formation. In very general terms, a theory can help us to understand the world (better). This is also the
idea behind the saying that there is nothing as practical as a good theory.

With this in mind, we will take a look at two particular theoretical problems which have been mentioned repeatedly in the preceding chapters, but which we have not solved in a principled manner. The first of these problems is the interaction of phonology and morphology, the second the form and nature of word-formation rules.

As we will see, there are a number of different criteria by which a theory can be judged, the most important of which are perhaps internal consistency, elegance, explicitness, and empirical adequacy. With regard to the criterion of internal consistency, it should be evident that a theory should not contradict itself. Furthermore, a theory should be elegant in the sense that it uses as little machinery (entities, rules, principles, etc.) as possible to explain an observed set of facts. And the explanations should be as explicit as possible, so that clear hypotheses can be formulated. This is important because hypotheses must be falsifiable, and only clear hypotheses can be clearly falsified. Finally, the theory should be empirically adequate in the sense that it can account for the observable data.

Equipped with this background information on theories in general, we are now in the position to examine the theory of 'Lexical Phonology and Morphology' or 'Lexical Phonology' for short, originating in the work of Kiparsky (1982), which tries to explain the relationship between phonology and morphology in a principled fashion.

7.2   The phonology-morphology interaction: Lexical Phonology

7.2.1   An outline of the theory of Lexical Phonology

In the previous chapters we have frequently seen that morphology and phonology interact. For example, we have observed that certain suffixes impose certain stress patterns on their derivatives (as in *prodúctive–productívity*) or are responsible for the deletion of segments (*feminine–feminize*). We also saw that compounds have a particular stress pattern. However, we have not asked ourselves how this interaction of phonology and morphology can be conceptualized in an overall theory of language.

In order to understand the main ideas of Lexical Phonology, it is helpful to take a brief look at the history of the school of linguistic thought called generative grammar. Somewhat simplifying the complex issues involved, we can say that in generative grammar, it was assumed that well-formed sentences as the output of the language system (the 'grammar') are generated in such a way that words are taken from the lexicon and inserted into syntactic structures. These structures are then interpreted semantically and pronounced according to the rules of the phonological component. A schematic picture of such an approach is given in (1). The schema abstracts away from particular details of the various models that have been proposed and revised over the years (see e.g. Horrocks 1987 for an overview):

(1)

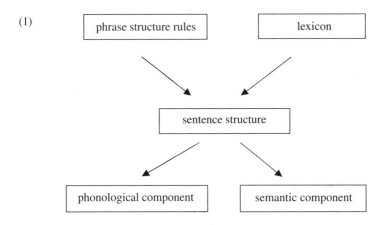

In this model, phonological processes crucially apply after all morphological and syntactic operations have been carried out, i.e. after all word-formation rules or inflectional rules have been applied and the words have been inserted into syntactic structures. A number of generativists soon realized, however, that, contrary to what the model predicts, there is significant interaction of phonology and morphology in the derivation of complex words, which led to the idea that certain phonological rules must apply before a given word leaves the lexicon and is inserted into a syntactic structure. In other words, parts of the phonology must be at work *in the lexicon*, and not only post-lexically, i.e. after the words have left the lexicon and are inserted into a syntactic tree. The theory that wants to account for the application of phonological rules in the lexicon is therefore aptly named **Lexical Phonology**.

The basic insight of Lexical Phonology is that phonology and morphology work in tandem. There are phonological rules that are triggered only by the affixation of a particular morpheme, and which apply in a **cyclic** fashion. The word 'cyclic' means here that whenever a new affix is added in a new derivational cycle, the pertinent rule can apply on that cycle. For example, each time we attach a given stress-shifting suffix to a given base, we must apply the pertinent stress rule (cf. *seléctive–selectívity*). If more than one affix is attached, **cyclic phonological rules** reapply at each step in the derivation of a particular word. Before we can see in more detail how this works we need to take a brief look at so-called **level-ordering**.

The concept of cyclic rule application has built heavily on work by Siegel (1974) and Allen (1978), who assume the existence of two **levels** or **strata** in English derivational morphology. In (2) I have listed a number of affixes according to the level to which they supposedly belong (cf. also Spencer 1991: 79):

(2)   Level I suffixes: +*al,* +*ate,* +*ic,* +*ion,* +*ity,* +*ive,* +*ous*
        Level I prefixes: *be*+, *con*+, *de*+, *en*+, *in*+, *pre*+, *re*+, *sub*+
        Level II suffixes: #*able,* #*er,* #*ful,* #*hood,* #*ist,* #*ize,* #*less,* #*ly,* #*ness,* #*wise*
        Level II prefixes: *anti*#, *de*#, *non*#, *re*#, *sub*#, *un*#, *semi*#

Affixes belonging to one stratum can be distinguished from the affixes of the other stratum by a number of properties (some of these properties were already discussed in section 4.2, but without reference to level-ordering).

First, level 1 affixes tend to be of foreign origin ('Latinate'), while level 2 affixes are mostly Germanic. Second, level 1 affixes can attach to bound roots and to words, while level 2 affixes attach to words only. For example, in *electric* the suffix attaches to the root *electr-*, while the adjective-forming level 2 suffix -*ly* only attaches to words (e.g. *earthly*). This difference in the strength of morphological boundaries is expressed by the '+' and '#' notation in (2), with '+' standing for a root boundary and '#' standing for a word boundary. The difference in boundary strength leads to the third difference between the two levels. Level 1 affixes tend to be phonologically more integrated into their base than level 2 affixes, with stratum 1 suffixes causing stress shifts and other morpho-phonological alternations, while stratum 2 suffixes do not affect their bases phonologically. Finally, stratum 1 affixes are generally less productive than stratum 2 affixes.

With reference to the two levels, an interesting property of English derivation can be captured, namely their combinability with other affixes. According to the so-called **level-ordering hypothesis**, affixes can easily combine with affixes on the same level, but if they combine with an affix from another level, the level 1 affix is always closer to the base than the level 2 affix. For example, level 1 suffix -*(i)an* may appear inside level 2 -*ism* but not vice versa (cf. *Mongol-ian-ism,* but **Mongol-ism-ian*). Level-ordering thus rules out many unattested combinations of affixes on principled grounds.

Coming back to cyclic rule application, the interaction of morphological and phonological rules can be schematized as in (3). The model as presented here is based on different studies in Lexical Phonology and ignores existing minor differences between the pertinent authors (e.g. Kiparsky 1982, Mohanan 1986) in order to bring out clearly the most important aspect of the theory, the interaction of morphological and phonological rules. For reasons that will become clear shortly, the model also includes regular and irregular inflection.

(3)   A model of Lexical Phonology

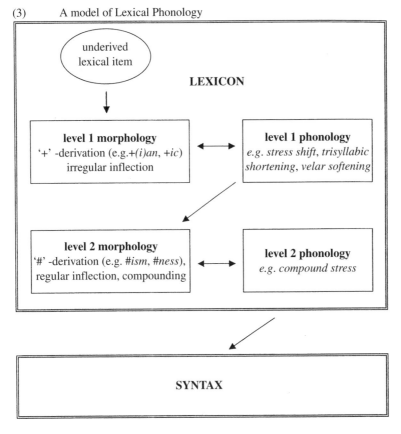

How does the model work? In the words of Mohanan, Lexical Phonology can be compared to a factory, with the levels as individual rooms in which words are produced: "There is a conveyor belt that runs from the entry gate to the exit gate passing through each of these rooms. This means that every word that leaves the factory came in through the entry gate and passed through every one of these rooms" (1986: 47). Let us illustrate this with the derivation of the potential compound word *Mongolianism debates*. This word would be derived by first subjecting the underived lexical item *Mongol* to +*(i)an* suffixation. Having attached *-ian*, the form *Mongolian* is transferred to the 'level 1 phonology' box, where stress is assigned on the syllable immediately preceding the suffix. *Mongólian* is then, on the next cycle, transferred to level 2 morphology where it receives the suffix *-ism* and is handed over to level 2 phonology. Not much happens here for the moment, because *-ism*, like all level 2 suffixes, is stress-neutral. The form is transferred back to level 2 morphology where it is inserted into a compound structure together with the right-hand element *debate*. The compound goes to level 2 phonology to receive compound stress and is then handed back to become pluralized, i.e. adopt regular inflectional *-s*. Back in level 2 phonology again, inflectional *-s* is interpreted phonologically (as one of the three possible regular allomorphs). The word is now ready to leave the lexicon and to be inserted into a syntactic structure. Fair enough, you might be tempted to say, but what do we gain with such a model? This is the topic of the next section.

7.2.2   Basic insights of Lexical Phonology

To answer the question of what Lexical Phonology has to offer, we can say that the model makes interesting predictions about the behavior of morphological units and helps us to explain a number of generalizations that emerge from the data and that we have dealt with in the previous chapters.

One prediction we have already mentioned above concerns the order of many affix–affix combinations. According to the level-ordering hypothesis, a given level 1 affix must attach before a level 2 affix, because level 2 output cannot feed level 1. Thus, the impossibility of, for example, **atom-less-ity* follows from the fact that *-less* is level 2, whereas *-ity* is level 1. Level 1 affixes inside level 2 affixes are fine (cf. *curi-ous-ness*), and so are combinations within a given level (cf. *electr-ic-ity, atom-less-ness*).

The model can also explain an interesting interaction between compounding and inflection, and between conversion and inflection. Consider, for example, the question of why compounds like *walkman* and converted nouns like *to grandstand* do not take irregular inflection, as would be expected on the basis of their right-most elements *man* and *stand* (cf. *walkmans* vs. **walkmen* and *grandstanded* vs. **grandstood*). In the above model these facts fall out automatically: assuming that irregular morphology is a level 1 process and further assuming that compounding and noun-to-verb conversion are both level 2 processes, irregular inflectional marking is no longer a possibility for these forms because there is no loop back from level 2 to level 1. Regular inflection (i.e. plural *-s* and past tense *-ed*), which, according to the model in (3), operates on level 2, is the only possible way of marking these grammatical categories on these items.

Talking about conversion, the model can also help us to solve the directionality problem of conversion, at least with noun-to-verb and verb-to-noun conversion. In section 5.1.1, we argued that stress shift in otherwise homonymous verb-noun pairs is an indication of verb-to-noun conversion (e.g. *to protést – the prótest*). In terms of Lexical Phonology, verb-to-noun conversion must be a stratum 1 process, because only on this level is there the possibility to change the stress of the base word. In contrast, noun-to-verb conversion is stress-neutral, hence a level 2 process. A look at the productivity of the two processes corroborates this. As we have said above, level 1 processes are generally less productive than level 2 processes, which would lead us to the hypothesis that level 1 verb-to-noun conversion must be significantly less productive than noun-to-verb conversion. And this is exactly what we find.

Finally, the model can account for a phenomenon we discussed in chapter 3, namely the blocking of regular derived forms by existing synonymous forms. In terms of Lexical Phonology, blocking can be accounted for by the idea that the application of a given rule at one stratum blocks the application of the same rule at a later stratum. For example, the suffixation of the irregular plural to form *oxen* blocks the application of the more general, regular plural suffix *-s*. This is an instance of the so-called **elsewhere condition**, which states that the special rule has to apply first, and the more general rule 'elsewhere' (cf. our formulation of morpho-phonological alternations in section 2.2). Extending this idea to derivational morphology, we could explain why nouns converted from verbs like *cook*, *bore*, *spy* block synonymous words with the agentive suffix *-er* (cf. **cooker*, **borer*, **spyer*). Verb-to-noun conversion (e.g. $cook_{VERB} \rightarrow cook_{NOUN}$) is level 1, while *-er* is attached at level 2. The application of the rule of agentive formation by verb-to-noun conversion at level 1 preempts the attachment of agentive *-er* on a later cycle. This does not mean that it is totally impossible to add *-er*, for example, to the verb *cook*. The point is that if an agentive meaning is chosen at level 1, this meaning is no longer available at level 2. Hence, the deverbal form *cooker* must receive another interpretation (e.g. an instrumental one).

In sum, Lexical Phonology sheds light on four different problem areas, namely the serial application of morphological processes and the co-occurring phonological operations, the productivity of different processes, the direction of conversion, and the phenomenon of blocking. Lexical Phonology has, however, been severely criticized on both empirical and conceptual grounds, and we will turn to this criticism in the next section.

7.2.3   Problems with Lexical Phonology

The obvious empirical problem is that the model does not say anything about possible and impossible combinations within a given stratum, thus leaving large amounts of data unaccounted for. Fabb (1988) finds that the 43 suffixes he investigates are attested in only 50 two-suffix combinations, although stratum restrictions would allow 459 out of the 1849 possible ones. In order to explain combinations within strata, individual selectional restrictions like those discussed in section 3.5.2 are needed in any case, and, as argued in Plag (1996, 1999), these selectional restrictions then also account for the would-be stratal behavior of affixes. This idea will be further illustrated in section 7.2.4 below.

Another empirical weakness of level-ordering is that there are a number of attested suffix combinations that are unexpected under the assumption of level-ordering. Thus stress-neutral *-ist* appears systematically inside stress-shifting *-ic* (e.g. *Calvin-ist* – *Calvin-ist-ic*), or stress-neutral *-ize* appears systematically inside stress-shifting *-(at)ion* (e.g. *colon-iz-ation*, see also exercise 3.1).

One major theoretical drawback of level-ordering is that the two strata are not justified on independent grounds. In other words, it is unclear what is behind the distinction between the two strata, and which property makes an affix end up on a given stratum. Originally, it has been suggested that the underlying distinction is one of etymology (borrowed vs. native, e.g. Saciuk 1969), but this does not explain why speakers can and do master English morphology without etymological knowledge. Others have argued that the stratum problem is in fact a phonological one, with differences between different etymological strata being paralleled by phonological differences. For example, Anshen et al. (1986) show that etymology correlates with the number of syllables: Latinate bases tend to be polysyllabic, Germanic bases mono- or disyllabic. This approach has the advantage that it would allow speakers to distinguish between the strata on the basis of the segmental and prosodic behavior of derivatives. However, explaining the nature of the strata as following from underlying phonological properties of suffixes does in fact weaken the idea of strata, because, as shown by Raffelsiefen (1999), not even two of the many suffixes of English trigger exactly the same type of morpho-phonological alternations, so that we would need as many substrata as we have suffixes that trigger morpho-phonological alternations.

Another serious problem is that a stratum cannot be defined by the set of affixes it contains, because many affixes must belong to more than one stratum: they show stratum 1 behavior in certain derivatives, whereas in other derivatives they display stratum 2 behavior. For example, there are forms where *-able* is stress-shifting, hence stratum 1, but in the majority of cases stress-shift is absent. Even doublets exist that show the stratum 1 and stratum 2 behavior: *compárable* vs. *cómparable*. Another example of double membership is *-ize*, which attaches to some roots (e.g. *baptize*), truncates its bases under certain circumstances (see section 4.4.2), and triggers so-called velar softening (*classi*[k] – classi[s]*ize*, see answer key, exercise 4.3). All three properties are typical of level 1, but *-ize* is not stress-shifting, attaches mostly to words, and is productive, all typical level 2 properties.

Giegerich (1999) discusses many cases of dual membership of affixes in great detail and – as a consequence – proposes a thoroughly revised stratal model, in which the strata are no longer defined by the affixes belonging to that stratum, but by the bases involved. In this revised model, both words and bound roots start out on level 1 as roots, i.e. as morphemes that do not have a part-of-speech specification yet. This can then nicely account for the fact that many affixes attach to bound roots and to words, because these affixes attach at level 1. According to Giegerich, such affixes can do so because they attach generally to roots, i.e. level 1 morphemes that are not specified for part-of-speech yet. For example, *ambiti-ous* and *courage-ous* are both formed at level 1, because -*ous* attaches to roots. But what about suffixes that only attach to words? In Giegerich's model, these attach only after the base morphemes have passed on to level 2, where they have received a part-of-speech specification.

There are, however, at least two severe conceptual problems with such a revised model. Giegerich explains the fact that some affixes attach to both bound roots and words by simply stipulating that the words are also roots. There is, however and crucially, no independent motivation for such a move, apart from the fact that it makes the model work. The problem of double membership of affixes is replaced by the problem of assigning a given word with the same form the status of a root at level 1 and the status of a word at level 2 without independent justification.

This leads us to the second conceptual problem. If we attach a suffix at level 1, the derived word still has no part-of-speech specification, because part-of-speech is only assigned by root-to-word conversion at level 2. In other words, suffixes like -*ous* would no longer have a part-of-speech specification, but would only receive it after attachment to a root and after having then reached level 2, where the derived form is subjected to the root-to-word conversion rule for which the suffix is specified. In the case of -*ous*, this would be the conversion of the form from a root into an adjective. This seems like an unnecessary and unjustified complication.

To summarize, there are major empirical and theoretical problems with Lexical Phonology and the idea of level-ordering. In the following subsection, we will therefore explore alternative models.

7.2.4   Alternative theories: Fabb (1988), Plag (1999), Hay (2002)

We have frequently seen throughout this book that any given affix or morphological process comes with its particular phonological, morphological, semantic, and syntactic properties. Plag (1996, 1999) shows that these diverse properties together are responsible for the possible and impossible combinations of a given affix both with roots and with other affixes. What has been analyzed as would-be stratal behavior automatically falls out from the phonological, morphological, and semantic properties of the affix. Since these properties must be stated anyway to account for the particular behavior of a given affix, no further stratal apparatus is necessary.

Plag (1996, 1999) also incorporates the idea of base-driven suffixation to explain apparent idiosyncrasies in suffix combinations. The idea of base-driven restrictions in suffixation is that it is not only a given suffix that requires, or 'selects,' a certain kind of base, but that bases, in particular those that contain certain suffixes, may select a certain kind of affix. For illustration of this idea, consider the deverbal suffixes in (4), which, according to Fabb (1988), do not attach to any suffixed word (this would be an affix-driven restriction):

(4)   Deverbal nominal suffixes not attaching to an already suffixed word
       -age   (as in *steerage*)
       -al   (as in *betrayal*)
       -ance   (as in *annoyance*)
       -ment   (as in *containment*)
       -y   (as in *assembly*)

Why should these suffixes behave in this way? And is this a property that has to be stated in the lexical entry of each of the nominal suffixes? In an approach that only looks at the question of which kinds of base a given affix selects this would be essential. Let us call such an approach 'affix-driven.' It is, however, possible to look at the problem from a different angle, i.e. from the perspective of the base. Which kinds of affix does a given base select? In such a base-driven approach, the impossibility of the above nominal suffixes to attach to already suffixed words could also be explained in terms of the bases, not only in terms of the nominal suffixes.

The argument with regard to the above nominal suffixes is this: the only suffixed words that could in principle appear before deverbal *-age, -al, -ance, -ment,* and *-y* are verbs ending in *-ify, -ize, -ate,* and *-en*. However, *-ify, -ize,* and *-ate* require (a suffix-particular allomorph of) the nominalizer *-(at)ion*:

(5)   magnification   verbalization   concentration
       *magnify-ation   *verbalize-ication   *concentrate-ation
       *magnify-ion   *verbalize-ion   *concentrate-ication
       *magnify-ance   *verbalize-ance   *concentrate-ance
       *magnify-al   *verbalize-al   *concentrate-al
       *magnify-age   *verbalize-age   *concentrate-age
       *magnify-y   *verbalize-y   *concentrate-y
       *magnify-ment   *verbalize-ment   *concentrate-ment

These facts suggest that the behavior of verbalizing and nominalizing suffixes is best analyzed as base-driven: combinations of the verbal suffixes *-ify, -ize, -ate* with *-age, -al, -ance, -ment,* and *-y* are ruled out because it is the bases (with their particular verbal suffixes) which select their (allomorph of the) nominalizing suffix *-ion*, and it is crucially not the nominal suffix which selects its base. Of course one could say that *-ion* selects *-ate, -ify,* and *-ize,* but this would not explain why the other nominalizing suffixes are systematically excluded. Hence a base-driven approach is superior in its explanatory power.

With *-en*, on the other hand, affix-driven restrictions are responsible for the (im)possibility of combinations. *-al* and *-ance* cannot attach to verbs in *-en*, because *-al* and *-ance* need to occur next to syllables that have main stress (*relúctance*, *refúsal*), which is impossible with *-en*, because *-en* is always unstressed. Hence forms like **deep-en-ance* or **deep-en-al* are impossible. The nominal suffixes *-age* and *-y* do not attach to *-en* because the distribution of these nominalizing suffixes is lexically governed, i.e. they only attach to lexically specified base words (see again section 2.3 for the notion of lexical government). The combination *-en-ment* is not ruled out by the structural restrictions of *-ment*, and is in fact attested, contra Fabb (e.g. *enlightenment*; see Plag 1999: 70–75 for a detailed analysis).

In sum, the example of deverbal nominal suffixes has shown how base-driven and affix-driven restrictions can account for possible and impossible affix-affix combinations and root-affix combinations. A model that focuses on suffix-particular affix-driven and base-driven restrictions is empirically more adequate and theoretically more parsimonious, because it can achieve empirical adequacy with the least possible machinery.

A model that relies solely on affix-particular restrictions could be criticized for the lack of generalizations across suffixes. After all, linguists want to believe that language in general and derivational morphology in particular is not just an accumulation of item-specific idiosyncrasies. This is the point where the psycholinguistically informed model of complexity-based ordering comes in.

In this model, developed in Hay (2000, 2001, 2002), morphological complexity is construed as a psycholinguistically real notion which heavily relies on the segmentability of affixes. The basic claim concerning the problem of affix ordering is that "an affix which can be easily parsed out should not occur inside an affix which can not" (Hay 2000: 23, 240). For reasons that will shortly become clear, I will refer to this approach as complexity-based ordering.

What does it mean for an affix to be "easily parsed out"? **Parsing** is a term which refers to the segmentation of speech, i.e. words and sentences, in its structural components. Morphological parsing is thus what listeners/readers do when they detect morphological structure (or isolate morphemes) in a string of words in order to make sense of complex words. Morphological parsing is not always easy. As is well known, there are words that are clearly composed of two or more morphemes (e.g. *concrete-ness*), there are words that are clearly monomorphemic (e.g. *table*), and there are words whose status as complex words is not so clear, as discussed in section 2.1.2 (e.g. *rehearse, interview, perceive*). Hay now shows that morphological complexity is a function of the psycholinguistic notion of morphological parsability, which in turn is largely influenced by at least two factors, frequency and phonotactics. In order to make things simpler, we will focus here on the role of frequency (considerations on the role of phonotactics can be found in Hay and Baayen 2003, and Plag 2002).

As already explained in chapter 3, in most current models of morphological processing, access to morphologically complex words in the mental lexicon works in two ways: by direct access to the whole-word representation ('whole-word route') or by access to the decomposed elements ('decomposed route'). Given that frequency plays a role in determining the resting activation of lexical items, it is clear that every access via the whole-word route strengthens the whole-word representation, whereas access on the decomposed route reinforces the representation of the decomposed morphemes and the decomposability of the complex word. How do we know which representation will be strengthened with a given word? It is usually assumed that the absolute frequency of a word correlates with its resting activation level. Hay suggests that, with regard to the storage of complex words, the **relative frequency** of the derived word and its base is significant. Relative frequency is defined as the ratio of the frequency of the derived word to the frequency of the base and measures how frequent the derivative is with respect to its base:

(6)   relative frequency:
        frequency of derived word divided by the frequency of the base

$$f_{\text{relative}} = \frac{f_{\text{derivative}}}{f_{\text{base}}}$$

With most complex words, the base is more frequent than the derived word, so that the relative frequency is smaller than unity. In psycholinguistic terms, the base has a higher resting activation than the derived word. This leads to a preponderance of the decomposed route, since due to its high resting activation, the base will be accessed each time the derivative enters the system. In the opposite case, when the derived word is more frequent than the base, there is a whole-word bias in parsing, because the resting activation of the base is lower than the resting activation of the derivative. For example, *business* is more frequent than its base *busy*, so that *business* will have a whole-word bias in access. Note that *business* (in the sense of 'company' and related meanings) is also semantically and phonologically opaque, which is often the case with derivatives that have strong, i.e. lexicalized, whole-word representations (see below). Conversely, *blueness* has a base that is much more frequent than the derived form, so that there will be a strong advantage for the decomposed route. The two cases are illustrated in (7), with frequencies taken from the BNC:

(7)

word	frequency	relative frequency	mode of access and representation
blueness	39	.0039	parsing bias
blue	10059		
business	35141	7.2	whole-word bias
busy	4879		

In sum, the higher the frequency of the derived word in relation to the base word, the less likely is decomposition. Alternatively, the lower the frequency of the derived word in relation to the base word, the more likely is decomposition.

Hay shows that relative frequency also patterns with other properties of complex words: low relative frequency correlates with high productivity and low relative frequency correlates with high semantic transparency. These correlations do not come as a surprise. We know that productive morphological processes are characterized by a high number of low-frequency words. The lower the frequencies of derived words the lower their relative frequencies (holding the frequency of the base constant). Thus productive processes should show a preponderance of low relative frequencies, whereas less productive morphological categories should be characterized by a preponderance of words with higher relative frequencies. We also know that productive categories are semantically transparent. That this is so can be seen as a consequence of processing, since productive processes favor the decomposed route, and decomposed storage strengthens the individual semantic representations of the elements. Decomposition leaves little room for semantic drift and opacity, which arise easily under whole-word access, because the meanings of the parts are less likely to be activated. Hence semantic opacity and low productivity go hand in hand with high relative frequencies.

From what we have said so far, interesting insights follow. The same suffix will be differently separable in different words depending on the respective frequencies of base and derivative. For example, *discernment* is more decomposable than *government*, because *discernment* has a much lower relative frequency (notably, *government* is also semantically more idiosyncratic and phonologically more opaque than *discernment*). Furthermore, suffixes represented by many words which are less frequent than their bases will tend to be more separable than suffixes represented by few words which are less frequent than their bases. For example, *-ish* has many derivatives with very low relative frequencies (such as *housewifish*, *out-of-the-way-ish*, or *soupish*), whereas *-ic* has many derivatives with higher frequencies (e.g. *democratic*, *fantastic*, *terrific*), to the effect that *-ish* tends to be more separable than *-ic*. And finally, we can predict that more separable affixes will occur outside less separable affixes (cf. also Burzio 1994: 354), because an easily decomposable suffix inside a non-decomposable suffix would lead to difficulties in processing, whereas a less easily decomposable inside a more easily decomposable suffix is easy to process. Based on these considerations, Hay proposes that "an affix which can be easily parsed out should not occur inside an affix which can not" (Hay 2000: 23, 240).

From this proposition, a further hypothesis follows. If the decomposability of suffixes is a gradient matter and suffixes can be assigned a certain separability, it should be possible to order suffixes in a hierarchy of boundary strength, such that affixes following an affix A on the hierarchy can be added to words containing A, but affixes preceding A on the hierarchy cannot freely attach to words containing A. This is illustrated in (8). Given the hierarchy in (8a), the combinations in (8b) should be possible, and the combinations in (8c) should be ruled out.

(8)   a. Hierarchy of suffixes: X-Y-Z-A-B-C-D
        b. Possible combinations: BASE-A-B, BASE-X-A-C, BASE-Y-Z-A
        c. Impossible combinations: *BASE-A-Z, *BASE-Y-A-Z, *BASE-X-A-Y

This hypothesis has been tested for fifteen suffixes of English for which level-ordering makes no predictions (Hay and Plag in press). On the basis of large amounts of data, it is shown that the affixes form the predicted hierarchy and that this hierarchy correlates with the parseability of the suffixes (as established by independent methods; see Hay and Baayen 2002).

To summarize, we have seen that we can cover a lot of ground in the analysis of word-formation by solely positing process-specific selectional restrictions as the central mechanism. Furthermore, we have seen that recent psycholinguistic research can help to build theories that are theoretically more interesting, empirically more adequate, and psychologically more real. Especially the last point comes out clearly if we briefly go back to two of the phenomena for which Lexical Phonology seems to provide an explanation, and which, as we will see, can be explained more satisfactorily in psycholinguistic terms.

First, blocking as conceptualized in Lexical Phonology has been shown to be riddled with exceptions. For example, many synonymous doublets like the two nouns *divide–divider*, both meaning 'something that divides,' are attested, which should not occur in a model such as Lexical Phonology, where blocking is a categorical, i.e. non-gradient, and exceptionless mechanism of the grammar. Alternatively, as discussed in detail in section 3.5.3, blocking can be more adequately explained as a psycholinguistic phenomenon, in particular as the effect of word-storage and word-processing mechanisms. Recall that, in brief, the higher the frequency of the blocking word, the higher the likelihood that it blocks competing forms. Thus, what appears to be an exceptional behavior in the stratal model is predictable in a psycholinguistic model in which gradient frequency-effects follow from the architecture of the system.

Second, Lexical Phonology explains the impossibility of irregular inflection as the effect of the cyclicity of rule application. However, in section 5.1.1, we have seen that irregular morphology depends on storage of the irregular word-forms in the lexicon. If such irregular word-forms do not exist for a (new) lexeme, it is necessarily inflected regularly. Again, we see that there is a psychologically more realistic explanation available without having to postulate any grammatical machinery.

Overall, the theory of Lexical Phonology may have been shown to be untenable. Lexical Phonology is to be commended, however, for having provided the crucial, and still valid, insight that phonological rules and morphological rules work in tandem. Furthermore, Lexical Phonology has generated a host of interesting hypotheses and has sparked off a lot of fruitful research. Having done so, it can be judged to be a good theory, even if not the most adequate one.

7.3   The nature of word-formation rules

In chapter 2 we introduced the notion of word-formation rules without discussing in detail the form of such rules or the overall concept of morphology in which they are embedded. I have often used the terms 'word-formation rule,' 'affix,' and 'morphological category' interchangeably as more or less synonyms, although, as we will shortly see, completely different theoretical conceptions of what morphology is or does underlie these notions. Such looseness in the use of terminology is generally to be avoided, but can be justified on two grounds. First, adopting a certain type of terminology often means committing oneself to a certain theoretical position (which I wanted to avoid in this book for didactic reasons), and second, adopting a particular theory is often unnecessary for the solution of particular empirical problems.

However, having solved many empirical problems in the course of ploughing through this book, one might want to dig deeper into the question of how the many observations and generalizations we have met fit into a coherent theory of word-formation. The central place in such a theory must be reserved for a mechanism or device that, speaking in very general terms, relates complex words to each other. This device can be conceptualized very differently according to different theories. In the following we will look at two theories in particular, the word-based and the morpheme-based approaches to word-formation.

7.3.1   *The problem: word-based versus morpheme-based morphology*

There is an important distinction to be drawn in the study of morphology (and of language in general), and this is the distinction between the syntagmatic and the paradigmatic axis. On the syntagmatic axis, we look at how linguistic elements are combined in a string of elements to form larger units. Thus, under the syntagmatic view, a word like *helpless* is analyzed as the concatenation of *help-* and *-less*, the derivative *decolonization* as the concatenation of the affixes *de-*, *-ize*, *-ation*, and the root *colony* in a particular sequential order. Under a paradigmatic approach, *helpless* is analyzed as a word belonging to a large set of morphologically related words, such as *boneless, careless, fruitless, pennyless, sleepless, speechless*, all containing *-less* as their second element and all sharing important aspects of meaning. Sets of morphologically related words are referred to by the term **paradigm**, a term that originated from the study of inflection in languages with rich morphology. For example, the present-tense forms of the Spanish verb *cantar* 'sing' can be arranged in the following verbal paradigm:

(9)　　　*canto*　　　'I sing'
　　　　cantas　　　'you (sg.) sing'
　　　　canta　　　'she/he sings'
　　　　cantamos　'we sing'
　　　　cantais　　'you (pl.) sing'
　　　　cantan　　　'they sing'

What is the problem with the distinction between the syntagmatic and paradigmatic views of morphology? After all, it seems as if the two views are simply two perhaps equally good ways of looking at complex words. However, from a theoretical standpoint, the two views entail completely different ideas about the nature of complex words and how they are formed. The two approaches can be subsumed under the headings of 'morpheme-based morphology' (for the syntagmatic approach) versus 'word-based morphology' (referring to the paradigmatic approach). Let us first turn to the morpheme-based model.

7.3.2   Morpheme-based morphology

In this model of morphology, morphological rules combine morphemes to form words in much the same way as syntactic rules combine words to form sentences. In section 2.1.2, we have already seen that there are often problems involved in determining morphemes. Such cases include the problem of zero-morphs, truncation, vowel mutation, and extended exponence. In other words, especially non-concatenative morphology seems to pose problems for a morpheme-based approach. In what follows, we will, however, not focus on how the tricky cases of non-concatenative morphology can be integrated into a morpheme-based framework, because it seems that, at least in languages like English, the majority of morphological phenomena are affixational and can therefore be straightforwardly analyzed in such a model. Rather, we will explore the theoretical consequences of a strictly morpheme-based morphology for the relationship between syntax and morphology.

Linguists like Selkirk (1982) or Lieber (1992) have claimed that a morpheme-based model would have the important advantage that the theory of language could be streamlined in such a way that no separate morphological component is needed. Syntactic rules and morphological rules would be essentially the same kinds of rule, with only the entities on which the rules operate being different. For obvious reasons, such an approach has been labeled **word syntax**. In order to understand how word syntax works, a little bit of syntactic theory is needed.

In sections 6.1.3 and 6.7 of the previous chapter we have already encountered syntactic phrases in the form of noun phrases. In addition to noun phrases, (10) gives examples of verb phrases, adjectival phrases, and prepositional phrases. These phrases are usually abbreviated as NP, VP, AP, and PP, respectively:

(10)   a. *noun phrases*:
          [the green carpet]$_{NP}$, [this new house]$_{NP}$, [Jane]$_{NP}$
     b. *verb phrases*:
          [moved into the city]$_{VP}$, [saw my mother]$_{VP}$, [hit the ground]$_{VP}$
     c. *adjectival phrases*:
          [extremely intelligent]$_{AP}$, [fond of her dog]$_{AP}$, [hardly expectable]$_{AP}$
     d. *prepositional phrases*:
          [into his face]$_{PP}$, [under the bed]$_{PP}$, [at home]$_{PP}$

The internal structure of such phrases can be described in terms of so-called **phrase structure rules**, which specify which kinds of elements a given phrase may consist of. Examples of phrase structure rules are given in (11), with non-obligatory elements given in parentheses:

(11)   a. NP $\rightarrow$ (article) (adjective) noun
     b. VP $\rightarrow$ verb (NP) (PP)
     c. AP $\rightarrow$ (adverb) adjective (PP)
     d. PP $\rightarrow$ preposition (NP)

The rules read like this. For (11a) we can say 'a noun phrase can consist of an article, and an adjective and an obligatory noun.' (11b) paraphrases as 'a verb phrase consists of an obligatory verb that may be followed by a noun phrase and/or a prepositional phrase,' and so on. The claim now is that similar rules can and should be written not only for syntactic phrases but also for complex words, as in (12):

(12)   a. word $\rightarrow$ root
     b. word $\rightarrow$ affix root
     c. word $\rightarrow$ root affix
     d. word $\rightarrow$ affix word
     e. word $\rightarrow$ word affix

The rules in (12) state that a word can consist of only a root (12a), of an affix and a root (12b, c), or of a word and an affix (12d, e). The difference between a root and a word has been discussed in section 1.2, and has turned out to be of considerable importance in the discussion of level-ordering, where we saw that some affixes were said to attach only to words, while other affixes attach also to roots. It may seem that nothing spectacular follows from rules such as those in (12). However, if we follow the ideas of the word syntax model and assume that the syntactic rules in (11) and the morphological rules in (12) are essentially of the same kind, a number of important things follow, two of which I want to discuss in the following.

The first important consequence for our model would be that affixes are lexical items on a par with words. Affixes would have their own independent meaning, a phonological specification, a syntactic category specification, and all other properties that lexical items have. For example, we know that the transitive verb *hit* takes a noun phrase as its object (*hit [the ground]*$_{NP}$; see (10b)), or that the adjective *fond* takes a prepositional phrase as its complement (*fond [of her dog]*$_{PP}$; see (10c)). Similarly, we know that *-ness* is a lexical item that attaches to the right of adjectives, or that *-able* is a lexical item that attaches to the right of verbs. The only difference between a word and an affix would thus be that an affix is a bound morpheme, whereas a word is a free morpheme. This is a welcome result, because it considerably reduces the complexity of the overall theory of language.

The second important consequence of the word syntax model is that if words are structured like phrases, words, like phrases, need to have a head. In the discussion of compounds in chapter 6 we have seen the usefulness of the concept of head in morphology, but the question is whether this notion is also pertinent in derivational morphology. In fact, the application of the notion of head to derived words is not straightforward.

In syntax it is generally assumed that all phrases have heads. In the syntactic phrases presented in (10), for example, the heads *carpet, home, Jane, moved, saw, hit, intelligent, fond, expectable, into, under, at* are the most important elements of their respective phrases, and it is their grammatical features that determine the features of the entire phrase. A noun phrase has a nominal head, a verb phrase has a verbal head, and so on. Now, extending the notion of head to derived words in general, and to the derived words in (13) in particular, we can make an argument that affixes also act as heads, because they determine the syntactic category of the derived word:

(13)

derived word	base	affix
sleepless$_A$	sleep$_N$	-less$_A$
emptiness$_N$	empty$_A$	-ness$_N$
colonialize$_V$	colonial$_A$	-ize$_V$
readable$_A$	ready$_V$	-able$_A$
starvation$_N$	starve$_V$	-ation$_N$
solidify$_V$	solid$_A$	-ify$_V$

As is clear from (13), no matter what kind of base word enters the derivation, it is always the suffix that determines the syntactic category of the whole word. This is parallel to phrases, whose head also determines the syntactic properties of the whole phrase. However, it seems that not all affixes are heads. With English prefixes, the category of the derivative is usually inherited from the base, so that we can state that prefixes, in contrast to suffixes, are not heads. Consider (14):

(14)

derived word	base	affix
unpleasant$_A$	pleasant$_A$	un-$_?$
retry$_V$	try$_V$	re-$_?$
microstructure$_N$	structure$_N$	micro-$_?$
inaccurate$_A$	accurate$_A$	in-$_?$
overestimate$_V$	estimate$_V$	over-$_?$
mini-camera$_N$	camera$_N$	mini-$_?$

The difference in behavior between prefixes and suffixes is straightforwardly explained if we simply assume that affixed words in English are always right-headed. Hence, if there is an affix in rightmost position, i.e. if the word is suffixed, the suffix determines the syntactic category of the word. If there is a word in the rightmost position of a derivative, as is the case in prefixed words, it is the category of that word that percolates to the derivative. This appears to be an elegant generalization, but it raises a number of problems.

To begin with, there are numerous exceptions to the alleged right-headedness of words. We find prefixes that behave like heads and suffixes that behave like non-heads. Consider (15) and (16):

(15)

derivative	base	category-changing prefix
debug$_V$	bug$_N$	de-$_V$
enable$_V$	able$_A$	en-$_V$
bedevil$_V$	devil$_N$	be-$_V$

(16)

derivative	base	non-category-changing suffix
greyish$_A$	grey$_A$	-ish$_?$
eightish$_{NUMERAL}$	eight$_{NUMERAL}$	-ish$_?$
kingdom$_N$	king$_N$	-dom$_?$
duckling$_N$	duck$_N$	-ling$_?$

The idea of morphological heads could perhaps be saved, as argued by Di Sciullo and Williams (1987), if we assume that features which are not present in the head are filled in from the non-head. Thus, if our affix does not bear any category features, these features can conveniently be inherited from the base. Technically, this works well with non-category-changing suffixes, but runs into serious problems with category-changing prefixes. Such prefixes obviously attach to fully specified bases (e.g. nouns), and simply overrule any pertinent specifications of the bases. Hence, even the idea of relativizing the notion of head does not help in all cases. Furthermore, by introducing relativized heads the putative parallelism between words and phrases is severely undermined, because in syntax there is no evidence that heads are ever relativized.

Another problem for the alleged parallelism between phrases and complex words is that in English most phrases are left-headed. For example, in English, we say [$_{VP}$ *go* [$_{PP}$ *to* [$_{NP}$ *the station*]]], with the verbal and prepositional heads being in initial (or leftmost) position, and not *[[[*the station*$_{NP}$] *to*$_{PP}$] *go* $_{VP}$], as you would in a language that has phrase-final heads, such as Japanese. If we assume that words are structured like phrases, it would be odd for words to have their heads consistently on the right while phrases are mostly left-headed in English.

Third, a phrase is usually a hyponym of the head, a state of affairs we know already from endocentric compounds. For example, the noun phrase [*the child with the blond hair*] denotes a kind of child, just like *pancake* denotes a kind of cake. While this criterion still works with compounds it is not obvious how it can be applied to all affixes. How can we claim, for example, that *completeness* is a kind of *-ness*, or *colonialize* a kind of *-ize*?

To summarize, we can say that word syntax, which is a particular type of morpheme-based approach to morphology, provides interesting insights into the nature of complex words, but many questions still remain unanswered. In essence, it seems that morphology cannot be totally reduced to syntax. Overall, morpheme-based approaches to morphology are especially suited for the analysis of affixational morphology, but run into problems with non-affixational processes. In view of these problems, a completely different approach is taken by proponents of word-based morphology, to which we now turn.

7.3.3   Word-based morphology

The theory of word-based morphology in generative grammar originated in Aronoff (1976). In this theory, affixes do not have an independent existence and do not have entries in the lexicon, only words do. And what is analyzed as a constituent morpheme in morpheme-based morphology is conceptualized as a particular phonological and semantic similarity between sets of words in word-based morphology.

Thus, word-based morphology expresses the relationship between morphologically related words not by splitting up words into their components but by formalizing the common features of sets of words in a **morphological schema**. For example, the relationship between the derived words and their bases in (17) can be expressed by the schema in (18) (see section 2.3 and section 4.5 for a more detailed discussion of the properties of *un-* words):

(17) | **base word** | **derivative** |
|---|---|
| able | unable |
| clear | unclear |
| common | uncommon |
| faithful | unfaithful |
| friendly | unfriendly |
| pleasant | unpleasant |

(18)
$$\begin{pmatrix} <X> \\ /X/ \\ A \\ \text{'X'} \end{pmatrix} \leftrightarrow \begin{pmatrix} <unX> \\ /\text{ʌnX}/ \\ A \\ \text{'not X'} \end{pmatrix}$$

The schema in (18) relates the base adjectives ('A') of the orthographic form <X>, the phonological form /X/ and the meaning 'X' to other adjectives of the orthographic form <*un*X> and the phonological form /ʌnX/, in that all /ʌnX/ adjectives have the meaning 'not X.' The double arrow means that in principle this is a non-directional relationship, so that the derivation could go both ways (a point to which we will return below).

Other examples of such derivational schemas are given in (19). Note that for the sake of simplicity, morpho-phonological restrictions of the kinds discussed in section 4.2 or in chapter 5 are not given in the schemas below, but could in principle be incorporated in a straightforward manner:

(19)

a.
$$\begin{pmatrix} <X> \\ /X/ \\ V \\ \text{'X'} \end{pmatrix} \leftrightarrow \begin{pmatrix} <Xable> \\ /X\text{əbl}/ \\ A \\ \text{'can be Xed'} \end{pmatrix}$$

b.
$$\begin{pmatrix} <X> \\ /X/ \\ A \\ \text{'X'} \end{pmatrix} \leftrightarrow \begin{pmatrix} <Xness> \\ /X\text{nəs}/ \\ N \\ \text{'property of being X'} \end{pmatrix}$$

c.
$$\begin{pmatrix} <X> \\ /X/ \\ \text{Numeral} \\ \text{'X'} \end{pmatrix} \leftrightarrow \begin{pmatrix} <Xish> \\ /X\text{ɪʃ}/ \\ \text{Numeral} \\ \text{'about X'} \end{pmatrix}$$

For the description of affixes, it seems that morpheme-based rules and word-based schemas would do equally well. Both rules and schemas are abstractions based on the analysis of related sets of words. The crucial difference between a schema and a morpheme-based word-formation rule is, however, that the schema does not make reference to individual morphemes, but only to whole words, to the effect that in such a model, morphemes are superfluous, and in fact inexistent. The word-based lexicon contains only words, no morphemes. What is analyzed as a morpheme in morpheme-based morphology is part of the phonological and semantic description of the set of derivatives in a word-based model. The word-based schema must therefore contain a variable, expressed by 'X' in (18) and (19), which stands for the possible bases.

The obvious advantage of word-based morphology is that it can deal in a uniform way with both affixation and non-affixational derivation. For example, instead of having to postulate a potentially ill-motivated zero-morph, conversion can be expressed in the form of a straightforward schema, as given in (20) for noun-to-verb conversion:

(20)
$$\begin{pmatrix} < X > \\ /N/ \\ \text{`X'} \end{pmatrix} \quad \leftrightarrow \quad \begin{pmatrix} < X > \\ V \\ \text{`event having} \\ \text{to do with X'} \end{pmatrix}$$

Personal name truncations, another potential embarrassment for a morphemic analysis, can be represented as in (21):

(21)
$$\begin{pmatrix} < X > \\ N_{\text{Name}} \\ \text{`X'} \end{pmatrix} \quad \leftrightarrow \quad \begin{pmatrix} /Y/c \\ N_{\text{Name}} \\ \text{`X, Familiar} \\ \text{to speaker'} \\ C \end{pmatrix}$$

As we have seen in chapter 5, the truncated form is subject to a number of phonological constraints, both concerning its structure and its relationship with the base. The notation '$/Y/_C$' is an abbreviation that stands for the truncated form of $/X/$, given as $/Y/$ and observing the phonological constraints C.

What is important here from a theoretical point of view is that the phonological constraints on truncations are best described as constraints on the derived form, i.e. on the output of morphological rules. That such output-oriented restrictions should exist is to be expected in a model in which outputs (i.e. the words conforming to the abstraction on the right of the arrow) have representations in the lexicon on a par with inputs (i.e. the words on the left-hand side of our schema). In a morpheme-based model, in which output forms have no independent status, phonological output constraints are unexpected.

Another class of derivatives that are best described as being formed on the basis of paradigmatic mechanisms are back-formations. Recall that in section 2.3 we introduced back-formation as a process by which a suffix is deleted to derive a more simplex word on the basis of a more complex one. An example of back-formation is the verb *edit*, which, historically, was formed on the basis of the complex form *editor*, modeled on other word pairs with a similar relationship (e.g. *act–actor*). Although back-formation can informally be described in terms of suffix deletion, such an analysis is not really convincing. In English there is no productive process of suffix deletion attested, hence it is strange to posit such a morpheme-deleting rule simply for cases of back-formation.

In contrast, back-formation emerges naturally from the kind of schemas we have just introduced. In such schemas a set of words is systematically related to another set of words and, given sufficient similarity to existing pairs, new relationships can be established between existing and newly created words. Thus given two related sets of words in a schema, we would naturally expect that the creation of new words on the basis of the schema can in principle go both ways. This is the reason why the arrows in the two schemas point in both directions. Coming back to back-formation, we can now say that the existence of back-formation is to be expected in a schema-based model, because there is no inherent directionality in the relationship between the two sets of words that are related by the schema.

This fact may give rise to a serious objection against schemas, because there is usually a preponderance of one direction. For example, in the case of the affixational schemas in (18) and (19) it is clear that the forms on the right of the double-headed arrow are overwhelmingly formed on the basis of the words to the left of the arrow. And even in the more problematic case of the directionality of conversion (see section 5.1.1), it seems clear that noun-to-verb conversion, i.e. the left-to-right direction, is much more productive than verb-to-noun conversion, i.e. the opposite direction. The crucial point remains, however, that both directions do indeed occur, and that this is predicted by the model. Back-formation can thus be defined as the application of a rule in the less productive direction (Becker 1993).

Another interesting prediction that emerges from the schema model is that we should find cases where both directions are equally well attested. Such cases, termed **cross-formations**, indeed exist. For example, every (potential) word with the suffix *-ist* has a corresponding (potential) word in *-ism*, see (22), and every word ending in adjectival *-ive* has a corresponding word ending in nominal *-ion*, as illustrated in (23):

(22)   a. **X-ism**   **X-ist**
        activism   activist
        anecdotalism   anecdotalist
        behaviorism   behaviorist

    bolshevism   bolshevist
    centrism   centrist
    cognitivism   cognitivist
    conformism   conformist
    contextualism contextualist

b.

$$\begin{pmatrix} < Xism > \\ /\text{X}\text{ızm}/ \\ \text{N} \\ \text{'ideology or attitude} \\ \text{having to do with X'} \end{pmatrix} \leftrightarrow \begin{pmatrix} < Xist > \\ /\text{X}\text{ıst}/ \\ \text{N} \\ \text{'follower of ideology} \\ \text{or attitude having to} \\ \text{do with X'} \end{pmatrix}$$

(23)   a. **X-ion**   **X-ive**
           action   active
           cognition   cognitive
           communication   communicative
           conclusion   conclusive
           distribution   distributive
           emulsion   emulsive
           induction   inductive
           locomotion   locomotive
           production   productive

b.

$$\begin{pmatrix} < X\text{-}ion > \\ /\text{X}\text{ıən}/ \\ \text{N} \\ \text{'act/result of} \\ \text{Xing'} \end{pmatrix} \leftrightarrow \begin{pmatrix} < X\text{-}ive > \\ /\text{X}\text{ıv}/ \\ \text{A} \\ \text{'characterized by} \\ \text{Xing'} \end{pmatrix}$$

Representing cross-formation as a schema has an additional theoretical advantage. Under a morpheme-based approach, nominal -*ion* and adjectival -*ive* are traditionally described as deverbal suffixes, which means that all words in -*ion* should be related to verbs, and all words in -*ive* should be related to verbs. A closer look at -*ion* and -*ive* derivatives reveals, however, that a number of them fail to have a base word, e.g. *emulse, *locomote. A similar problem occurred in exercise 4.1, where we saw that *colligable* 'capable of forming part of a colligation' does not have a verbal base and is obviously coined directly on the basis of *colligation*.

  The lack of a base word is a severe problem for a morpheme-based view of morphology, whereas in word-based morphology, derivatives of one kind (in our case -*ive* derivatives) can be related directly to derivatives of some other kind (in this case -*ion* derivatives).

7.3.4   Synthesis

To summarize our discussion of morpheme-based and word-based morphology, we can state that word-based morphology can account in a straightforward fashion for a wider range of phenomena than seems possible in a morpheme-based approach. But does that mean that morphemes are inexistent or superfluous? It seems not. There is some evidence that word-internal morphological structure is needed to account for a number of phenomena, which are not easily accounted for otherwise.

For example, the past tense of the verb *understand* is *understood* (as in *stand–stood*), which means that past-tense formation must have access to the root *stand*. In other words, it can be argued that some kind of morphological segmentation of *understand* is the prerequisite for applying the correct ablaut.

Or consider the choice of the allomorphs of *-ion* with derived verbs, discussed in section 4.4.1. The choice between *-ation*, *-ion*, and *-ication* is determined by the suffix of the derived verb (*-ize* takes *-ation*, *-ate* takes *-ion*, and *-ify* takes *-ication*). This means that the internal morphological structure of the base determines further suffixation, which in turn means that the derived verbs must have internal morphological structure that must be visible in further affixation processes.

A third type of phenomenon not easily compatible with a morphological theory abandoning morphemes comes from phonotactics. Certain combinations of sounds are illegal within morphemes, but freely occur across morpheme boundaries. For example, [pf] never occurs inside any morpheme of English, but does so across morphemes, as in *hel*[pf]*ul* or *Kee*[pf]*at out of your diet*.

Finally, psycholinguists have found abundant evidence for the existence of morphemes as entities of processing and storage (cf. also the discussion in section 7.2.4 above).

What then can be a reasonable conclusion arising from this apparently inconclusive state of affairs? Which model is the 'right one'? Taking all the evidence and arguments together, it seems that both ways of looking at complex words are needed to account for the full range of phenomena in human language. Evidence from psycholinguistic studies also points in the direction of a compromise position. Practically all current psycholinguistic models of morphological storage and processing acknowledge that complex words can in principle be stored and processed as whole words and in a decomposed fashion. The two seemingly conflicting syntagmatic and paradigmatic approaches may be less in a conflicting than in a complementary relationship.

Coming back to our criteria for judging theories as developed in section 7.1, we can say that eliminating either morphemes or schemas from our morphological theory leads to a more elegant theory, because the overall machinery is reduced.

However, this elegance is obviously bought at the cost of a significant loss in empirical adequacy. And if theories are meant to help us to understand reality, it seems that we have to value empirical adequacy more highly than theory-internal elegance.

Further reading

For different models of Lexical Phonology concerning English the reader should consult Kiparsky (1982, 1985), Strauss (1982), Halle and Mohanan (1985), Mohanan (1986), Kaisse and Shaw (1985), and Giegerich (1999). Critical treatments of Lexical Phonology abound, particularly useful are Aronoff and Sridhar (1987), Fabb (1988), and Booij (1994). For the role of selectional restrictions see Plag (1999), (2002). Detailed justification for complexity-based ordering can be found in Hay (2000, 2001, 2002), while Hay and Plag (2002) investigate the interaction of processing factors and grammatical restrictions in constraining suffix combinations.

For approaches to word syntax, see Selkirk (1982), Williams (1981a, b), Di Sciullo and Williams (1987), and Lieber (1992). Aronoff (1976) is seminal for the development of a word-based view on derivational morphology. The most radical proponent of 'a-morphous morphology' is Anderson (1992) with his monograph of that title, a detailed critique of which can be found in Carstairs-McCarthy (1993). McQueen and Cutler (1998) and Stemberger (1998) are state-of-the-art articles on the psycholinguistic aspects of morphology, dealing with morphology in word recognition and word production, respectively.

Exercises

Basic level

Exercise 7.1

On the basis of the criteria given in section 7.2.1, give arguments for the stratal membership of the suffixes involved in the following pairs of words:

porous–porosity	*follow–follower*
derive–derivation	*woman–womanhood*
Aristotle–Aristotelian	

Exercise 7.2

This exercise concerns the empirical predictions of level-ordering. The following data can be interpreted as evidence against the level-ordering hypothesis. Analyze the internal structure of the words below, providing either a tree diagram or a bracket representation. Identify the stratal membership of the affixes involved, referring to the list of affixes given in (2) in this chapter. For the purposes of the exercise, assume that *-ical* in *ungrammaticality* is only one suffix (i.e. a variant of *-ic*), not two suffixes (see section 4.4.3 for details on *-ic* vs. *-ical*).

On the basis of the stratal identification, give arguments why the data below are evidence against the idea of level-ordering.

ungrammaticality	*Machiavellistic*
reorganization	*controllability*

Exercise 7.3

It is generally assumed that the suffix *-ate* attaches to nouns to create verbs (expressing, for example, an ornative meaning, as in *hyphenate* 'provide with a hyphen'). Furthermore, it is assumed that all verbs in *-ate* can take *-ion* as a nominalizing suffix in order to form nouns expressing an action, process or result meaning (e.g. *hyphenation* 'the action of hyphenating,' 'the result of hyphenating'). Provide two morpheme-based word-formation rules (as exemplified in section 2.3) expressing these generalizations.

As an alternative to the morpheme-based analysis we could think of a word-based analysis of the relationship between *-ate* and its base words, and between *-ate* derivatives and *-ation* derivatives. Provide two schemas along the lines of the schemas in section 7.3.3.

With your two alternative ways of handling the pertinent words in hand, move on to exercise 7.4.

Advanced level

Exercise 7.4

For the majority of the data, both approaches as outlined in the answer to the previous exercise work equally well. However, there are facts which may be better accounted for under one of the approaches.

Consider first the observation made by Marchand (1969: 260) that nouns in *-ation* that go together with verbs in *-ate* are very often attested earlier than the respective verbs. The following data, taken from the *OED*, are a case in point:

nominal base	derived verb	action/process/result noun
sediment	not attested	*sedimentation*
epoxide	not attested	*epoxidation*

Discuss which of the two approaches can better cope with such data.

Exercise 7.5

Hay and Baayen (2002) have calculated the parseability of suffixes using different types of measures, i.e. type and token parsing ratios, number of parsed tokens, number of parsed types, number of hapaxes, and the productivity measure P. Parsing ratios indicate the amount of forms with a given affix that are segmented into their constituent morphemes relative to the amount of all forms with that affix. A parsing ratio of 0.3, for example, would mean that 30 percent of all forms would be parsed into their morphological constituents. With all other forms (i.e. 70 percent) whole-word access and representation would be favored.

The following table from Hay (2002: 535) summarizes the results of these calculations for a number of affixes that have traditionally been considered level 1 and level 2 affixes, respectively.

	Level 1 affixes	Level 2 affixes
Average number of types parsed	34.64	143.81
Average type-parsing ratio	0.3	0.61
Average number of tokens parsed	1139.21	3711.44
Average token-parsing ratio	0.12	0.34
Average number of hapaxes	22.79	77.31
Average productivity (P)	0.002	0.030

What can these figures tell us about ordering restrictions? Try to answer the following questions in particular:

a.   In what way do level 1 and level 2 affixes differ according to the figures in the table?

b.   What does that difference mean for a processing-based account of level-ordering à la Hay ("an affix which can be easily parsed out should not occur inside an affix which can not," Hay 2000: 23, 240)?

c.   What are the consequences of these considerations for the theory of Lexical Phonology as described in sections 7.2.1 and 7.2.3?

Answer key to exercises

Chapter 1

Exercise 1.1

A grammatical word is a word that is specified for grammatical categories and can occur as such in a sentence. Thus, *walked* in (a) is a grammatical word because it is a verb that is specified for tense, in this case past tense. In (b), *walk* is also a grammatical word, because it is a verb used in the second person (even though second person is not overtly marked on the verb). *Walked, walk,* and *walking* are all different forms, i.e. 'word-forms,' of one underlying word, the so-called lexeme, WALK. The word-forms *walked, walk,* and *walking* are also orthographic words, because they occur between blank spaces. The word-form *walking* is part of a larger grammatical word, the compound *walking stick* ('a stick for walking'). This compound is represented by two orthographic words.

Exercise 1.2

Morpheme: the smallest meaningful unit, e.g. *walk* and *-ed* in *walked*.
Prefix: a bound morpheme that is attached in front of a base, e.g. *de-* in *decolonialize*.
Suffix: a bound morpheme that is attached after a base, e.g. *-ed* in *walked*.
Affix: the cover term for prefix, suffix, infix, e.g. *de-, -ed, -bloody-* are all affixes.
Compound: a word made up of two bases, e.g. *apartment building*.
Root: the smallest, central, meaningful element of the word, e.g. *colony* in *decolonialize*.
Truncation: a morphological process by which the derived word is created by subtracting material from the base, as in *Rob* (← *Robert*).

Exercise 1.3

computerize: *compute* (free, root), *-er* (bound, suffix), *-ize* (bound, suffix)
bathroom: *bath* (free, root), *room* (free, root)

numerous: *numer-* (bound, root), *-ous* (bound, suffix)
unthinkable: *un-* (bound, prefix), *think* (free, root), *-able* (bound, suffix)
intersperse: *inter-* (bound, prefix), *-sperse* (bound, root)
actors: *act* (free, root), *-or* (bound, suffix), *-s* (bound, suffix)

Exercise 1.4

a. 18 morphemes (bound morphemes are marked by hyphens following or preceding the morpheme)

text	*some*	*comment*
book	*time*	*-s*
write	*-s*	*and*
-er	*grate-*	*scholar*
-s	*-ful*	*-ly*
are	*for*	*advice*

b. morphological processes

textbook	compounding
textbook writer	compounding
writer	derivation
writers	inflection
are (BE+plural+present)	inflection
sometimes	compounding and inflection
comments	inflection
scholarly	derivation

Exercise 1.5

An orthographic word is defined as a string of letters occurring between blank spaces or before a punctuation mark. If apostrophes are not considered punctuation marks in the sense of the definition, there are nine orthographic words in the sentence. If apostrophes are considered punctuation marks, we can count eleven words, two of which contain an apostrophe followed by final *s*. Both alternatives are somewhat unsatisfactory because in the case of *party's* we are dealing with two grammatical words, i.e. realizations of the two lexemes PARTY and BE, whereas in the case of *brother's* we are dealing with only one grammatical word, i.e. the lexeme BROTHER in its genitive form.

The next problem is that the two orthographic words *birthday party* should be considered one lexeme, a compound word. This reduces the number of words in this sentence to eight if we count words in terms of lexemes: MY, BIRTHDAY

PARTY, BE, CANCEL, BECAUSE, OF, BROTHER, ILLNESS. Note that we have assumed that *because of* represents two lexemes. This assumption, however, is controversial, because one could argue that *because of* is a compound preposition. After all, if *because of* were a phrasal unit, its meaning should be compositional and predictable, which it is not. Under the assumption that *because of* is one lexeme, our sentence features seven lexemes.

With regard to grammatical words, the same problem arises, so that we can count either seven or eight grammatical words, with the grammatical word *my* occurring twice. Here is a list of the grammatical words: *my, birthday party, is, cancelled, because, of* (or *because of*), *brother's, illness.*

Exercise 1.6

Since *-ly* is a suffix, it can be either inflectional or derivational in nature. Working our way down through the criteria in (16), the first problem is whether adverbial *-ly* encodes a lexical meaning or a grammatical category. Considering the meaning of *slow* vs. *slowly*, *aggressive* vs. *aggressively*, for example, there is no difference in meaning observable, *-ly* does not contribute anything to the meaning of the word. This is the kind of behavior we expect from inflectional suffixes. However, *-ly* does not seem to indicate a grammatical category (tense, aspect, voice, number, etc.) either.

Is *-ly* syntactically relevant? Yes. Whether *-ly* is attached to an adjective solely depends on the adjective's position in the sentence. If the adjective modifies a noun, it never takes adverbial *-ly*, if the adjective modifies a verb or an adjective, the adjective must take *-ly*. Thus, it is the syntax, i.e. the grammatical rule system, that demands the occurrence or non-occurrence of *-ly*, just as the syntax demands when third person singular must be marked on the verb.

The ordering of *-ly* with regard to derivational adjectival suffixes (*-ive-ly, -ent-ly, -ful-ly*) also indicates that *-ly* behaves rather like an inflectional suffix: *-ly* is always outside all derivational suffixes and is the last suffix to be attached. (The only exception to the latter generalization are the comparative and superlative suffixes *-er* and *-est*, which occur outside adverbial *-ly*, as in *quick-li-er/-est*. These suffixes are generally considered inflectional, however.)

Let us consider the next criterion, change in part of speech. One might argue that *-ly* makes adverbs out of adjectives, which means that *-ly* is category-changing, hence derivational. This analysis depends, however, on the assumption that adjectives and adverbs are really distinct categories. It has however been argued that adjectives and adverbs are just instances of only one single underlying category. Depending on where in a sentence the members of this category occur, they either have *-ly* or they don't. Thus, we could rename adjectives as 'adnominal adjectives' (because they stand with nouns) and adverbs as 'adverbal adjectives' (because they stand with verbs). This analysis would be in line with the observation that *-ly* attachment is syntactically triggered.

Are *-ly* derivatives often semantically opaque? As already mentioned above, *-ly* does not add any meaning to its base word's meaning, hence we would not expect any semantic opacity effects. An example violating this expectation is *hardly*, which is an adverb whose meaning is not the same as the meaning of the base *hard*, hence we are dealing with a case of semantic opacity. There are very few cases like that, however.

The last point to consider concerns restrictions in productivity. It seems that most adjectives can take *-ly*, with less than a handful of exceptions (e.g. **fastly, *goodly*).

Let us summarize our findings. Although it has to be admitted that the picture is not always clear, it seems that most of the criteria speak against classifying *-ly* as a derivational suffix. I have inserted 'yes' and 'no' into table 1A below to illustrate the results of our discussion. The last criterion is given in parentheses because, *-ly* being a suffix, it does not say anything about *-ly* being derivational or inflectional.

Table 1A *Adverbial -ly: derivation or inflection?*

derivational property	inflectional property
– encodes lexical meaning – **no**	– encodes grammatical categories – **no**
– is not syntactically relevant – **no**	– is syntactically relevant – **yes**
– can occur inside derivation – **no**	– occurs outside all derivation – **yes**
– changes part of speech – **yes/no**	– does not change part of speech – **yes/no**
– is often semantically opaque – **no**	– is always semantically transparent – **yes**
– is often restricted in its productivity – **no**	– is fully productive – **yes**
(– is not restricted to suffixation)	(– is always suffixational)

We can learn from the discussion of adverbial *-ly* that the distinction between derivation and inflection is not categorical. Rather, we are dealing with a continuum on which the different processes can be located. Some are clearly inflectional, some are clearly derivational, some lie somewhere in between the two extreme poles of the continuum.

Chapter 2

Exercise 2.1

The words in (a) are related to each other by conversion, i.e. the words on the left are derived from the words on the right without any visible marking.

Conversion is a problematic phenomenon for the notion of morpheme since it forces us to accept the existence of morphemes which possess no overt morphs. This is a strange state of affairs if we consider our definition of morpheme as a unit of form and meaning. The standard way out of this dilemma is to assume that zero-forms are possible elements in a language. Thus we could say that the verbs *father* and *face* are produced from the nouns *father* and *face* by means of attaching a zero-morph.

The words in (b) are cases of truncation. The truncated names *Dave* and *Trish* are derived from *David* and *Patricia* respectively, but where is the morph that forms these derivatives in a compositional manner? Again we run into problems with the idea that morphemes are a unit of form and meaning. One could say that the form of the morpheme is the process of deletion but this would necessitate a broader definition of morpheme which would allow processes to be counted as morphs.

The examples in (c) are verbs on which the past-tense morpheme is expressed by a vowel alternation plus an additional [t] (and loss of [ŋ] in the case of *brought*). This is the problem of extended exponence, where one morpheme is represented by more than one form, with the additional complication that we have one form and one process as exponents of the plural morpheme. This problem can only be solved by again including the notion of 'process' into our definition of morpheme and by allowing discontinuous morphs.

Exercise 2.2

Since all the words in question begin with the orthographic string <re> a first assumption would be that all of these words are morphologically complex and contain the prefix *re-*. To prove this assumption we have to show that each of the putative constituent morphemes in these words has a meaning, that the meaning of *re-* in these words is roughly the same (or, alternatively, we would have to postulate more than one prefix *re-*), and that the meaning of *re-* and the meaning of the respective root together yield the correct meaning of the derivative.

Basically, the given list can be divided into two groups – words where the prefix *re-* has some meaning (these are enumerated on the left) and those where this meaning is difficult to identify or is absent (these are listed on the right):

re + state	*re + port*
re + phrase	*re + frain*
re + try	*re + gard*
re + format	*re + tain*
	re + main
	re + st

A first analysis shows that there are four words where *re-* is attached to an independently occurring word, and the rest of the words do not contain an independently attested form when *re-* is stripped off (*-port* in *report* is obviously not the same entity as the noun *port*). If we try to analyze the potential meaning(s) of *re-* in the above words, we make little progress with the words on the right, whereas the words on the left can be quite easily analyzed as containing an element *re-* that has the meaning 'again' or 'anew.' The elements *phrase, try, format* and *state* are all verbs and have meanings of their own which are the same as in combination with *re-*. Together, the prefix and the respective bases have the predictable meanings: *restate* means 'state again,' *rephrase* means 'phrase again,' and so forth. From all this we can conclude that the verbs on the left are complex words, containing the prefix *re-* and a base, while the verbs on the right are simplex. The proposed analysis is corroborated by the different stress patterns of the verbs in the two columns. All verbs with the prefix *re-* have a secondary stress on *re-*, those that are not prefixed have either no stress on *re-* or primary stress (*rést*).

Exercise 2.3

In all the four cases we deal with morphologically conditioned base allomorphy, i.e. the realization of one and the same morpheme by means of different morphs in a morphologically defined context. Thus, in the first case the attachment of the suffix *-ity* causes a change in the stress pattern: primary stress is shifted from the first syllable of the base *áctive* to the syllable preceding the suffix: *actívity*. In the second case the attachment of the suffix *-ity* to the adjectival base *curious* causes the following effects. The primary stress is shifted from the first syllable of the base *cúrious* to the syllable immediately preceding the suffix and the first syllable of the base receives a secondary stress instead (*cùriósity*). Furthermore, the vowel of the second syllable of the base changes from [ə] to [ɒ]: *curi*[ə]*s–curi*[ɒ]*sity*. In the last two examples the attachment of the suffix *-ion* causes a change in the base-final consonants: [t] and [s] turn into [ʃ]: *affec*[ʃ]*ion, posse*[ʃ]*ion*.

Exercise 2.4

All three words are complex words that consist of more than two elements, i.e. they are cases of multiple affixation or multiple compounding, respectively. Following the lines of argumentation given in chapter 2 for such cases, the structure of *uncontrollability* can be analyzed as follows. The word consists of four morphemes, the verbal root *control*, the suffixes *-able* and *-ity*, and the prefix *un-*.

The meaning of the word 'quality of not being able to be controlled' suggests that it derives by a cyclic stacking of affixes: first, *-able* is attached to the root, yielding *controllable* 'able to be controlled.' This derivative is then prefixed by *un-*, giving us *uncontrollable* 'not being able to be controlled.' Finally, the attachment of the nominalizing suffix *-ity* produces the derivative *uncontrollability*, with the appropriate meaning. This analysis is represented in the following tree diagram:

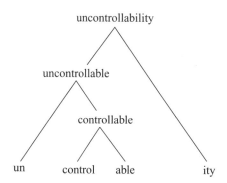

Alternatively, *un-* might be considered as the final affix being attached to the nominalization of *controllable*, *controllability*, as in the following tree:

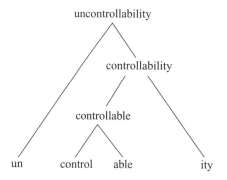

However, we said in chapter 2 that if *un-* is attached to abstract nouns, it usually creates the meaning 'lack of N.' Therefore, in the latter case the interpretation should be 'lack of controllability.' This is a possible, but slightly different meaning from the actual meaning of the word *uncontrollability* which is 'quality of being uncontrollable.' Both analyses correspond to the general behaviour of these affixes as deverbal (*-able*), de-adjectival (*-ity*), and de-adjectival/denominal (*un-*), and both structures yield possible semantics of the word in question.

The second multiply affixed word poses similar problems. The word *post-colonialism* is principally ambiguous: it can either designate a kind of colonialism that comes after the established colonialism, giving us the structure [[*post*]-[*colonialism*]], or it designates a political syndrome that is postcolonial, giving us the structure [[*postcolonial*]-[*ism*]] (a slight semantic difference, I admit). Since *post-* attaches to adjectives and nouns, and *-ism* can attach to adjectives, both analyses are also structurally possible.

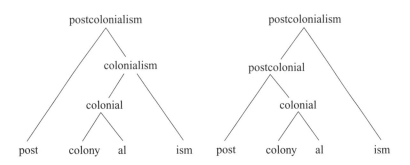

The rest of the derivation as given in the diagrams above should be uncontroversial, although there is one more alternative conceivable, namely to attach *-al* to a putative noun *post-colony* and then to attach *-ism* to the resulting adjective. However, it is not really clear what the word *postcolony* would mean, and how this meaning would fit into the meaning of the whole derivative.

Finally, the word *anti-war-movement* consists of the four morphemes, *anti-*, *war*, *move* and *-ment*. Given that *anti-* can attach to nouns, two structures are in principle possible, the first being [*anti*-[*war-movement*]], which would refer to something or someone that is against a war-movement. Alternatively, *anti-war-movement* can denote a movement that is against a war, in which case the word can be represented as [[*anti-war*]-*movement*]. The noun *movement* can of course additionally be analyzed as containing the verbal base *move* and the suffix *-ment*, giving us [*anti*-[*war*-[*move-ment*]]] or [[*anti-war*]-[*move-ment*]].

In sum, we see that with all three words, different internal structures go together with different meanings.

Exercise 2.5

There are five groups of words, each of which has a different allomorph of *in-*. Table 2A lists the words accordingly, with the pertinent allomorph in the first row.

Table 2A

[ɪn]	[ɪn] or [ɪŋ]	[ɪm]	[ɪl]	[ɪr]
inharmonic	*incomprehensible*	*impenetrable*	*illiterate*	*irresponsible*
ingenious	*incompetent*	*impossible*	*illegal*	*irresistible*
inoffensive	*inconsistent*	*immobile*	*illogical*	*irregular*
indifferent				
inevitable				
innumerable				

What governs the distribution of the allomorphs is the first sound of the base word, to which the final consonant of the prefix assimilates. Thus, before a labial consonant like [m] or [p], we find [ɪm], before base-initial [l] we find [ɪl], before [r] we find [ɪr], before the velar consonant [k] we find in rapid speech [ɪŋ] (with a velar nasal), and in careful speech [ɪn]. In all other cases [ɪn] is obligatory. Assuming an underlying form /ɪn/, the morpho-phonological rule for the prefix *in-* looks as follows:

/ɪn/ → {[ɪn], [ɪŋ]} | __ [velar]
/ɪn/ → [ɪm] | __ [labial]
/ɪn/ → [ɪl] | __ [l]
/ɪn/ → [ɪr] | __ [r]
/ɪn/ → [ɪn] | elsewhere

The above rule system could be further streamlined by eliminating the first rule, because, strictly speaking, the realization [ɪŋ] is optional. Unlike the other rules, this alternation is not demanded by the morpho-phonology of the prefix, but is due to a more general mechanism of assimilation in fast speech. For example, *in Cambridge* is also optionally pronounced with a velar nasal in fast speech registers.

We can test the predictions made by the rules by looking at base words which provide the pertinent environments and can take the prefix *in-*, such as *correct, moveable, legible, rational, adequate*. When prefixed, the forms are pronounced [ɪn]*correct* (or [ɪŋ]*correct*), [ɪm]*moveable*, [ɪl]*legible*, [ɪr]*rational*, and [ɪn]*adequate*, supporting the above rules.

Exercise 2.6

The first step in setting up an experiment is to think about the kind of task the experimental subjects could be asked to perform. Possible tasks involving complex words are word-decision tasks or other kinds of judgment task. You could for example have the subjects decide whether they think a given word is a possible word of the language or not, or have subjects rate words as being better or worse possible words. One could also present subjects with incomplete sentences and have the subjects fill the gaps with words they have to create on the basis of given morphemes and the given context. Depending on which experiment we choose, we have to construct appropriate data sets for presentation to our subjects.

Let us opt for the rating experiment. In order to test whether the hypothesis is correct we need at least two data sets. The first set would be a list of verbs that express an action or a process which can be reversed. These verbs would then be prefixed with *un-*. The second set of data would be a list of verbs that do not express such an action or such a process, and which would equally be prefixed by *un-*. According to the hypothesis, the verbs in the first set should be rated significantly better than those of the second set.

Alternatively, we could use the two lists of yet unprefixed verbs and ask our subjects to say which verbs on the list they think *un-* can possibly be attached to. According to the hypothesis, more verbs of the first list should end up with the prefix.

To facilitate these tasks for the subjects one could provide questionnaires with sentences that provide a more or less natural context in which the forms occur (for rating), or in which the forms need to be inserted by the subjects.

Note also that the frequency of words can play a decisive role in such experiments, to the effect that, all other things being equal, highly frequent verbs may behave differently from verbs that are much less frequently used. It is therefore important to match the test items as far as possible with regard to their frequencies. The frequency of words can be looked up in various sources, e.g. in Leech et al. (2001), or by accessing electronic corpora such as the BNC (see the discussion in section 3.3 for more details).

For a better understanding of the semantic problems involved and some useful ideas for the construction of test items, you may consult Buck (1997), a non-experimental study of morphological negation of locative verbs (e.g. *to weed*, *to bark*, *to oil*, *to water*, *to bag*).

Chapter 3

Exercise 3.1

I have used *Webster's Third* and Funk and Wagnalls (1963, 450,000 entries), with the following result: of the 16 hapaxes given, six (i.e. 38 percent) are not listed in *Webster's Third*, and nine (56 percent) are not listed in Funk and Wagnalls (1963). These figures confirm the hypothesis that among the hapaxes we find a significant proportion of neologisms.

Table 3A

item	*Webster's Third*	Funk and Wagnalls
academicize	**No**	Yes
aerobicize	**No**	**No**
aerosolize	**No**	**No**
aluminiumize	**No**	**No**
anthologize	Yes	**No**
anthropomorphize	Yes	Yes
apostasize	Yes	**No**
arabize	Yes	**No**
archaize	Yes	Yes
astrologize	Yes	Yes
attitudinize	Yes	Yes
austrianize	**No**	**No**
bilingualize	**No**	**No**
botanize	Yes	Yes
canadianize	Yes	**No**
carbonize	Yes	Yes
	6/16	9/16

Exercise 3.2

Productivity in the narrow sense can be expressed by the following formula:

$$P = \frac{n_1^{\text{aff}}}{N^{\text{aff}}}$$

P stands for 'productivity in the narrow sense,' n_1^{aff} for the number of hapaxes with a given affix, and N^{aff} stands for the number of all tokens with that affix. If we now calculate the missing P measure for the suffixes in table 3.1 the results will be as follows:

-ion:	$524 : 1369116 = 0.00038$
-ish:	$262 : 7745 = 0.0338$
-ist:	$354 : 98823 = 0.0036$
-ity:	$341 : 371747 = 0.00092$
-less:	$272 : 28340 = 0.0096$

These P measures are inserted in bold print in the modified table 3B overleaf.

Table 3B *(table 3.1 completed) Frequency of affixes in the BNC (from Plag et al. 1999) and* OED *(from Plag 2002)*

	V	N	n_1	P	*OED* neologisms
-able	933	140627	311	0.0022	185
-ful 'measure'	136	2615	60	0.023	22
-ful 'property'	154	77316	22	0.00028	14
-ion	2392	1369116	524	**0.00038**	625
-ish	491	7745	262	**0.0338**	101
-ist	1207	98823	354	**0.0036**	552
-ity	1372	371747	341	**0.00092**	487
-ize	658	100496	212	0.0021	273
-less	681	28340	272	**0.0096**	103
-ness	2466	106957	943	0.0088	279
-wise	183	2091	128	0.061	12

Exercise 3.3

The data show the process of nominalization of the three verbs, *magnify*, *verbalize*, and *concentrate*. These three verbs take three different nominal suffixes: the verb *magnify* takes the suffix *-cation* (undergoing simultaneously a change in the base final segments from [aɪ] to [ɪ]), the verb *verbalize* takes the suffix *-ation*, and the verb *concentrate* takes the suffix *-ion* (again accompanied by a change, though a different one, in the base-final segment). It is also clear from the data set that the verbs in question do not take any other of the synonymous nominal suffixes.

Obviously some kind of restriction must operate on these verbs, but what kind of restriction is it? If we take into account the phonological properties of these verbs, no solution emerges: all three verbs have three syllables and their stress pattern is also the same: main stress on the first syllable, secondary stress on the final syllable (*mágnifỳ*, *vérbalìze*, *cóncentràte*). So the restriction is probably not a phonological one. If we now turn to the morphological structure of the verbs in question, we can observe that all the three verbs contain suffixes: *-ify*, *-ize*, and *-ate*, and that the nominal suffix *-cation* attaches not only to the verb *magnify*, but to all verbs ending in this suffix. The nominal suffix *-ation* attaches not only to the verb *verbalize* but to all verbs ending in the suffix *-ize*, and the nominal suffix *-ion* attaches not only to the verb *concentrate*, but to all verbs ending in *-ate* (cf., for example, *stratify–stratification*, *organize–organization*, *agitate–agitation*). This observation suggests that the nominal suffixes *-ication*, *-ation*, and *-ion* are sensitive to the morphological structure of their base words. The obvious advantage of such an account is that it explains why the verbs in question (and all other derived verbs with the three suffixes) do not take any of the other nominalizing suffixes: it is the particular kind of base word (i.e. a derived verb ending in a particular suffix) that demands attachment of one particular nominalizing suffix, automatically ruling out all other nominalizing suffixes. This is a so-called 'base-driven' restriction. For elaboration and discussion of the concept of base-drivenness you may consult Plag (1996) or Giegerich (1999).

Exercise 3.4

We have seen in this chapter that different measures can be used for calculating how productive (or unproductive) an affix may be. They can be summarized as follows. Productivity can be measured by counting the number of attested different words with a particular suffix at a given point of time (i.e. type frequency of the affix). The greater the type frequency, the higher the productivity of a given affix. Alternatively, productivity can be measured by counting the number of neologisms at a given period using, e.g. such a dictionary as *OED*. The greater the number of neologisms, the higher the productivity of a given affix. Productivity can also be measured by counting how often derivatives with a given affix are used (i.e. by counting token frequency) in a corpus, e.g. in the BNC. The higher the token frequency the greater the productivity. Yet another method is to count the number of hapaxes with a given affix in a corpus. The higher the number of hapaxes the greater the productivity. Finally, by dividing the number of hapaxes by the number of tokens, we arrive at *P*, which indicates the probability of finding new words within all the tokens of a particular morphological category.

Using the data from table 3B we can group the suffixes in question according to each measure in the descending order of their values.

Table 3C

Rank	*V*	N	n_1	number of neologisms	*P*
1	**-ion**	**-ion**	**-ion**	**-ion**	-ish
2	**-ity**	**-ity**	**-ist**	**-ist**	-less
3	**-ist**	**-ist**	**-ity**	**-ity**	**-ist**
4	-less	-less	-less	-less	**-ity**
5	-ish	-ish	-ish	-ish	**-ion**

An interesting picture arises from table 3C: according to the first four measures, i.e. type frequency, token frequency, number of hapaxes, and number of neologisms, the suffixes -*ion*, -*ity*, and -*ist* (printed in bold) must be regarded as most productive, and the suffixes -*less* and -*ish* as much less productive. However, according to the *P* measure, the situation is exactly the opposite: the suffixes -*ish* and -*less* must be regarded as most productive, and the suffixes *-ion, -ity*, and *-ist* as much less productive. There seems to be a contradiction between the *P* values and the other values.

However, if we assume that productive morphological processes are characterized by large numbers of low-frequency words and small numbers of high-frequency words, the said contradiction can be resolved. Thus, the suffixes *-less* and *-ish* do not occur in very many different words, and these words are also not so frequently used, hence the low *V* and *N* figures, and the comparatively small number of hapaxes and *OED* neologisms. However, if we only consider the words within those two morphological categories, we find that the *proportion* of hapaxes among all tokens is very high, which means that there is a high probability of finding new forms among all the words with these suffixes. And this high probability is expressed by a high *P* measure. In less technical terms, the apparent contradiction can be explained by saying that we obviously don't use *-less* and *-ish* words a lot, but it's very easy to create new ones.

One methodological problem may also play a role in the discrepancy of the behavior of *-less* and *-ish* as against the other suffixes, namely the dependency of productivity on different genres. For example, certain kinds of complex words abound in certain kinds of discourse but are extremely rare in other types. For example, *-ish* (as in *twentyish*) is quite frequent in everyday conversation, but hardly productive in academic prose. This means that the composition of the corpus will have an important influence on the productivity to be measured. In a representative corpus that includes data from various domains (as does the BNC), genre-specific effects are sought to be leveled out, but even the BNC itself contains only about 10 percent data from spoken language, the remaining 90 percent being from written sources.

With regard to the neologisms listed in the *OED* we can assume that, if only for practical reasons, written genres are also over-represented, which introduces a bias into measuring productivity with this tool. For a more detailed discussion of genre-related effects on productivity, see Plag et al. (1999).

Exercise 3.5

Following the hint given in the exercise, we first analyze the stress patterns of all derivatives and count the syllables. We insert acute accents on the syllables that carry main stress:

a. -ize derivatives

académicize	*accéssorize*	*ábsolutize*	*ácronymize*	*ádjectivize*
áerosolize	*ánodize*	*anthropólogize*	*bácterize*	*Báskonize*
Bólshevize	*Bónderize*	*bóvrilize*	*cánnibalize*	*cápsulize*
*ártize	**mássize*	**bourgeóisize*	**Japánize*	**spéechize*

b. *-ify* derivatives

ártify	*bourgeóisify*	*géntrify*	*jázzify*	*kárstify*
mássify	*múcify*	*mýthify*	*Názify*	*négrify*
*rándomify	**féderalify*	**áctivify*	**módernify*	**Gérmanify*

We now see the following pattern: *-ize* is always preceded by one or more unstressed syllables, whereas *-ify* is always preceded by a stressed syllable. From this generalization it follows that *-ify* can only attach to bases that are monosyllabic (such as *art, jazz, karst, mass*, etc.) or to bases that have more than one syllable but stress on their last syllable, as is true for *bourgeóisify*. Furthermore, it follows that *-ize* can only attach to words of more than one syllable, because monosyllabic bases would place their stress immediately adjacent to *-ize*, which is ruled out by the above constraint.

The only, but systematic, exception to these generalizations are words that end in unstressed /ɪ/, such as *gentry* or *Nazi*. Obviously, such words can take *-ify*, but one of the /ɪ/'s is deleted (either the base-final one or the suffix-initial one). Our phonological constraint would, however, predict that words ending in unstressed /ɪ/ would also be able to take *-ize*. That this prediction is on target is evidenced by words such as *dandyize*. In sum, *-ize* and *-ify* are nearly in complementary distribution.

For a more detailed analysis of the intricacies of the phonology of *-ize* and *-ify* see Plag (1999: chs 6 and 7).

Chapter 4

Exercise 4.1

To extract the words from the *OED* the following queries have to be entered into the system (the names of the files into which the results are written, e.g. 'able-17.ent,' are arbitrarily chosen):

- 'ENT wd=(*able) & fd=(1600–1699) into (able-17.ent)' for the seventeenth century
- 'ENT wd=(*able) & fd=(1700–1799) into (able-18.ent)' for the eighteenth century
- 'ENT wd=(*able) & fd=(1950–1985) into (able-20.ent)' for the second half of the twentieth century.

The result file for the seventeenth century is much larger than that for the eighteenth century (1127 words vs. 283 words), which can be taken as an indication of the general fact that the productivity of this suffix has changed considerably over time.

For a verification of this hypothesis we would, of course, have to clean the lists of raw data.

The file covering the first thirty-five years of the second half of the twentieth century contains 81 entries, which will now be further analyzed. We open this result file by clicking on the 'file' menu, choosing the option 'open' and clicking on the 'able-20.ent' file. By double-clicking on the individual highlighted lines in the result file we can open the respective entries and can now scan each entry in order to see whether it contains a relevant *-able* derivative. Another way of checking whether all items in the result file really belong to the morphological category in question is to export information from the result file into a regular text file. This can be done by clicking on the 'file' menu again, and then choosing the option 'output to text.' Then we choose the result file from which we want to extract information, in our case 'able-20.ent.' A new window pops up that gives us the opportunity to choose which type of information we want to extract. In our case, it is convenient to choose 'word' and 'definition.' Clicking 'ok' gives us the next window, in which we give a name to the text file into which the information will be written. The command 'ok' creates the desired text file. This file can now be read and further processed with any standard editing or text-processing software.

In the following, we will clean up the first seven entries as an example for illustration. After the exportation procedure just described, the entries appear in our text file as given below. Each entry is followed by a comment on how the pertinent word is treated in our cleaning-up procedure.

> *addressable, a.**Allowing the assignment of an address and therefore capable of being individually accessed. Of (a) memory: in which all locations can be separately accessed.*

This appears to be an unproblematic neologism: *addressable* fits the general pattern of other *-able* derivatives ('capable of being addressed').

> *astable, a.**Not stable. In Electr. (see quot. 1960).*

This is clearly not a derivative on the basis of *-able* but a prefixed from of *stable*. It must therefore be excluded from our file of twentieth-century *-able* neologisms.

> *colligable, a.**Capable of forming part of a colligation (sense 4).*

Semantically this is a well-behaved *-able* derivative, but there is the problem that there is no form **collig* from which *colligable* could be derived. However, there are forms such as *colligate*, *colligation*, etc., and it is from (one of) these forms that *colligable* must be derived. We therefore leave *colligable* in our file. Additionally, however, we make a note that new forms are derived not only on the basis of existing forms of verbs, but also on the basis of other complex words, in this case *colligation*. See section 7.3.3 for further discussion of this point.

> \collocable, a.\Capable of forming part of a collocation (sense 1 c).

This form creates a problem analogous to that of *colligable* and is therefore treated according to the same reasoning. Leave in file.

> \contactable, a.\=Capable of being contacted.

A wonderfully regular form.

> \corrodable, a.\= corrodible a. Also co"rroda'bility.

Apparently just a new (regularized!) orthographic variant of the older *corrodible*. Hence it is not a neologism and needs to be erased from the file. The form could be entered into a separate file which may later be used for a study of the productivity of the two orthographic variants.

> \deproletarianize, v.\trans. To free of proletarian character or qualities; to cause to lose proletarian nature. Also absol. Hence deprole "tariani'zation; dep-role'tarianized ppl. a.; deproletaria'nizable, deprole'tarian adjs.

The headword of this entry (*deproletarianize*) is not an *-able* word. However, if we search the whole entry we see that there is a list of derivatives included at the end, including *deproletarianizable*, which is a regular *-able* derivative. This example shows that the 'word' search in the *OED* covers not only main headwords but also words that are derived from the headword and listed at the end of the respective entry.

If we continue this kind of procedure, we will finally end up with a cleaned list of *-able* neologisms which can then be further analyzed.

Exercise 4.2

Part 1 The suffixes *-ion* and *-ure* both attach to verbal bases of Latin origin. This is important because we have seen in section 4.3 that certain suffixes, especially those which are of non-native origin and begin with a vowel, can trigger phonological alternations. This is also the case with the suffixes under analysis.

First, let us have a look at the final consonants of the verbal bases and the derivatives. All verbal bases in (a) end in either an alveolar voiced fricative [z] or an alveolar voiced plosive [d], whereas the derivatives have the alveolar-palatal voiced fricative [ʒ] instead. This means that both suffixes trigger a change in the segmental make-up of the base word. This observation could be captured by the following morpho-phonological rule:

(i)   a. /z/ → [ʒ] | ___ {*-ion, -ure*}
        b. /d/ → [ʒ] | ___ {*-ion, -ure*}
        (read: /z/and /d/are realized as [ʒ] before the suffixes *-ion* and *-ure*)

Second, if we take syllable structure of the bases into consideration, we can observe that all verbal bases in (a) consist of two syllables, whereas all derivatives have three syllables. This means that both suffixes add one more syllable to the base. In doing so, they incorporate the final consonant of the base into the onset of the new last syllable (e.g. *e.rode* vs. *e.ro.sion*).

Finally, if we take a look at the stress pattern of the verbal bases in (a), we see that all of them are stressed on the last syllable. All the nominal derivatives in (a) are stressed on the same syllable. This means that both nominal suffixes are either stress-neutral, or that they attract stress to the syllable immediately preceding them. The data given in (a) are in accordance with both hypotheses and we would need additional data to test whether the suffixes have the capacity to shift stress. In sections 4.3 and 4.4, it was argued that *-ion* indeed requires main stress on the syllable immediately preceding it. Hence, in the case of the verbs under discussion the base stress is already in place, and we cannot observe any stress shift.

Part 2 Similar to the suffixes of part 1, *-ity, -ize, -ify* and *-ism* are also suffixes that attach to bases of Latin origin, and all are vowel-initial. And again the suffixes trigger a phonological alternation. All base words end in the consonant [k], while all derivatives have [s] instead. Again this could be captured by a morphophonological rule:

(ii)   /k/ → [s] | ___ {*-ify, -ity, -ism, -ize*}
        (read: /k/ is realized as [s] before the suffixes *-ify, -ity, -ism,* and *-ize*)

It remains to be shown whether the above rule only holds for established words or is in fact also productive with new formations.

All suffixes add one or two syllables to the base, and, being vowel-initial, the suffixes incorporate the base-final consonant into the onset of their (first) syllable (e.g. *a.to.mi.ci.ty, o.pa.ci.fy, e.ro.ti.cize, ro.man.ti.ci.sm*).

Exercise 4.3

In all three words we have [k] preceding the suffix *-ism*. This is obviously not in accordance with the rule we have just established, and which demands that [k] is realized as [s] (the [k]/[s] alternation in morphologically complex words is also known as 'velar softening'). Is it possible to reformulate our rule, so that it makes better predictions?

The first conceivable solution would be to simply state that the words *anarchism*, *monarchism*, and *masochism* are arbitrary exceptions, a somewhat unsatisfactory solution, since we have at least three (and perhaps more) words that behave alike.

A second possibility could be to further specify the context in which rule (ii) applies. Thus, in addition to demanding that [k] occur immediately to the left of the suffix, [k] would also be required to be the base-final segment. This reformulation would work nicely for *anarchy* and *masochist*, which are not [k]-final words. However, *monarchism* can be derived from *monarch*, which is [k]-final (cf. also the less commonly used word *anarch* 'anarchist' (*OED*), from which *anarchism* might be derived). An additional problem for this solution is that *anarchism* and *masochism* could be argued to be derived from bound stems as bases (*anarch-* and *masoch-*), which would leave us again with [k]-final bases.

The last possibility is to take a closer look at the mapping of orthographic symbols onto pronunciations. While in general spelling can be seen as a secondary system that tries to represent important aspects of the phonological structure of a language, for example its sounds in the form of letters, we might hypothesize that here we might be dealing with a peculiar case where the orthography is needed to account for phonological alternations. The argument might run as follows.

All three words are spelled with <ch>, while the words in exercise 4.2 are all spelled with <ic> or <que>, respectively. This suggests that we might be dealing with alternations that are best captured by referring to the spelling of these words. Disregarding <que>, and following a suggestion by Raffelsiefen (1993), we could reformulate rule (ii) in terms of orthography–pronunciation mapping:

(iii)   a. <k>   →   [k]
         b. <c>   →   [s] | __ <iC>
         c. <c>   →   [k] | __ #
         d. <ch> →   [k]

In plain language, rule (iiia) states that an orthographic <k> is always pronounced [k]. Apart from words beginning in <kn>, this holds for all words of English: <kick>, <kind>, <snake> etc. According to (iiib), <c> is always pronounced [s] if it occurs before <i> and a following orthographic symbol representing a consonant. Notably, this also holds for all words of English, independent of their morphological make-up (cf., for example, <city>, <cell>, <seducing>). If <i> is followed by a vowel, the pronunciation [ʃ] occurs (cf. e.g. <appreciate>). All <c>'s occurring in word-final position (for which the symbol '#' is used in (iiic)) are pronounced [k]. Finally, <ch> is always pronounced [k].

This account has the considerable advantage that the regular sound-spelling mappings given in (iii) need to be stated anyway to account for the ability of literate speakers to pronounce words with these orthographic symbols correctly. Furthermore, it shows that the alternation in (ii) is not due to these suffixes, but due to general principles of orthography-phonology mappings in English.

There is, however, one serious problem. While the rules (iiia, b, and c) make no wrong predictions, rule (iiid) cannot explain why in the majority of words where <ch> occurs, it is pronounced [tʃ], e.g. <church>, <chin>, <choke>, <such>. Hence, a more adequate account of the behavior of <ch> would have to look like (iv):

(iv)   a. <ch>   →   [k]
        b. <ch>   →   [tʃ]

How would speakers/readers know which rule to choose with a given word? Words such as <psychology>, <hierarchy>, <hypochondric> behave according to rule (iva), but many other words do not (e.g. <church>). The difference in pronunciation often corresponds to a difference in origin. The [k] words are usually of Greek origin, while the [tʃ] words are usually of Germanic origin. However, since most speakers do not know the etymology of most words, they simply have to learn which words are spelled and pronounced in which way. The word *masochist* is a case in point. It is ultimately based on the name of an Austrian novelist (Leopold von Sacher-Masoch), and is thus not of Greek origin, but still behaves according to rule (iva).

Coming back to our initial question of how the pronunciation of *anarchism, monarchism*, and *masochism* can be reconciled with rule (ii) above, we have seen that no principled account is possible. In fact, having explored conceivable alternatives, we are back at our first possible solution, namely to assign our three words *anarchism, monarchism*, and *masochism* the status of arbitrary exceptions. This may be somewhat unsatisfactory, but in the light of the alternatives we have discussed it is the most convincing solution.

For a more detailed discussion of the relationship between morphology and orthography see Raffelsiefen (1993: 73–74, on the [k]/[s] alternation) and Giegerich (1999: ch. 5, on vowel alternations).

Exercise 4.4

On the basis of the information given in chapter 4, table 4A can be set up, showing the mapping of meaning, category of derived word, and prefix.

The table shows that there is a considerable overlap between the prefixes in question. In most cases a single meaning can be expressed by several prefixes,

Table 4A

meaning	derived word	prefix
'not X'	adjective	*in-/dis-/non-/un-*
'not X'	verb	*dis-*
'absence of X'	noun	*un-/non-/dis-*
'not having the proper characteristics of X'	noun	*un-/anti-/non-*
'the opposite of an X'	noun	*anti-*
'against, opposing'	noun	*anti-*
'reversative'	verb	*un-/dis-/de-*
'privative'	verb	*un-/de-*

e.g. the reversative meaning can be expressed by the three prefixes *un-*, *dis-*, and *de-*. On the other hand, there are meanings that can be expressed by one particular prefix only, without any overlap. For example, the notion 'against, opposing' can be expressed by the prefix *anti-* only (cf. *anti-war*), and the function of clausal negation can only be taken over by the verbal prefix *dis-* (as in *not agree – disagree*)

Let us look more closely at one of the cases where the domains of the pertinent prefixes overlap. With adjectival derivatives expressing 'not X,' it seems that, contrary to what table 4A may suggest, the domains of the four possible prefixes do not completely overlap. Table 4B illustrates this: we see that the actual overlap of the domains is not as large as we might have suspected beforehand. Whether this also holds for the other cases of overlap could be further investigated by the reader in a similar fashion.

Table 4B

meaning	derived word	further specifications	prefix
'not X'	adjective	Latinate bases only	*in-*
'not X'	adjective	lexicalized combinations only	*dis-*
'not X'	adjective	without evaluative force, contradictories or complementaries	*non-*
'not X'	adjective	evaluative force possible, preference for contraries	*un-*

In general, this exercise has shown that an investigation of the semantic and combinatorial restrictions of each individual prefix can reveal that these restrictions considerably reduce the potential overlap of the domains of rival prefixes. See Plag (1999: ch. 8) for a more general discussion of affixal rivalry.

Exercise 5.1

Chapter 5

Table 5A

complex word	base	type of word-formation process
Amerindian	*American Indian*	blend
Caltech	*California Institute of Technology*	clipping and blending
deli	*delicatessen (shop)*	clipping
frogurt	*frozen yogurt*	blend
Greg	*Gregory*	truncation
intro	*introduction*	clipping
laser	*light amplification by stimulated emission of radiation*	acronym
OED	*Oxford English Dictionary*	initialism
to boycott	*boycott* (common noun, derived from the proper noun *Boycott*)	conversion (proper noun → common noun, common noun → verb)
UFO	*unidentified flying object*	two kinds of pronunciation are attested, it is either an acronym [jufoʊ] or an initialism [juɛfoʊ].

Note that you may not have been familiar with all the words, and that it may even have been impossible to find all base words with the help of very good dictionaries. This shows that such coinages may often be highly context-dependent or group-specific, which supports the idea that especially clippings and truncations are used to mark familiarity.

Exercise 5.2

[No model answer is provided for this exercise. See section 5.1 for discussion.]

Exercise 5.3

Prosodic morphology differs from other types of morphology in that it makes crucial reference to prosodic categories for the expression of meaning. The term 'prosody' refers to phonological phenomena and units that extend beyond the individual phoneme, such as stress, intonation, syllables, and feet. The morphological category of name truncations, for example, is expressed entirely through prosodic means, i.e. there is nothing that signals the membership of a given form in this morphological category apart from the prosodic structure of that form and its relation to the prosody of the base. Thus, crucially, name truncations are monosyllabic, they have a certain syllable structure, and they anchor on either the initial or a stressed syllable of their base words.

In contrast to this, -*ness* suffixation can be described without reference to prosodic categories, apart from the fact that it attaches to prosodic words (see section 4.3 for discussion of the notion of prosodic words). There are other suffixes that involve prosodic manipulation of their bases (e.g. stress-shifting suffixes like -*ity* or -*ation*), but these prosodic effects are not the only or primary means of expression, hence these suffixes do not fall under the rubric of prosodic morphology.

Exercise 5.4

We have seen in chapter 5 that the criteria of stress, semantic complexity and frequency can be used in order to determine the direction of conversion. We will systematically apply these criteria to each pair of words.

In the word pair *release*$_N$–*release*$_V$ we might be dealing with noun-to-verb conversion because there is no stress shift observable, which would be expected if the pair were a case of verb-to-noun conversion. However, we have to be careful about the nature of the stress criterion. We saw in section 5.1.1 that in those cases where there *is* a stress shift, we are dealing with noun-to-verb conversion. We did not find evidence that *all* noun-to-verb conversions indeed show stress shift. Thus only the presence of stress shift can tell us something about the directionality (namely noun to verb), while the lack of stress shift is inconclusive.

Turning to the criterion of semantic complexity, we may consult a dictionary in order to see how these two words are paraphrased. The *OED*, for example, tells us that the noun denotes an 'act of freeing' (s.v. *release n 1*), while the verb is paraphrased as 'to make or set free' (s.v. *release v 1*). This indicates that the noun is more complex than the verb. This impression is further strengthened by the fact that we find *liberation* among the synonyms for the noun *release* and *to liberate* among the synonyms for the verb *release*. And if we agree that *liberation* is semantically (and morphologically!) more complex than *liberate*, we have good reason to say that the noun *release* is more complex than the verb *release*.

Looking at the frequency of the verb and the noun, we see that *to release* is significantly more frequent than the noun *release*. This is also an indication that the verb is basic and the noun is derived. In sum, the stress criterion is inconclusive, but the other two criteria point in the direction of verb-to-noun conversion.

With the word pair *to name*$_V$–*the name*$_N$ the stress criterion is useless because we are dealing with monosyllabic forms. The criterion of semantic complexity gives us a clearer idea. The verb *name* can be paraphrased as 'give a name,' which shows that the verb is more complex, hence that we are dealing with noun-to-verb conversion. This analysis is supported by the respective frequencies of the two words: the noun *name* is used much more frequently than the verb.

A similar reasoning applies to the pair *clear*$_V$–*clear*$_N$. Stress is useless, and the semantics point in the direction of adjective-to-verb conversion, since *to clear* means 'to make clear,' which includes the meaning of the adjective and is therefore semantically more complex. The frequency data provide further evidence for the adjective-to-verb conversion analysis.

The application of the stress criterion to the pair *smoke*$_N$–*smoke*$_V$ is again impossible. The semantic criterion can be applied as follows: the verb *to smoke* can be paraphrased as 'to produce smoke,' which suggests that it is semantically more complex than the noun *smoke*. Hence we should be dealing with noun-to-verb conversion. However, the frequencies seem to indicate that it is rather the other way round. The verb *to smoke* has a higher frequency than the noun *smoke*, which would speak for verb-to-noun conversion. However, the difference in frequency is not very significant: *to smoke* has the frequency of 3516, whereas the noun occurs 2823 times in the BNC. In the cases discussed above the differences were much more pronounced. Furthermore, we have to take into consideration that the verb *to smoke* has in fact at least one more meaning that is relevant here. In addition to 'produce smoke,' there is the much more specialized meaning 'inhale and exhale fumes (of tobacco, for example).' We would perhaps want to argue that the latter meaning did not arise through noun-to-verb conversion, but via metaphorical extension of the meaning of the verb *to smoke* 'to produce smoke.' Thus, in order to use frequency to establish the directionality of the pair *smoke*$_N$–*smoke*$_V$ we would first have to determine the frequency of the verb *to smoke* when used with the meaning 'to produce smoke,' and then compare the frequencies again. Given that *smoke* meaning 'inhale fumes' is presumably much more commonly used than *smoke* meaning 'produce smoke,' we would arrive at the conclusion that both frequency and semantics point in the direction of noun-to-verb conversion for the pair *smoke*$_N$–*smoke*$_V$ 'produce smoke.'

Turning finally to *jail*, we may argue that the verb *jail* is semantically more complex than the noun *jail*, since it can be paraphrased by 'to put into jail.' This confirms the hypothesis that we are possibly dealing with an instance of noun-to-verb conversion. The frequencies suggest the same, even though the frequency of the noun *jail* is not dramatically higher than that of the corresponding verb.

Overall, it seems that, if applied carefully, the different criteria for establishing the directionality of conversion work reasonably well, even though individual criteria may sometimes not be applicable or might not yield conclusive evidence.

Exercise 5.5

There is an important prosodic difference between the data in (a) and (b) on the one hand, and the data in (c) on the other. The examples in (a) and (b) either have an onset in their first syllable, as in (a), or, if they don't have an onset, the first syllable is stressed, as in (b). The examples in (c) have neither: the first syllable of the base is both onsetless and stressless. Obviously, the combination of these two properties disqualifies the first syllable as an anchor for the truncation. Only one property (onset *or* stress) may be missing from the first syllable in order for it to be eligible for survival in the truncation.

Thus we have to refine our generalization further by stating that name truncations are generally formed on the basis of a stressed syllable of the base. Unstressed first syllables may also serve as anchors if they contain an onset.

Note that of the data mentioned in section 5.2.1, one form is a counterexample to the pattern just described. *Al* is formed on the basis of *Alonzo*, although the base has an unstressed, onsetless first syllable. Such counterexamples are very rare and this particular form may be licensed by the existence of *Al* as an established truncation of *Alfred* and *Albert*. For a more detailed analysis see Lappe (2003).

Exercise 5.6

Let us first examine which part of the base is reduplicated. We can classify the examples given into two groups as shown in table 5B.

Table 5B

complete reduplication of base	reduplication of everything but the first onset of the base
Andy-W**andy** **Annie**-P**annie**	p**iggie**-w**iggie** b**oatie**-w**oatie** h**ousey**-w**ousey** Ch**arlie**-P**arlie** l**ovey**-d**ovey** R**oddy**-D**oddy** Br**innie**-W**innie** St**evie**-W**eavy**

If the first syllable of the base has an onset, the whole base without the onset of the first syllable is reduplicated. That it is indeed the onset which is left behind and not simply the first consonant is evidenced by the forms with complex onsets, *Brinnie-Winnie, Stevie-Weavy*. If there is no onset, the whole form is reduplicated (e.g. *Andy-Wandy*). The two cases can be unified by the generalization that everything of the base but the onset of the first syllable is reduplicated.

Furthermore, it can be observed that in the data set only words that are disyllabic trochees occur as bases of reduplications (see section 4.6 for the notion of trochee). We would have to test whether this is an artifact of the data presented here or whether this is indeed a significant generalization over larger sets of pertinent words.

The next question that arises is what happens to the reduplicated part of the base. All reduplicants in the data begin with a consonant. In those cases where the base had no onset, an onset is added (e.g. *Andy-Wandy*), and in those cases where the base had an onset, this onset is replaced in the reduplicant by a different onset. The new onset is always simplex, so that, if the onset of the base consisted of a consonant cluster (CC, as in *Stevie*), the cluster is replaced by a simple onset (consisting of one consonant only, as in *Stevie-Weavy*).

With regard to the kinds of onset of the reduplicants, three groups of words can be distinguished, as shown in table 5C.

Table 5C

w-initial reduplicant	*p*-initial reduplicant	*d*-initial reduplicant
Andy-Wandy	Annie-Pannie	lovey-dovey
Brinnie-Winnie	Charlie-Parlie	Roddy-Doddy
piggie-wiggie		
boatie-woatie		
Stevie-Weavy		
housey-wousey		

We see that the set of onsets possible in the reduplicant is severely restricted, only /w/, /p/, and /d/ are attested. /w/ is the most common onset, and /d/ occurs only with liquid-initial bases (/l/ and /r/ belong to the class of sounds called 'liquids').

In sum, we have found a number of interesting patterns, which shows that even in this seemingly irregular domain prosodic and segmental restrictions play a role. More data are of course needed to substantiate (or indeed falsify) the above analysis.

Chapter 6

Exercise 6.1

The word *blackboard eraser* consists of two elements that are words, *blackboard* and *eraser*, hence it must be a compound. Other evidence for its being a compound lies in the fact that it has its main stress on its first member: *bláckboard eraser*. It is an endocentric compound, since *blackboard eraser* denotes a kind of eraser. The first element of the compound, *blackboard*, is again a compound. The second element, *eraser*, is a noun which is derived from the verb *erase* by the suffixation of instrumental/agentive *-er*.

The item *broad-shouldered* may first look like a compound: it consists of the two orthographic and phonological words *broad* and *shouldered*. However, *shouldered* also has an internal structure of its own: it consists of the root *shoulder* and the suffix *-ed*, which raises the question of whether *broad-shouldered* is really a compound or rather a derivative with the phrase [*broad shoulder*] as its base. Given that *broad-shouldered* means 'provided with broad shoulders,' and given that there is the ornative suffix *-ed* in English which produces exactly that meaning, we have to conclude that this is a case of derivation, with a phrase as the base (see also the description of *-ed* in section 4.4.3).

The word *unacceptability* is the result of derivation: it consists of the prefix *un-*, the root *accept*, and the two suffixes *-able* and *-ity*. *Hard-working* is an adjectival compound with a participle as right-hand element, which is modified by *hard*. *Flowerpots* exhibits two processes, compounding and inflection. The compound *flowerpot* is inflected for plural.

Speaking can be the result of two different processes: derivation or inflection. On the one hand, the word *speaking* can be regarded as a present participle of the verb *speak*, in which case it is the result of inflection. On the other hand, *speaking* can be regarded as a deverbal noun denoting a process. In this case the form should be viewed as a result of derivation. There is also a third possibility: *speaking* may occur as an adjective, as in *a speaking elephant*. In this case the suffix *-ing* might be regarded as derivational as well, changing verbs into adjectives. See also the discussion of nominal and adjectival *-ing* in sections 4.4.1 and 4.4.3.

Movie monster is a nominal, endocentric compound, while *developmental* is a derivative consisting of the root *develop* and the two derivational suffixes *-ment* and *-al*.

Exercise 6.2

English compounds can be said to have the following three characteristics. First, compounds are binary structures that may consist of roots, words, or phrases. Thus, all words in the data available are such binary structures: the compounds *oak tree, drawbridge, sky-blue*, and *mind-boggling* consist of two constituents each, and these constituents are words: *oak* and *tree, draw* and *bridge, sky* and *blue, mind* and *boggling*.

Second, compounds in English are right-headed and they inherit their major properties from the head. Thus, in the data given all compounds can be interpreted in such a way that the left-hand member modifies the right-hand member, which serves as the head of a compound: an *oak tree* is a kind of tree, a *drawbridge* is a kind of bridge, and *sky-blue* is a kind of blue. In the case of *mind-boggling* the first member is an argument of the second member, hence it is a synthetic compound. The syntactic properties in the compounds in question are also inherited from the right-hand members, to the effect that the compounds have the part-of-speech of the right-hand element, and that the plural marking occurs on the head (e.g. *oak-trees*, and not *oaks-tree*).

Third, most compounds in English exhibit a regular stress pattern that is typical of compounds and different from the stress pattern of phrases: compound stress falls on the left-hand member of a compound (in two-member compounds). This pattern is exemplified by *óak-tree, dráwbridge*, and *mínd-boggling*. Adjectival compounds may often have final stress, and *sky-blúe* is an example of this aberrant pattern.

Exercise 6.3

I will first give a classification based on the types of meaning of the different compounds.
Exocentric compound:

> *bootblack*, 'a person who blackens boots'

Endocentric compounds:

> *frying pan*, 'a kind of pan,' *silkworm* 'a kind of worm,' *gas-light* 'a kind of light'

Possessive compounds:

> *redhead* 'a person who possesses red hair,' *hard-top* 'a car with a metal roof'

Appositional compounds:

> *maidservant* 'a person who is both maid and servant,' *actor-manager* 'a person who is both an actor and a manager,' *Austria-Hungary* 'country that consists of both Austria and Hungary,' *German-English* 'entity which is both German and English'

Coordinative compounds:

> *author-reader (exchange)* 'a particular relation between reader and author,' *man-machine (interaction)* 'a particular relation between man and machine'

The paraphrases given above already indicate the rationale behind the classification, but a few additional remarks may be in order.

German-English can be either an appositional compound or a coordinative compound, depending on the context. Thus, e.g. in the phrase *German-English family*, this compound is appositional because it denotes an entity which is characterized by both members of the compound. In the phrase *German-English contact* the compound *German-English* is coordinative because it denotes a relation between two entities, in this case two groups of people.

The compounds *hard-top* and *redhead* could be classified as both possessive and exocentric, because their semantic heads are outside the compounds and they denote an entity that is characterized by the property expressed by the compound. *Actor-manager* is also ambiguous, since, depending on the context, it could also act as a coordinative compound, for example in *actor-manager exchange*.

The compound *silkworm* might be tricky as well, because a silkworm is strictly speaking not a worm, but a four-legged caterpillar. However, in everyday language, *worm* can refer to any small, creeping animal with a slender, elongated body and no, or only small, limbs. Hence, we are dealing with a rather ordinary endocentric compound.

Exercise 6.4

Coordinative compounds denote two entities that stand in a particular relationship with regard to the following noun. Let us hypothesize that they are phrases of some kind rather than words. This hypothesis can be tested as follows.

First, we can investigate the syntactic behavior of the compounds in question: compounds function as syntactic atoms, they cannot be interrupted by some other element – be it a word or a phrase. If the data in question are compounds, they cannot be interrupted. Let us try the interruptability test by inserting adjectives between the two members:

the doctor-patient gap	*the doctor-**old** patient gap
the nature-nurture debate	*the nature-**good** nurture debate
a modifier-head structure	*a modifier-**adjectival** head structure
the mind-body problem	*the mind-**straight** body problem

Under a phrasal analysis we would expect that the second noun could be modified by a preceding adjective, since adjectives can generally precede nouns in phrases. The data above show, however, that the insertion of adjectives does not work well for the structures in question, which indicates that they are compounds rather than phrasal in nature.

Second, we can investigate the stress pattern of the compounds in question. We have said in section 6.1.3 that copulative compounds, i.e. both appositional and coordinative compounds, have rightward stress and are thus systematic exceptions to the compound stress rule. Under the hypothesis that coordinative compounds are not compounds at all, we would not need to posit an exceptional pattern, which makes the phrasal analysis of coordinative compounds appear more elegant, at least with regard to stress. The problem is, however, that we must take into account exceptional stress patterns in compounds also in cases other than coordinative compounds, e.g. with many adjectival compounds, so that even the phrasal account needs to postulate sets of exceptions. Overall, the stress criterion does not really provide substantial evidence for either analysis.

An additional argument in favor of the compound status of these examples might however be that coordinative relations of the kind shown in the data are usually expressed in syntax by means of a conjunction, as in *the relation between doctor **and** patient*, or *the problem of mind **and** body*. Furthermore, unlike in the corresponding phrases, we can never find inflectional endings in coordinative compounds: **the doctors-patients gap* vs. *the gap between doctors and patients*. The obligatory lack of the conjunction and the obligatory absence of inflection are strong indicators for the morphological nature of coordinative compounds, which is further supported by the uninterruptability observed above.

In sum, although the evidence is not entirely conclusive, it seems that a compound analysis is superior.

Exercise 6.5

In order to be able to decide on the status of the elements *under-* and *over-* in the words *underdog, undercoat, overtax*, and *overripe*, we should have a look again at the definition of an affix. It has been stated in section 4.1 that affixes are bound morphemes that can only occur if attached to some other morpheme. If we apply this definition, it seems that the elements *under-* and *over-* in the words in question also occur as free morphemes, namely prepositions, as in *under the table* and *over the rainbow*. This would then mean that the data in question are compounds and not prefixed derivatives.

However, we also saw in the said section that sometimes the meaning of the free form is so different from the meaning of the homophonous bound form that it does not make sense to say that they are one and the same item. For example, the free morpheme *wise* was shown to be very different in meaning from the adverb-forming morpheme *-wise*, so that the latter must be analyzed as a suffix, and not as part of a compound.

Therefore, in order to substantiate our hypothesis from above that *underdog, undercoat, overtax*, and *overripe* are compounds, we would have to show that the bound forms *under-* and *over-* have basically the same meaning as the free forms *under* and *over*.

The meaning of *under-* in *underdog* can be characterized as 'in a state of inferiority or subjection' (note also that *underdog* is semantically exocentric, because it usually does not refer to dogs). This meaning is also attested for the preposition *under*, as in *under the present regulations* or *under her guidance*. In *undercoat*, which can be paraphrased as 'a coat worn beneath another,' *under-* has the meaning 'beneath,' which is also well attested for the preposition *under* (cf. *He sleeps under the bridge*, or *The dog is under the table*). This means that the meaning of the free form *under* and the bound form *under-*, as it occurs in the words *underdog* and *undercoat*, is the same, which clearly speaks for an analysis of the words in question as preposition-noun compounds. It is not necessary to postulate the existence of a prefix *under-*.

Let us now turn to *over*. The word *overripe* means 'too ripe,' and *overtax* can be paraphrased as 'to tax too heavily,' so that the meaning of the morpheme *over-* in both words is 'too much, excessively, more than is appropriate.' Although the preposition *over* is primarily used in its spatial sense ('above,' as in *over the rainbow*), there are also usages that closely match that of *over-* in *overripe* and *overtax*. For example, in *a distance of over 100 miles* or *she paid over 2000 dollars*, we find the idea of excessiveness which can also be observed for *over-* ('the distance exceeds 100 miles,' and 'the amount to pay exceeds the sum of 2000 dollars'). We may therefore conclude that the meaning of *over-* in *overripe* and *overtax* is sufficiently similar to that of the preposition *over* to justify the analysis of *overripe* and *overtax* as preposition–noun compounds. (For a discussion of a wider variety of complex words involving *under-* and *over-* see, for example, Adams 2001: 71–76.)

Chapter 7

Exercise 7.1

Some criteria for distinguishing between level 1 and level 2 suffixes are listed in table 7A.

Table 7A

Level 1 suffixes typically . . .	Level 2 suffixes typically . . .
. . . cause stress shift	. . . are stress neutral
. . . cause segmental alternations	. . . do not cause segmental alternations
. . . attach to Latinate bases	. . . attach to Latinate and Germanic bases

If we apply these criteria to the given words, we see that the complex words in the left-hand pairs all show stress shift: *pórous–porósity, deríve–derivátion, Aristótle–Aristotélian*. They all display segmental alternations (e.g. *por*[ə]*s–por*[ɒ]*sity*) and take Latinate bases. The complex words on the right, however, do not cause the said phonological alternations and have Germanic bases. Therefore, *-ity, -ation*, and *-ian* are level 1, while *-er* and *-hood* are level 2.

Exercise 7.2

Let us first determine the internal structure of each word and identify the stratal membership of each affix involved. Below, the word structures are represented by brackets, and the affix levels are indicated by '1' (for level 1) and '2' (for level 2). The stratal membership was taken from the list of affixes and strata in (2), chapter 7:

ungrammaticality	*Machiavellistic*
[[un-[grammat-ical]]-ity]	[[Machiavelli-ist]-ic]
[[2-[base-1]]-1]	[[base-2]-1]
reorganization	*controllability*
[[re-[organ-ize]]-ation]	[[control-able]-ity]
[[2-[base-2]]-1]	[[base-2]-1]

The words involving prefixes can both be analyzed and interpreted in such a way that the nominal suffix is the last to attach: *ungrammatical → ungrammatical-ity, reorganize → reorganiz-ation*. This means that the level 1 suffix is attached outside the level 2 prefix. This should, however, be impossible according to the level-ordering hypothesis.

Note that there are of course also alternative interpretations possible, according to which the prefixes are last to attach (*grammaticality → un-grammaticality, organization → re-organization*). Under this analysis, no violation of level ordering can be observed. Crucially, however, the former analysis is not only possible, it is even more plausible than the alternative, because *un-* and *re-* standardly attach to adjectives and to verbs, respectively, giving us *ungrammatical* and *reorganize* as the bases for the attachment of *-ity* and *-ation*, respectively.

The nouns *Machiavellistic* and *controllability* are instances of a similar problem. Here, the level 2 suffixes *-able* and *-ist* do occur inside level 1 suffixes, which, contrary to the facts, is ruled out under the assumptions of level ordering. Alternatively, we could assign *-able* or *-ist* membership in two strata, which would, however, seriously weaken the overall model.

Exercise 7.3

The following morpheme-based word-formation rules can be established:

WORD-FORMATION RULE FOR THE SUFFIX *-ate*
phonology:	/eɪt/
semantics:	'provide with X'
syntax:	verb
base:	noun

WORD-FORMATION RULE FOR THE SUFFIX *-ion*
phonology:	/ən/
	base-final alternation /t/ → /ʃ/
semantics:	'action of Xing, process of Xing, result of Xing'
syntax:	noun
base:	verb in *-ate*

In a word-based approach the relationships could be represented as follows:

$$
\begin{pmatrix} <X> \\ /X/ \\ N \\ \text{'X'} \end{pmatrix} \leftrightarrow \begin{pmatrix} <Xate> \\ /Xeɪt/ \\ V \\ \text{'provide with X'} \end{pmatrix}
$$

$$
\begin{pmatrix} <Xate> \\ /Xeɪt/ \\ V \\ \text{'provide with X'} \end{pmatrix} \leftrightarrow \begin{pmatrix} <Xation> \\ /Xeɪʃən/ \\ N \\ \text{'action/process/result of Xating'} \end{pmatrix}
$$

Exercise 7.4

The obvious problem with the lack of base verbs is that in a morpheme-based model the existence of a base word is crucial, because the suffix *-ion* needs a base word to which it can attach. In a word-based account, this problem does not occur. The relationship between the three types of words can be depicted as a trilateral one as shown in the diagram overleaf.

$$
\begin{pmatrix}
< X > \\
/X/ \\
N \\
`X'
\end{pmatrix}
$$

$$
\begin{pmatrix}
< Xate > \\
/\text{Xeit}/ \\
V \\
`\text{provide with X'}
\end{pmatrix}
\longleftrightarrow
\begin{pmatrix}
< Xation > \\
/\text{Xeiʃən}/ \\
N \\
`\text{action/process/result of Xating'} \\
\text{Xating'}; \\
`\text{action/process/result of} \\
\text{action having to do} \\
\text{with X'}
\end{pmatrix}
$$

The schema does not make any reference to individual morphemes and the internal structure of words, but expresses the relation between the three sets of words. Since there is no directionality in the relation between sets of words in a schema, the creation of new words can go in various ways: *-ate* derivatives can be formed on the basis of *-ation* derivatives, and *-ation* derivatives can be formed on the basis of nouns without the intermediate step of verbal derivation. In this model it is therefore predictable that some *-ation* words might not have corresponding *-ate* verbs, and that some *-ate* verbs may come into existence later than the corresponding *-ation* words. In sum, the word-based approach allows a more adequate analysis of the data in question.

Exercise 7.5

a.   Level 1 affixes differ significantly from level 2 affixes. Level 1 affixes score lower on each of the measures that indicate the separability of the affix from its base. With level 1 affixes, fewer types and fewer tokens are morphologically segmented and fewer hapaxes can be found. Furthermore, the productivity of level 1 affixes is much lower.

b.   We can say that the distinction between level 1 and level 2 affixes reflects Hay's processing account of level ordering. Under the assumption that affixes which stand closer to the base are less easily parsed out, we would predict that level 1 affixes should be the ones that are less easily parsed out than level 2 affixes. The data in the table are in perfect accordance with this prediction.

c. In a way, the results presented in the table corroborate the idea of level ordering, since the figures show that level ordering is not merely a theoretical construct but has clear psycholinguistic correlates. However, this must be interpreted – somewhat ironically – as the fatal blow for the theory of level ordering, because the existence of a psycholinguistic explanation makes level ordering superfluous. What looks like level ordering is in fact the outcome of the mechanisms of morphological processing. Level ordering as an independent device in our theory can be discarded, because the facts which the idea of level ordering seeks to explain fall out automatically from our – independently needed – theory of morphological processing.

References

Adams, Valerie 2001, *Complex Words in English*, Harlow: Longman.

Allen, Margaret 1978, 'Morphological Investigations,' PhD dissertation, University of Connecticut, Ann Arbor: University Microfilms.

Anderson, Stephen R. 1992, *A-morphous Morphology*, Cambridge: Cambridge University Press.

Anshen, Frank, Mark Aronoff, Roy Byrd, and Judith Klavans 1986, 'The role of etymology and word-length in English word-formation,' MS, SUNY Stonybrook/IBM Thomas Watson Research Center, Yorktown Heights, NY.

Aronoff, Mark 1976, *Word Formation in Generative Grammar*, Cambridge, MA: MIT Press.
1980, *Juncture*, Saratoga, CA: Anma libri.

Aronoff, Mark and S. N. Sridhar 1987, 'Morphological levels in English and Kannada,' in Gussmann (ed.), pp. 9–22.

Baayen, Harald 1993, 'On frequency, transparency and productivity,' in Booij and van Marle (eds.), pp. 181–208.

Baayen, Harald and Antoinette Renouf 1996, 'Chronicling *The Times*: productive lexical innovations in an English newspaper,' *Language* 72: 69–96.

Baayen, Harald and Rochelle Lieber 1991, 'Productivity and English word-formation: a corpus-based study,' *Linguistics* 29: 801–843.

Baeskow, Heike 2002, *Abgeleitete Personenbezeichnungen im Deutschen und Englischen*, Berlin and New York: Walter de Gruyter.

Barker, Chris 1998, 'Episodic -*ee* in English: a thematic role constraint on a new word formation,' *Language* 74: 695–727.

Bauer, Laurie 1983, *English Word-formation*, Cambridge: Cambridge University Press.
1988, *Introducing Linguistic Morphology*, Edinburgh: Edinburgh University Press.
1990, 'Be-heading the word,' *Journal of Linguistics* 26: 1–31.
1998a, 'Is there a class of neoclassical compounds and is it productive?,' *Linguistics* 36: 403–422.
1998b, 'When is a sequence of two nouns a compound in English?,' *English Language and Linguistics* 2: 65–86.
2001, *Morphological Productivity*, Cambridge: Cambridge University Press.

Bauer, Laurie and Rodney Huddleston 2002, 'Lexical word-formation,' in Huddleston and Pullum (eds.), pp. 1621–1721.

Bauer, Laurie and Antoinette Renouf 2001, 'A corpus-based study of compounding in English,' *Journal of English Linguistics* 29: 101–123.

Becker, Thomas 1990, *Analogie und Morphologische Theorie*, Munich: Wilhelm Fink.

1993, 'Back-formation, cross-formation, and "bracketing paradoxes" in paradigmatic morphology,' in Booij and van Marle (eds.), pp. 1–25.

Berg, Thomas 1998, 'The (in)compatibility of morpheme orders and lexical categories and its historical implications,' *English Language and Linguistics* 2: 245–262.

Bolinger, Dwight 1948, 'On defining the morpheme,' *Word* 4: 18–23.

Booij, Geert E. 1993, 'Against split morphology,' in Booij and van Marle (eds.), pp. 27–49.

1994, 'Lexical Phonology: a review,' in Wiese (ed.), pp. 3–29.

Booij, Geert E. and Jaap van Marle (eds.) 1988, *Yearbook of Morphology 1988*, Dordrecht: Foris.

1990a, *Yearbook of Morphology 1989*, Dordrecht: Foris.

1990b, *Yearbook of Morphology 1990*, Dordrecht, Boston, and London: Kluwer.

1992, *Yearbook of Morphology 1991*, Dordrecht, Boston, and London: Kluwer.

1993, *Yearbook of Morphology 1993*, Dordrecht, Boston, and London: Kluwer.

1995, *Yearbook of Morphology 1994*, Dordrecht, Boston, and London: Kluwer.

1998, *Yearbook of Morphology 1997*, Dordrecht, Boston, and London: Kluwer.

1999, *Yearbook of Morphology 1998*, Dordrecht, Boston, and London: Kluwer.

2000, *Yearbook of Morphology 1999*, Dordrecht, Boston, and London: Kluwer.

2001, *Yearbook of Morphology 2000*, Dordrecht, Boston, and London: Kluwer.

2002, *Yearbook of Morphology 2001*, Dordrecht, Boston, and London: Kluwer.

Booij, Geert E., Christian Lehmann, and Joachim Mugdan (eds.) 2000, *Morphologie/Morphology: ein internationales Handbuch zur Flexion und Wortbildung/An International Handbook on Inflection and Word-formation*, Vol. 1, Berlin: Mouton de Gruyter.

Borer, Hagit 1990, 'V+*ing*: it walks like an adjective, it talks like an adjective,' *Linguistic Inquiry* 21: 95–103.

Brekle, Herbert Ernst 1970, *Generative Satzsemantik und transformationelle Syntax im System der Englischen Nominalkomposition*, Munich: Fink.

Buck, R. A. 1997, 'Words and their opposites. Noun to verb conversion in English,' *Word* 48: 1–14.

Burzio, Luigi 1994, *Principles of English Stress*, Cambridge: Cambridge University Press.

Bybee, Joan 1985, *Morphology*, Amsterdam: Benjamins.

Carstairs-McCarthy, Andrew 1992, *Current Morphology*, London: Routledge.

1993, 'Morphology without word-internal constituents: a review of Stephen R. Anderson's *A-morphous Morphology*,' in Booij and van Marle (eds.), pp. 209–233.

Cetnarowska, Bożena 1993, *The Syntax, Semantics and Derivation of Bare Nominalizations in English*, Katowice: Uniwersytet Śląski.

Chomsky, Noam and Morris Halle 1968, *The Sound Pattern of English*, New York: Harper and Row.

Clark, Eve and Herbert Clark 1979, 'When nouns surface as verbs,' *Language* 55: 767–811.

Dalton-Puffer, Christiane and Ingo Plag 2001, 'Categorywise, some compound-type morphemes seem to be rather suffix-like: on the status of -*ful*, -*type*, and -*wise* in Present Day English,' *Folia Linguistica* 34: 225–244.

Di Sciullo, Anne-Marie and Edwin Williams 1987, *On the Definition of Word*, Cambridge, MA: MIT Press.

Doleschal, Ursula and A. M. Thornton (eds.) 2000, *Extragrammatical and Marginal Morphology*, Munich: Lincom.

Don, Jan 1993, *Morphological Conversion*, Utrecht: Led.

Downing, Pamela 1977, 'On the creation and use of English compound nouns,' *Language* 53: 810–842.

Dressler, Wolfgang U. 2000, 'Extragrammatical vs. marginal morphology,' in Doleschal and Thornton (eds.), pp. 1–10.

Dressler, Wolfgang U. and Lavinia Merlini Barbaresi 1994, *Morphopragmatics. Diminutives and Intensifiers in Italian, German, and other Languages*, Berlin: Mouton de Gruyter.

Fabb, Nigel 1988, 'English suffixation is constrained only by selectional restrictions,' *Natural Language and Linguistic Theory* 6: 527–539.

1998, 'Compounds,' in Spencer and Zwicky (eds.), pp. 66–83.

Farnetani, Edda, Carol Taylor Torsello, and Piero Cosi 1988, 'English compound versus non-compound noun phrases in discourse: an acoustic and perceptual study,' *Language and Speech* 31: 157–180.

Farrell, Patrick 2001, 'Functional shift as category underspecification,' *English Language and Linguistics* 5: 109–130.

Fisiak, Jacek (ed.) 1985, *Historical Semantics, Historical Word-formation*, New York: Mouton de Gruyter.

Fradin, Bernard 2000, 'Combining forms, blends and related phenomena,' in Doleschal and Thornton (eds.), pp. 11–59.

Frauenfelder, Uli and Robert Schreuder 1992, 'Constraining psycholinguistic models of morphological processing and representation: the role of productivity,' in Booij and van Marle (eds.), pp. 165–183.

Fudge, Erik 1984, *English Word-stress*, London: Allen and Unwin.

Funk, Isaac K. 1963, *Funk and Wagnalls New Standard Dictionary of the English Language*, New York: Funk & Wagnalls.

Gibbon, Dafydd and H. Richter (eds.) 1984, *Intonation, Accent and Rhythm*, Berlin: Mouton de Gruyter.

Giegerich, Heinz J. 1999, *Lexical Strata in English. Morphological Causes, Phonological Effects*, Cambridge: Cambridge University Press.

Gussmann, Edmund (ed.) 1987, *Rules and the Lexicon*. Lublin: Catholic University.

Halle, Morris and K. P. Mohanan 1985, 'Segmental phonology of Modern English,' *Linguistic Inquiry* 16: 57–116.

Hammond, Michael 1999, *The Phonology of English*, Oxford: Oxford University Press.

Hammond, Michael and Michael Noonan (eds.) 1988, *Theoretical Morphology*, San Diego and London: Academic Press.

Haspelmath, Martin 1996, 'Word-class changing inflection and morphological theory,' in Booij and van Marle (eds.), pp. 43–66.

2002, *Understanding Morphology*, London: Arnold.

Hatcher, Anna G. 1960, 'An introduction to the analysis of English compounds,' *Word* 16: 356–373.

Hay, Jennifer 2000, 'Causes and Consequences of Word Structure,' PhD thesis, Northwestern University.

2001, 'Lexical frequency in morphology: is everything relative?,' *Linguistics* 39.4: 1041–1070.

2002, 'From speech perception to morphology: affix-ordering revisited,' *Language* 78.3: 527–555.

Hay, Jennifer and Harald Baayen 2002, 'Parsing and productivity,' in Booij and van Marle (eds.), pp. 203–235.

2003, 'Phonotactics, parsing and productivity,' MS, University of Canterbury and MPI für Psycholinguistik Nijmegen.

Hay, Jennifer and Ingo Plag in press, 'What constrains possible suffix combinations? On the interaction of grammatical and processing restrictions in derivational morphology,' *Natural Language and Linguistic Theory*.

Hopper, Paul J. (ed.) 1977, *Studies in Descriptive and Historical Linguistics*, Amsterdam and Philadelphia: Benjamins.

Horrocks, Geoffrey 1987, *Generative Syntax*, London: Longman.

Huddleston, Rodney and Geoffrey Pullum 2002, *The Cambridge Grammar of the English Language*, Cambridge: Cambridge University Press.

Ingram, John, Thi Anh Thu Nguyen and Rob Pensalfini in press, 'An acoustic analysis of compound and phrasal stress patterns in Australian English,' *Journal of Phonetics*.

Jespersen, Otto 1942, *A Modern English Grammar. On Historical Principles. Part VI Morphology*, London: Allen and Unwin.

Jones, Daniel 1997, *English Pronouncing Dictionary*, Cambridge: Cambridge University Press.

Jucker, Andreas H. 1994, 'New dimensions in vocabulary studies: review article of the *Oxford English Dictionary* (2nd edition) on CD-ROM,' *Literary and Linguistic Computing* 9: 149–154.

Kaisse, Ellen and Patricia Shaw 1985, 'On the theory of lexical phonology,' *Phonology Yearbook* 2: 1–30.

Kastovsky, Dieter 1986, 'The problem of productivity in word formation,' *Linguistics* 24: 585–600.

Katamba, Francis 1993, *Morphology*, Basingstoke: Macmillan.

Kaunisto, Mark 1999, '*Electric/electrical* and *classic/classical*: variation between the suffixes -*ic* and -*ical*,' *English Studies* 80: 343–370.

Kiparsky, Paul 1982, 'Lexical morphology and phonology,' in The Linguistic Society of Korea (ed.), 1–91.

1985, 'Some consequences of Lexical Phonology,' *Phonology Yearbook* 2: 85–138.

Krott, Andrea, Harald Baayen, and Robert Schreuder 2001, 'Analogy in morphology: modeling the choice of linking morphemes in Dutch,' *Linguistics* 39: 51–93.

Kubozono, Haruo 1991, 'Phonological constraints on blending in English as a case for phonology-morphology interface,' in Booij and van Marle (eds.), pp. 1–20.

Ladd, Dwight Robert 1984, 'English compound stress,' in Gibbon and Richter (eds.), pp. 253–266.

Lappe, Sabine 2003, 'English Prosodic Morphology,' PhD thesis, University of Siegen.

Leech, Geoffrey N., Paul Rayson and Andrew Wilson 2001, *Word Frequencies in Written and Spoken English*, Harlow: Longman.

Lees, Robert B. 1960, *The Grammar of English Nominalizations*, The Hague: Mouton.

Lehnert, Martin 1971, *Rückläufiges Wörterbuch der englischen Gegenwartssprache*, Leipzig: Verlag Enzyklopädie.

Levi, Judith N. 1978, *The Syntax and Semantics of Complex Nominals*, New York: Academic Press.

Liberman, Mark and Alison Prince 1977, 'On stress and linguistic rhythm,' *Linguistic Inquiry* 8: 249–336.

Liberman, Mark and Richard Sproat 1992, 'The stress and structure of modified noun phrases in English,' in Sag and Szabolcsi (eds.), pp. 131–181.

Lieber, Rochelle 1992, *Deconstructing Morphology*, Chicago and London: University of Chicago Press.

The Linguistic Society of Korea (ed.), *Linguistics in the Morning Calm*, Seoul: Hanshin Publishing Co.

Ljung, Magnus 1970, *English Denominal Adjectives. A Generative Study of the Semantics of a Group of High-frequency Denominal Adjectives in English*, Lund: Studentlitteratur.

Longman Dictionary of Contemporary English 2000, Munich: Langenscheidt-Longman.

Lüdeling, Anke, Tanja Schmid and Sawwas Kiokpasaglou 2002, 'Neoclassical word-formation in German,' in Booij and van Marle (eds.), pp. 253–283.

Malkiel, Yakov 1977, 'Why *ap-ish* but *worm-y*?,' in Hopper (ed.), pp. 341–364.

Marchand, Hans 1969, *The Categories and Types of Present-day English Word-formation*, 2nd edition, Munich: Beck.

Matthews, Peter 1991, *Morphology*, 2nd edition, Cambridge: Cambridge University Press.

McQueen, James M. and Anne Cutler, 1998, 'Morphology in word recognition,' in Spencer and Zwicky (eds.), pp. 406–427.

Meyer, Ralf 1993, *Compound Comprehension in Isolation and in Context. The Contribution of Conceptual and Discourse Knowledge to the Comprehension of Novel Noun-Noun Compounds*, Tübingen: Niemeyer.

Mohanan, Karuvannur P. 1986, *The Theory of Lexical Phonology*, Dordrecht: Reidel.

Muthmann, Gustav 1999, *Reverse English Dictionary. Based on Phonological and Morphological Principles*, Berlin and New York: Mouton de Gruyter.

Nevis, Joel N. and John T. Stonham 1999, 'Learning morphology: what makes a good textbook?,' *Language* 75: 801–809.

OED 1994, *The Oxford English Dictionary (2nd edition), on Compact Disc*, Oxford: Oxford University Press.

Olsen, Susan 2000a, 'Composition,' in Booij et al. (eds.), pp. 897–916.

  2000b, 'Compounding and stress in English: a closer look at the boundary between morphology and syntax,' *Linguistische Berichte* 181: 55–69.

  2001, 'Copulative compounds: a closer look at the interface between syntax and morphology,' in Booij and van Marle (eds.), pp. 279–320.

Plag, Ingo 1996, 'Selectional restrictions in English suffixation revisited. A reply to Fabb (1988)', *Linguistics* 34: 769–798.

  1999, *Morphological Productivity. Structural Constraints in English Derivation*, Berlin and New York: Mouton de Gruyter.

  2002, 'The role of selectional restrictions, phonotactics and parsing in constraining suffix ordering in English,' in Booij and van Marle (eds.), pp. 285–314.

Plag, Ingo, Christiane Dalton-Puffer and Harald Baayen 1999, 'Morphological productivity across speech and writing,' *English Language and Linguistics* 3: 209–228.

Plank, Frans 1981, *Morphologische (Ir-)Regularitäten: Aspekte der Wortstrukturtheorie*, Tübingen: Narr.

Raffelsiefen, Renate 1993, 'Relating words. A model of base-recognition,' *Linguistic Analysis* 23: 3–164.

1999, 'Phonological constraints on English word formation,' in Booij and van Marle (eds.), pp. 225–288.

Rainer, Franz 1988, 'Towards a Theory of Blocking,' in Booij and van Marle (eds.), pp. 155–185.

Riddle, Elizabeth 1985, 'A historical perspective on the productivity of the suffixes -*ness* and -*ity*,' in Fisiak (ed.), pp. 435–461.

Rose, James H. 1973, 'Principled limitations on productivity in denominal verbs,' *Foundations of Language* 10: 509–526.

Rúa, Paula López 2002, 'On the structure of acronyms and neighbouring categories: a prototype-based account,' *English Language and Linguistics* 6: 31–60.

Ryder, Mary Ellen 1994, *Ordered Chaos: the Interpretation of English Noun-Noun Compounds*, Berkeley: University of California Press.

'Bankers and blue-chippers: an account of -*er* formations in Present-day English,' *English Language and Linguistics* 3: 269–297.

Saciuk, Bogdan 1969, 'The stratal division of the lexicon,' *Papers in Linguistics* 1: 464–532.

Sag, Ivan A. and Anna Szabolcsi (eds.) 1992, *Lexical Matters*, Stanford: Center for the Study of Language and Information.

Sanders, Gerald 1988, 'Zero Derivation and the Overt Analogon Criterion,' in Hammond and Noonan (eds.), pp. 155–175.

Schneider, Klaus Peter 2003, *Diminutives in English*, Tübingen: Niemeyer.

Selkirk, Elisabeth 1982, *The Syntax of Words*, Cambridge, MA: MIT Press.

Siegel, Dorothy 1974, 'Topics in English morphology,' PhD thesis, MIT.

Skousen, Royal 1995, 'Analogy: a non-rule alternative to neural networks,' *Rivista di Linguistica* 7.2: 213–231.

Spencer, Andrew 1991, *Morphological Theory: an Introduction to Word Structure in Generative Grammar*, Cambridge: Cambridge University Press.

Spencer, Andrew and Arnold M. Zwicky (eds.) 1998, *The Handbook of Morphology*, Oxford: Blackwell.

Stemberger, Joseph 1998, 'Morphology in language production with special reference to connectionism,' in Spencer and Zwicky (eds.), pp. 428–452.

Stockwell, Robert, and Donka Minkova 2001, *English Words: History and Structure*, Cambridge: Cambridge University Press.

Strauss, Steven 1982, *Lexicalist Phonology of English and German*, Dordrecht: Foris.

Walker, John 1924, *The Rhyming Dictionary*, revised by L. Dawson, London: Routledge.

Webster, Noah 1971, *Webster's Third New International Dictionary of the English Language*, Springfield, MA: Merriam.

Wiese, Richard (ed.) 1994, *Recent Developments in Lexical Phonology* (Arbeiten des Sonderforschungsbereichs 'Theorie des Lexikons' Nr. 56), Düsseldorf: Heinrich-Heine-Universität.

Williams, Edwin 1981a, 'On the notions "lexically related" and "head of a word,"' *Linguistic Inquiry* 12: 245–274.

1981b, 'Argument Structure and Morphology,' *The Linguistic Review* 1: 81–114.

Zimmer, Karl E. 1964, *Affixal Negation in English and other Languages: an Investigation of Restricted Productivity* (Supplement to *Word* 20), London: Clowes.

Subject index

Figures in **bold print** indicate pages where the respective terms are introduced or more closely defined.

Affix index

Page numbers in **bold print** refer to the concise descriptions of individual affixes given in chapter 4.

Author index